Durham City and Cathedral from the South-East

Family, Lineage, and Civil Society

A STUDY OF SOCIETY,
POLITICS, AND MENTALITY
IN THE DURHAM REGION,
1500-1640

BY

MERVYN JAMES

CLARENDON PRESS · OXFORD

1974

Oxford University Press, Ely House, London W.1

GLASGOW   NEW YORK   TORONTO   MELBOURNE   WELLINGTON
CAPE TOWN   IBADAN   NAIROBI   DAR ES SALAAM   LUSAKA   ADDIS ABABA
DELHI   BOMBAY   CALCUTTA   MADRAS   KARACHI   LAHORE   DACCA
KUALA LUMPUR   SINGAPORE   HONG KONG   TOKYO

ISBN 0 19 822408 7

PRINTED IN GREAT BRITAIN
BY WILLIAM CLOWES & SONS, LIMITED
LONDON, BECCLES AND COLCHESTER

PREFACE

This book attempts to outline a preliminary framework for the study of a region whose history during this period has been surprisingly little written about; and this in spite of the intrinsic interest of one of the oldest industrial societies in Europe, where the roots of the modern world drive deep down into the past. A study of this kind ought never to be merely 'local', and it is to be hoped that the matters discussed will be relevant to the wider pattern of English society, politics, and culture.

J. P. Cooper, Christopher Hill, Keith Thomas, and B. R. Wilson read all or some of the chapters, and I am most grateful to them for their comments and criticisms. David Burnett, Ian Doyle, and R. C. Norris of the University Library at Durham gave most kind and helpful assistance in securing access to books and other materials.

The book was completed at All Souls College, Oxford, where I owe a debt of gratitude to the Warden and Fellows for having elected me to a Visiting Fellowship.

Mervyn James

Oxford,
September 1972.

CONTENTS

viii   *Contents*

CONCLUSION: FROM LINEAGE SOCIETY TO CIVIL SOCIETY

APPENDICES

BIBLIOGRAPHY

LIST OF PLATES

turies, and given symmetrically arranged mullion-and-transome windows. See Pevsner, p. 218. Photograph Ursula Clark [*Facing page 87*

7. Humanism becomes visible. (a) Lord Lumley's splendid renaissance fireplace in the hall of Lumley Castle, placed there *c.* 1580; many other similar fireplaces, if on a more modest scale and of more eclectic design, adorned the halls of the new manor houses of Jacobean Durham. (b) The spectacular entrance to Walworth Castle, *c.* 1600, with its classical detail. The superimposed pillars are Tuscan, Ionic, and Corinthian (see p. 16). Photographs Ursula Clark   [*Facing page 102*

8. Horden Hall (see p. 15), a well-preserved example of the new-style gentry housing, built for the Conyers family in 1600. The north front, which appears in the illustration, is two-storied, and shows the porch with its coupled Tuscan columns. There is a third storey in the gables to the east and west, and in the south wing extending behind the house. Photograph Eric de Maré   [*Facing page 103*

9. Walworth Castle, the most impressive of the new-style houses built in Durham during the period, and the seat of the Jenison family. The semi-circular angle towers give the building a romantic castellated effect (see p. 16). Photograph Ursula Clark [*Facing page 103*

10. John Cosin's Gothic revival: the architectural setting for the 'Arminian' liturgical ideal. The Billings engraving of the chancel of Brancepeth church (see below, pp. 112, 124, 130), showing the refurnishing begun during the 1630's, when Cosin was rector, the craftsman employed being Robert Barker. In the seating Gothic form and detail is combined with the Jacobean strap-work decoration of the two stall-ends. The most consciously and elaborately Gothic feature is the chancel screen, which is probably post-Restoration. Here the polygonal posts to the right and left of the entrance have incised zigzag ornamentation copied from the pillars of Durham cathedral, and the Gothic perpendicular ornamental detail has been reproduced with great accuracy. From R. W. Billings, *Illustrations of the Architectural Antiquities of the County of Durham,* 1846   [*Facing page 190*

11. The chalice, candlestick, and flagons here illustrated form part of the communion plate with which Cosin adorned the chapel at Auckland Castle upon his appointment as Bishop of Durham in 1660. The splendour and quality of this liturgical plate is due to Cosin's access to goldsmiths employed by the Crown, like the 'M. Houser' who made the candlestick and flagons. These objects express the realized ideal of splendour in the performance of the liturgy with which Cosin had been associated at Durham in the 1620's and 1630's. See Oman, p. 184 ff., and below, p. 111 ff. Reproduced with the kind permission of the Right Rev. The Bishop of Durham, and of The Curator, The Bowes Museum, Barnard Castle   [*Facing page 191*

INTRODUCTION: THE REGION

HIGHWAYS AND WATERWAYS

OUTSIDERS who have left impressions of Durham during the sixteenth and seventeenth centuries usually crossed it,[1] going north to Newcastle and Edinburgh or else south to York, by the Great North Road. In the sixteenth century the earl of Northumberland's officers, coming from Alnwick, usually took four or five days to reach London from Durham city.[2] But if post-horses were used (by the seventeenth century these were available at ten-mile stages of the route from London to Edinburgh) and if the traveller 'have a body able to endure the toil' a speed of about twelve miles an hour could be kept up, and the journey north or south considerably shortened. When in 1603 Sir Robert Carey made his extraordinary journey from London to Edinburgh to announce the death of Queen Elizabeth to her successor King James, he must have used such a system of relays. As a result he rode 150 miles on each of two successive days, reaching Doncaster the first night, Widdrington in Northumberland the second, and Edinburgh the third. Durham must have been reached in the course of the second day.[3] Stage coaches, when at last they began to be introduced in the reign of Charles II, made travel more widely available and softened the rigours of long journeys on horseback, but could not equal the speed of post-horses. In the early eighteenth century it was still a journey of four days from London to York, and another two from York to Newcastle.[4]

Land communications were supplemented by shipping and the seaways. Danzig grain and that of East Anglia reached Durham by way of Newcastle for the most part,[5] and maritime

Note. Abbreviated references will be found fully set out in the Select Bibliography.

[1] e.g. John Aston, who recorded his journey in his *Journal*, 1639 (*Diaries I*), as Sir William Brereton did his in his *Journal* of 1635 (*Diaries II*); see also Celia Fiennes's *Diary* of the 1690s (Fiennes).

[2] Sy. H. MS. (Aln) X/II/6.   [3] Hinde, 237 ff.   [4] Ibid.
[5] *Ag. Hist.*, p. 20.

contacts with the Netherlands had a cultural as well as commercial importance. Recusant literature and agents from this source reached Durham through South Shields, or through Newcastle by way of the chain of Recusant bases which linked the north to the south banks of the Tyne.[1] Inevitably the spectacular rise of the coal export trade from Newcastle and later Sunderland, which got under way during the last quarter of the sixteenth century, greatly increased the volume of maritime contacts with London and the east coast ports.[2] Until late in Elizabeth's reign coal was shipped in ordinary merchantmen designed for trade in cloth, corn, beer, and wine; but these were narrow and light of keel, and so ill adapted for the carriage of coal. Consequently they were superseded, at least as far as the Newcastle traffic was concerned, by the 'collier', a type of ship which was wide and heavy of keel, built to hold a maximum cargo of coal, and to be operated by a small crew, so economizing in running costs.[3] As a result, between the 1590s and 1630s the average size of coastal coal cargoes shipped from the Tyne rose from 56 to 139 tons, while in the course of the seventeenth century the amount of labour needed to operate a collier was reduced by at least a half.[4] One of the drawbacks which restricted the growth of the coal trade from the Wear during the seventeenth century was the inadequacy of Sunderland as a port. For until the harbour was deepened in the eighteenth century it was impossible for very large vessels to enter the Wear, so that Sunderland could not share as fully as Newcastle in the economies resulting from large-scale transportation. The average size of cargoes loaded there increased to an average of no more than 60 tons in the course of the seventeenth century.[5]

The length and discomfort of the fortnight's voyage to London prevented the sea route from superseding that by land, except for passengers with bulky baggage, like furniture to transport. This would be difficult and expensive to send overland, and for this reason the Lilburne family, moving house in 1619 from Greenwich to their Durham home at Thickley

---

[1] See e.g. *C.S.P. Dom. Ch. I, 1625–6*, pp. 310–11, 325, 358; *Barnes*, pp. 309–12; Caraman, chs. 4–5.
[2] See below, pp. 86 ff.   [3] Nef, i.390.   [4] Ibid.
[5] Ibid., p. 392.

Punchardon, came by sea to Newcastle.[1] But although the fleets of colliers were unsuited for passengers and could scarcely have much facilitated direct contact between the Durham society and London, there can be no doubt that the rise of the coal trade did bring Durham closer to the mainstream of national life and politics. For it gave the government a quickened interest in an area on which the capital was increasingly dependent for its supplies of fuel, and in a commodity which became increasingly important as a source of revenue. Government in turn, with the politics of Court and Parliament, acquired a corresponding relevance for the growing Durham coal interest. This was greatly strengthened between 1570 and 1640 by the recruitment into the gentry of leading Newcastle families enriched by coal,[2] and it was under the leadership of the coal-owners that a sharpened interest in the affairs of the House of Commons began to shape itself in Durham after the accession of James I. A demand arose for the representation there of the Palatinate, which made no headway against the resistance first of Bishop James, then of Bishop Neile.[3] In the reign of Charles I the coal-owners and shippers at Sunderland came to reflect most obviously the oppositionist religious and political tastes of the capital. They were able to rely on support and comfort, when need arose, from business associates amongst the London coal merchanting community who shared the convictions of the Sunderland men.[4] But not all the consequences of this closer involvement of Durham and London resulting from the rise of the coal industry were advantageous. In 1640 the dependence of London on the north-east for its fuel supplies led to military occupation and exploitation by a Scots army, as the most obvious and immediate means to bring pressure to bear on the government of Charles I.

Even before the coal trade had strengthened and extended the links with London and the south, Durham in spite of its remoteness had not been marooned in any northern isolation. During the Tudor period, since the city straddled the easiest route from London to Berwick and Edinburgh, through it passed a lively succession of diplomats, military men, politicians, and divines on the way to or from one or other of these places.

---

[1] Lilburne, *Innocency*, p. 8.   [2] See below, p. 69ff.   [3] See below, p. 166–7.
[4] See e.g. *C.S.P. Dom. Ch. I, 1640*, pp. 50–1 (No. 116).

These were frequently put up at the deanery or castle. The bishops of Durham, in the sixteenth century as well as in the seventeenth, had close contact with the Court, while many had held high office under the Crown; and the society which centred on the Cathedral (which included the episcopal lawyer establishment as well as the preponderantly university-trained cathedral clergy) reflected the cultural and religious tendencies of Oxford, Cambridge, and London. Metropolitan tastes and opinions were also represented in the great aristocratic households like that of Lumley castle, or of Raby under the earls of Westmorland, where for example manuscripts of the works of the poet Lydgate circulated in the earlier years of the sixteenth century.[1] And until the accession of James I brought about the union of the Crowns of England and Scotland contacts with the Court and national politics were made closer by the proximity of the Border. There military and administrative posts opened the service of the Crown to many of the Durham lords and gentry, some of whom also became members of the Council in the North. Two bishops of Durham (Tunstall and Hutton) became presidents of the latter body during the Tudor period, and a Durham peer, the fifth earl of Westmorland, rose to be Queen Mary's lieutenant general in the North.[2] There is no reason to believe that the Palatinate was particularly cut off, as far as the governing class was concerned, from the mainstream political and religious currents of the age. The real barrier here was social not spatial, the cultural horizons of the peasantry, the parish gentry, and the shopkeepers in the little towns defining a religious and folk sub-culture connected with, but different from the world-view of their betters. This was still the case even in the seventeenth century, after the spread of literacy and education had carried the approved and dominant attitudes further down the social scale.[3]

UPLAND AND LOWLAND

The many travellers who made the journey along the Great North Road from York to Northallerton entered Durham at

---

[1] MSS. of Lydgate's *Troy Book, Siege of Thebes,* and *The Fall of Princes* are associated with Catherine countess of Westmorland and her daughter Margaret Neville countess of Rutland, and with John, Lord Lumley. See Lydgate, *Fall,* Pt. 4, pp. 14, 26, 28; Lydgate, *Troy Bk.,* p. 19.

[2] See below, pp. 45, 49, 155.   [3] See below, pp. 125 ff.

the crossing of the Tees at Croft Bridge, proceeding from there by way of Darlington and the city of Durham to Gateshead and over the Tyne. This was the northern border of the Durham Palatinate as far as its confluence with the Stanley Burn, which carried the boundary line south-westward to join the course of the Derwent, and so on to the head waters of the Tees. The road passed through the Tees and Wear lowland, skirting the East Durham plateau, where villages rather than hamlets and scattered farmsteads (as in the upland) were the rule, and where until the extensive enclosures of the earlier seventeenth century the large open fields with their mixed husbandry, with crops of wheat as well as rye, would have reminded the traveller of the kind of countryside and agriculture which prevailed further south in the Yorkshire plain and midlands.[1] The only one of these visitors from the south who penetrated into the remoter and wilder western parts of Durham seems to have been the antiquarian and topographer John Leland, who journeyed through the Palatinate sometime between 1535 and 1543. He made his way up Weardale at least as far as Saint John's Chapel, noting that the area was still largely forest, which also persisted around Bishop Auckland; and that upper Weardale was still a haunt of the red deer. Teesdale similarly was dominated by the royal forest of Marwood, which extended far up the dale, just as the Bishop's Roughside Forest covered much of Derwentdale.[2] Human settlement however was already extensive in this upland forested area, and Leland noted that although Weardale was not fertile in corn, there was fine grass 'in the dale self where the ryver passith',[3] so that the area, like Teesdale and Derwentdale, was mainly one of pastoral farming. Here scattered farmsteads and isolated home-steads gave a different style to society from that of the lowland, with the kinship group centred on the farmstead hearth pro-viding the strongest social tie. The market towns (Stanhope, Wolsingham, or Barnard Castle) were the only considerable nucleated settlements, a state of affairs which contrasted with the settled manorial village communities of the plain and plat-eau. The upland farms grew meagre crops of oats and barley,

---

[1] See *Ag. Hist.*, pp. 16–28 for the contrasting upland and lowland environments of the north-east and north-west.

[2] *Leland*, i.70–1, 77–8.   [3] Ibid., p. 71.

insufficient to provide adequate reserves against dearth. But the
acreage of meadow and pasture often exceeded that of arable,
and the main emphasis in the economy was on cattle-breeding
(the stock being sold for fattening in the lowland and further
south), and sheep-raising. Throughout the period this pastoral
agriculture continued to encroach on the forest. In Weardale by
1598 cattle had occupied the frith at Burnhope, which had
previously fed 40 red deer, 'besides many others which haunted
in the sundry hopes and pastures within the said Forest'.
Similarly the grazings of Stanhope had been taken over by
horses, and the number of deer in the park had fallen from
200 to 40. By 1700 the forest had given way to pasture and
moorland.[1]

The upland farming economy afforded only a precarious
living to those who depended on it, particularly in view of a
growing population which pressed against scarce resources.
The margin of reserves was too narrow to tide the upland communities over recurring wet summers and bad harvests. In such
circumstances no available asset was likely to be neglected, and
the rise of the lead-mining industry of Teesdale, Weardale, and
Derwentdale was made possible by the surplus human, as well
as mineral, resources of the upland.[2] Coalmining, on the other
hand, was more a feature of the lowland, establishing itself along
the Tyne at such centres as Gateshead and Whickham, as well
as in the Wear valley downstream from Chester-le-Street towards Sunderland. Both rivers developed as commercial high-
ways on which plied the fleets of 'keels' which carried the coal
downstream from the collieries, with their riverside 'staithes'
or wharfs, to the harbours at Newcastle and Sunderland. In
the reign of Charles I the number of keels which plied on the
Tyne was estimated at between 200 and 300, with a very much
smaller fleet on the Wear, which as late as the early eighteenth
century employed no more than between 100 and 200 of these
vessels.[3] Coalmining, with such other and partly related
activities as the manufacture of sea-salt and quarrying, were
already by the early seventeenth century creating a new style
of landscape at the mouths and along the banks of the Tyne
and Wear. 'Here at Shields', wrote Sir William Brereton in

---

[1] *Ag. Hist.*, pp. 21–5; Church Comm. Durh. MS. 277863, Survey of Stanhope.
[2] See Raistrick, pp. 51 ff.   [3] Nef, i. 389.

---

1.   *The Durham Upland:* the high moors of Weardale from Cowshill ▶

2(a). *The Durham lowland:* Egglescliffe

2(b). *The Durham lowland:* Heighington

1635, 'are the vastest saltworkes I have seen . . . by reason of the conveniencye of coal and the cheapness thereof . . . here is such a cloude of smoake, as amongst these workes you cannot see to walke. . . .'[1] At the great coal-producing manor of Whickham the open fields of the traditional agrarian order were already pitted with mine-shafts, the arable pasture and meadow criss-crossed with wayleaves from the pits to the river, and the crops spoilt by coal-dust, much to the detriment of the tenants' husbandry.[2] In this community it seems that the majority were householders or mere inhabitants with little or no land in the manorial fields, occupied as pitmen or hauliers, keelmen or lodging-house keepers. Mining or industrial villages of this kind multiplied particularly in the Tyne valley in the course of the seventeenth century.

PLAGUE AND POPULATION

In the regrettable absence of an adequate study of the excellent Durham series of parish registers, any discussion of the demography of the period can only be a matter of rough estimates, round figures, and general impressions. Such scraps of information as are available seem to point to a perceptible upward demographic trend. For example, in 1569 a general muster was held of all the inhabitants of the Palatinate between the ages of 16 and 60, a routine resorted to from time to time to establish the numerical strength and degree of military preparedness of the region. The total of the muster was 7,773, and using a multiplier of four this gives a population of just over 30,000. The corresponding figures for the general muster of 1615 are 8,320 and 33,280, showing a modest increase in spite of the famine and plague crises of the 1590s with their many casualties.[3] Other scraps of information also suggest an upward trend. For example, the growth in the number of tenancies in many places on the bishop of Durham's estates between 1588, when the estates were surveyed, and the parliamentary surveys made in 1647; while the many warrants granted by the Bishop's officers authorizing tenants to make

---

[1] Brereton, *Diaries II*, p. 18.
[2] Church Comm., Durh., MSS. 244227, 244229. See also below, p. 96.
[3] P.R.O., S.P.12/51/14; Sur. *Hist.*, i. cxxxvii–cxxxviii.

intakes from moors and forests also point to a mounting pressure of population against the cultivable land available.

The main counteracting factor to population growth was provided by the recurring crises of plague recorded in the region throughout the period, the onset of plague being often preceded by a period of high food prices carrying the undernourishment of the poor to the point where resistance to the onset of infectious disease was reduced on a mass scale. The first such crisis of which details are available was the catastrophic visitation of 1520–2, whose severity was no doubt in part due to the extraordinary coincidence of three bad harvests in succession during the years 1519, 1520, and 1521, bringing a protracted dearth which eased the course of the epidemic. According to William Frankleyn, archdeacon of Durham, writing in September 1522, more than 4,000 persons had been struck down by the plague in the Palatinate during the previous two years, 3,000 of them in Durham city and in Darlington. As a result of this 'great death' the mobilization of the bishopric to meet the threatened Scottish invasion of the duke of Albany was severely hampered, armour and weapons being immobilized in infected dwellings 'with which no one will meddle'. 'Most of those who should have been the chief captains' were dead, the plague having struck down the heads of some half-dozen leading Durham families.[1]

Unless Frankleyn exaggerated the number of casualties (and he may have done so to justify his difficulties in raising troops) no subsequent sixteenth-century onset of plague quite equalled the catastrophic outbreak of 1522. Perhaps that of 1597–8 comes closest to the latter in severity, following as it did on a protracted four years' dearth which coincided with a European Great Famine. This cut off the imports of Danzig rye through Newcastle, which normally provided the most important source of relief on such occasions. Scattered statistics survive to hint at the extent of the disaster, like the record of 975 deaths in Durham (probably not the full total) and of 340 in Darlington.[2] A crisis of comparable severity did not recur until 1636, when the plague brought fearful casualties to Newcastle, the 5,037 deaths possibly halving the town's population. Less is

---

[1] *L.P. Hen. VIII*, iii.2531; Hoskins, 'Harvest', pp. 28 ff.
[2] Ibid., p. 38; Sykes, i.81–2; Shrewsbury, p. 173.

known about how hard Durham was hit, beyond the 515 dead in Gateshead.[1] Three other documented outbreaks, those of 1545, 1586, and 1623, coincided with or followed on years of dearth. The 1545 outbreak forced the earl of Hertford to pull his troops out of the bishopric into Yorkshire; that of 1586 broke out at Stranton in the Palatinate against a background of high food prices which attest the bad harvest of the previous year. Thereafter it raged in the region of Hartlepool, spreading to Newcastle in 1589 (where 1,727 persons died) and breaking out again in Durham in 1590. The plague of 1623 was less severe, and centred on Newcastle.[2] The terrible years when the plague raged without restraint through whole communities, ravaging countrysides and particularly the towns, were only the spectacular high-points in the history of the disease. It was a permanent smouldering presence which periodically flared up into an epidemic.

Not very much could be done to combat these recurring crisis situations. In a populous town like Newcastle particularly, near-panic conditions tended to prevail once the mortality began to climb beyond a tolerable level. In the crisis of 1589 hundreds of Newcastle townspeople left their homes and took refuge in the towers and platforms of the town walls or in the surrounding fields, and the mayor refused to perform his duties. But as the casualties mounted, the futility of pro-phylactic measures became increasingly obvious, and a mood of resignation developed; death came to be viewed familiarly, almost casually. Some (like widow Alison Lawes of Gateshead in 1571) adopted a mood of religious acceptance, seeing the plague as the occasion when 'I thank God of the saym . . . it shall please Almighty God of his great goodness and mercie to call me and all my children . . . unto his great mercie.' Others were content, without any but conventional expressions of religious feeling, to dispose by will of their possessions, neglecting (until pressure was brought to bear by the priest and their neighbours) even those charitable bequests which might have improved their prospects in the other world they were shortly to enter. For the Puritans, on the other hand,

---

[1] Sykes, i.89; Richardson, p. 27; Howell, pp. 6–8; Shrewsbury, pp. 382–4.
[2] *L.P. Hen. VIII*, xx(2).524; Sykes, i.79, 80, 86; Hoskins, 'Harvest', pp. 45, 46.

visitations of plague were the signs of God's anger at collective sins.[1]

In such circumstances it was usual for the rich to flee from infected places and take refuge in the countryside, like Bishop Matthew, who hastily quitted Durham for his manor at Stockton during the infection of 1597.[2] The authorities expelled immigrants, discouraged travel, and warned ships away from infected ports. A cess was usually levied to assist the sick, who in the case of poor families were moved out to booths on the town moors, or shut up in their houses, where most of them died.[3] But the likeliest prophylactic was to quit the gregarious squalor of the towns for the space and relative isolation of the countryside. The worst ravages of the plague were always felt in urban communities, where the poor were huddled closely together, and where (on the analogy of London) about one-sixth to a quarter of the population might die in a plague year; the countryside, on the other hand, might scarcely be affected at all.[4]

It is probably significant, therefore, from the point of view of that modest but perceptible population increase which we have noted, that the region had no great town, like Newcastle to the north, or York to the south, to offset its predominantly rural character. In the early sixteenth century Leland dismissed the towns of the Palatinate with a sentence or two. He thought that at Durham the town 'is but a small thing' compared with 'the stately close', and all he had to say of Darlington was that it had a stone bridge of three arches and was 'the best market town in the bishoprick, saving Duresme'. He devoted much more attention and space to describing the cathedral and its close, and the castles at Durham, Raby, Brancepeth, and Barnard Castle, than to the urban centres. It is plain that he regarded the former, rather than the latter, as the significant centres of the region.[5] At the end of the seventeenth century, when Celia Fiennes rode through Durham, she

---

[1] Welford, iii.56; *Wills & Inv.*, i.326, 351; John Fenwick, *Christ ruling in the Midst of his Enemies*, quoted in Richardson, p. 27.

[2] Sykes, i.82.

[3] Welford, ii.385, 486, 514; Sykes, i.80, 101. These measures were probably modelled on those of London which were codified and published by the Privy Council for general use. See Wilson, *Plague*, pp. 14 ff.

[4] Wrigley, pp. 96–7.   [5] Leland, i.74, 69.

paid more attention to the city, calling it 'the noblest' she had yet seen, with 'cleane and pleasant buildings, streetes large, well pitch'd'. But Darlington was still only 'a little market town', although she noted that the market was a large one.[1] Probably even by 1700 none of the Durham towns, including the city itself, had a population of much more than 3,000. The most spectacular urban development of the century had been the rise of Sunderland from an insignificant fishing settlement to be the port of the Wear valley coal industry and the centre for the local quarrying and salt-producing enterprises. Nevertheless by 1681 the population was no more than 2,490.[2] In spite of the occasional industrial settlement the Palatinate remained a region of fields and moorlands, of villages, hamlets, and lonely farmsteads.

THE DOMESTIC LANDSCAPE: HOUSES AND HABITATIONS

As Leland entered the third court at Raby, he noted that this was 'the heart of the castel'. Here he inspected the hall, which was 'large and stately', together with the 'houses of office', i.e. the kitchen and other service rooms. He saw too the great chamber, 'exceeding large', which had in its original conception been an impressive room, open to the roof, adorned with windows of coloured glass depicting the pedigree of the Nevilles. It was in these great public apartments, the setting for the communal meals of the castle, that the solidarity of such a great household of officers and servants as that of the earl of Westmorland, with its 'affinity' of gentry families, received visible, ceremonial expression. The client gentry dined with the superior officers and the earl at the high table, or else in the more intimate and exclusive setting of the great chamber; servants and lowlier dependents occupied the benches in the body of the hall. The towers of the outer courts (at Brancepeth and Barnard Castle, as well as Raby) provided the 'lodgings', i.e. the sleeping accommodation, chambers and stabling which were the complement of the public rooms. But by the time Leland made his visit to Raby, the gregarious pattern of life, centred on hall and great chamber, which the great lords had been accustomed to live out in the midst of their dependents, had already been modified with a view to greater privacy and

[1] Fiennes, pp. 181, 182.   [2] Hutch., ii.525.

comfort for the lord and his family. The topographer took note
that the great chamber had been divided into two or three
smaller rooms, and that the painted glass of the Neville pedigree had been taken down and clear windows put in its place.[1]

The great castles of the region afforded the most elaborate
domestic environment available during the period, one in
which many different kinds of specialized rooms and accommodation were assembled in the characteristic quadrangular
plan of several conjoined courtyards. In this way architectural
expression was given to the needs of the communities of servants
and followers which depended on the great aristocratic houses.
The farmhouse, on the other hand, whether the dwelling of
the yeoman or minor gentleman, or of the more humble
husbandman, was the setting for a very different style of living,
being planned to provide shelter and storage for family, livestock, implements, and stores, rather than accommodation for
a numerous clientele of servants and dependents. But in the
farmhouse too, as in the castles and seats of the rich upper
gentry, the same development asserts itself. The emphasis on
the hall (or 'hall-house') as a single large all-purpose apartment, the gregarious centre around which most domestic
activities circulated, declines. Instead a trend asserts itself
towards a greater compartmentalization of the domestic space
into separate rooms used for specialized purposes, making for
greater privacy and the more efficient organization of domestic
and farming routines. Even as late as the end of the sixteenth
century the primitive 'hall-house', with its undifferentiated
inner space still survived, as in the case of the grange at
Haswell, which stood in 1570 side by side with a later house of
several specialized rooms (probably built by the coal-owning
Newcastle Anderson family, which had recently settled there)
but which itself consisted simply of a hall-house and barn.[2] Or
there is the instance of the affluent Shincliffe yeoman John
Carter, whose house in 1590 had only two parts, the hall-house
and the backhouse. The latter was a service room, but of no
defined use beyond that of an all-purpose storage area, perhaps
because in this style of dwelling the backhouse had originally
provided shelter for cattle, and might still be used for this purpose in a specially hard winter.[3]

[1] Leland, i.75.   [2] *Wills & Inv.*, i. pp. 335 ff.   [3] Barley, p. 120.

A common (and perhaps the earliest) development of the hall-house was towards the kind of dwelling in which the hall remained as an undifferentiated domestic area in which food was stored and cooked, and in which the household was warmed and fed. But side by side with it (or above it) separate rooms were provided known as 'chambers' or 'parlours' which seem to have been used primarily as sleeping accommodation. Houses of this sort persisted until the end of the century amongst the more conservative or less well-off even of the gentry. The home of Nicholas Blakiston at Norton, for example, conformed in 1562 to this type, and consisted simply of a hall and chamber, with apparently no kitchen or storage rooms. The inventory to the will of Bartholomew Lilburne, great-grandfather of the Leveller, John, suggests a similarly simple house-plan. Like that of Richard Conyers in Gilesgate parish, Durham, it mentions separate chambers, but no differentiated kitchen facilities. An urban variant of the type was the house of William Walton, a draper, at Durham. This consisted of a hall-house, a parlour and chamber, and the shop from which Walton plied his trade.[1] Where such dwellings, as in the case of the gentry and yeomen, sheltered relatively large households, a still highly socialized style of living is suggested, centred on the hall, perhaps still with an open hearth, with family and servants inevitably brought into close proximity with each other.

But in the houses of the richer and more sophisticated gentry, merchants, and yeomen, the process of differentiation in rooms and their uses had been carried much further. A common development was the provision of a separate kitchen and storage rooms (pantry and buttery, for dry and wet stores respectively, being the most common) on the far side of a cross passage through the house which divided them from the hall; and it may have been at this stage that a fireplace and flue against the passage wall displaced the traditional central and open hearth. By the turn of the seventeenth century these arrangements had become general amongst the upper classes, and the standard plan for the houses of the gentry and those near to them in wealth and status. As such they were to be found at Burn Hall, at Lambton, at the Hedworth house at Harraton, at Crook Hall near Durham, at the Claxton house at

[1] *Wills & Inv.*, i.205, 193, 253. *Wills & Inv.*, ii.221.

Old Park, to take only a few examples.[1] Other developments in
the specialized use of domestic space were also to be found in
houses of this sort, particularly the provision of defined accommodation for servants, which set the latter apart from the family,
in their own storey or wing. Thus as early as 1558 the parsonage
at Sedgefield had its 'hinds' house' and its 'wardwife house',
and in 1563 there was a 'maidens' chamber' in the Hutton
house at Walworth. In the 1570s we encounter the 'servants'
chambers' at the house of the prosperous farmer of Church
lands Leonard Temperley at Sacriston Heugh, at the Bellasis
house at Morton, and in many other such dwellings.[2] As the
servants were increasingly relegated to the service rooms and
their own quarters, so the hall-space tended to atrophy, the
family taking meals in the more private and comfortable setting
of a dining room, the hall becoming the servants' mess, or a store
room, or simply an impressive entrance chamber to the house.
In the latter case the fireplace was often given a carved over-
mantel displaying the family arms. These arrangements were
to be found at the house of the Brickwell family, farmers of the
lands of the deanery at Darlington, who had probably brought
relatively advanced ideas of domestic comfort with them from
the south. Here there was a 'dining parlour', furnished with
table, six stools, two chairs, and a side-board. It is unlikely that
the family often abandoned this comfortable apartment for
the hall, with its long table and settle, and the old chest and
two spinning wheels which were its only other contents.[3]
Further developments in the progression from gregariousness
to privacy were the provision of special accommodation for
children (the Parkinson house at Beaumont Hill had a nursery
as early as 1567)[4] and for individuals. The latter no doubt first
made its appearance in parsonages, where the 'study' was a
usual feature. But apartments set apart for individual use are
also to be encountered in lay houses, particularly the larger
and grander ones, in the course of the period. Thus Lambton
had its 'lord's chamber', and Harraton 'my lady's chamber'
and 'Brian's chamber'; and Henry Brickwell at Darlington
had 'his own chamber', with its hangings, its little round table
and two green chairs, its chests, a candlestick, and in one cor-

---

[1] Ibid., i.152, 252, 280, 417.   [2] Ibid., i.160, 209, 420; ii.315.
[3] Ibid., ii.168.   [4] Ibid., i.271.

ner a halberd and battle-axe—an intimate and personalized setting.[1]

It is this trend towards greater privacy and a closer intimacy that the domestic architecture of the period most significantly expresses. With the servants and their affairs less closely entwined with those of the family, the latter was increasingly turned in on its own inner life, preoccupied with the flow of relatives and friends for whose use each house needed an ample provision of guest-chambers. Externally too by the seventeenth century the houses of the gentry tended increasingly to display a decent symmetry and orderliness, contrasting in this respect with the older type of hall, an example of which once survived at Holmside, originally the seat of the Tempests who had thrown away their estates and future in the Rising of 1569. Of this house Surtees observed[2] early in the nineteenth century that it 'belonged to a class of mansion inferior to the peel or castle, yet built with a view to defence. Part of the old courtyard is remaining; the Chapel forms the north side. . . . The original lights of the Hall are narrow, strongly guarded with mullions and bars, . . . it now presents a confused mass of buildings of many dates.' The inconvenience of such a 'confused mass' of buildings, the result of many additions and much adaptation, must have been behind the complete rebuilding of so many gentry houses which took place during the half-century before the Civil War. The rambling assemblages of rooms and chambers inherited from a previous age were replaced by stone houses with symmetrical fronts and mullioned windows, giving more complete and effective expression to the new styles of domesticity. Typical of these was Horden Hall, built for the Conyers family about 1600. This had a symmetrical north front and a porch with coupled Tuscan columns. Above this a seven-light window. The main entrance gave on to a hall dominated by a heavy oak mantel, with busts, foliage, and the arms of Claxton and Conyers. The main staircase was also an impressive feature of carved oak, decorated with figures and tracery. The ground floor presumably housed the parlours and service rooms, with the bed-chambers above, and servants' accommodation in the gables.[3] These symmetrical and orderly

[1] Ibid., i.281; ii.62, 168.   [2] Sur. *Hist. Durh.*, ii.324.
[3] Pevsner, p. 169; Sur. *Hist. Durh.*, i.24.

arrangements were reproduced with suitable modification but in the same idiom, and with the same novel humanist touches in the pillared classical entrance-ways, at the new halls of Gibside, Gainford, Headlam, Washington, West Auckland, and elsewhere.

Of a different order of things was the great house (the only one of its kind put up in the region) built for the Jenison family at Walworth in 1600, and paid for out of the administrative fortune made by an auditor of Ireland of Newcastle merchant connection. The continued pressure of traditional values (now given a romanticized and nostalgic architectural expression) is suggested by the design of this house which expresses the persisting notion that a castle is the appropriate kind of dwelling for the wealthy and prestigious. Walworth was given a front of three storeys with thick semi-circular angle towers, producing an impressive castellated effect. But the house was remote from the world of Raby, Brancepeth, Lumley, or Hylton, and had nothing to do with feudal connections and affinities. More expressive of the background of the Jenisons was the spectacular classical porch, related to but much more splendid than its counterpart at Horden. It rose in three superimposed orders of coupled columns, Tuscan, Ionic, and Corinthian. This stood at the far end of an entrance court originally flanked by two-storeyed wings, with two-storeyed bay windows at their ends, which may perhaps have contained the 'galleries' which were so often the mark of the new-style 'courtier' great houses. Stained glass windows characteristically displayed the arms of the Jenison patrons, including those of the Cecils and Queen Elizabeth.[1] Houses of this kind effectively symbolized the drastic changes still working themselves out in the composition and way of life of the gentry class.

[1] Pevsner, p. 235; Sur. *Hist. Durh.*, iii.316n; Hutch. iii.208. John Smythson, son of the famous Elizabethan architect Robert Smythson, designed the Jacobean 'castles' at Slingsby, Yorks., and Ogle, Northumberland, and may have had a hand in designing Gainford Hall for the Cradock family. See Girouard, pp. 143–4, 144n. Could he also have been responsible for Walworth?

PART I

The Sixteenth Century
1500–1570

I

SOCIETY: THE INHERITED PATTERN

THE SOCIAL FOUNDATION: FAMILY TYPES AND VARIANTS

THEN as now society was founded on the family, and in many and important ways the small, intimate family world projected basic symbols and standards reflected back from the wider whole of society, the state, and the Church. The magistrate, the king, and God himself were seen in the image of a father, to be feared as well as loved, and who 'chasteneth his children' as well as caring for them. For the emphasis in family life was patriarchal. It was on the father, its head and representative, that the persistence and viability of the family institution rested. But also on the stability of the monogamous marriage, in which the wife was the necessary, but also subordinate, partner. Opinion, morality, and legal sanctions combined to enforce the cohesion of the family, through which alone skills, values, and possessions could be transmitted from one generation to the next. The family was also the circle within which what was most deeply felt in the affective life of the time was played out. No bonds were stronger than those between husband and wife, parents and children, just as the bitterest feuds could arise from family quarrels. Much of the social life of the period revolved around family reunions of aunts, uncles, cousins, and grandparents, held particularly at the critical points of family history, joyous or mournful; as when children were born and baptized, marriages celebrated, or the dead buried.[1]

Most of these features of the family were a part of the social inheritance, and at least as far as the lowland is concerned, family organization in sixteenth-century Durham seems much what it had been in the 'champion' England of the thirteenth

---

[1] On the family in the early modern period (mainly the seventeenth century), see *Filmer*, intro.; Hill, *Society*, pp. 443 ff.; Laslett, chs. 1 and 4; Macfarlane, particularly pts. II and III; Thirsk.

century, as described by Homans.[1] In the case of Durham however the documentation is more ample, and something can be said about other kinds of family than that of the 'husbandman' or substantial tenant who dominates Homans's picture. For example the family situation of John Copland of Witton Gilbert, who made his will[2] in 1564, takes us at once into a world inferior to that of the husbandman. Copland gave himself no title or designation, as it was usual to do in wills, not even the lowest of all, that of 'husbandman'. The reason is plain enough: he had no claim to land, not even to an unexpired lease or tenancy at will, which he could transmit to an heir, except for 'a ridge' (i.e. a single strip of ground in the open fields) sown with wheat 'in Northumberland'. His twenty sheep and two cows were probably depastured on the common; or perhaps he rented a plot of ground from some prosperous farmer for whom he worked as a labourer. Copland's status seems to have been that of a labourer-smallholder, and his substance was meagre. When his goods were valued after his death the total sum they would raise after debts had been paid was only £3 13s. 2d.

As far as his family was concerned, he was a widower with two sons, John and Thomas, the former with four daughters, the latter with one. An interesting feature of his relations with his children is that he placed no particular emphasis on the eldest son; and this although primogeniture was universal amongst the peasantry of the lowland (as well as amongst the gentry) where there was land to be transmitted. Copland however treated his sons more or less equally. John got ten sheep, a cow, and a large brass pot; Thomas also got ten sheep and a cow, but since he received only a small brass pot, the ridge of sown wheat went to him as well. A pewter dish was left to each of five granddaughters. Neither son appears to have lived with his father, as was usual in husbandman or yeoman families, where it was customary for the ageing father to hand over the management of the family farm to the heir, and withdraw to a restricted part of the homestead, most of which was then occupied by the son and his family. John Copland's debts included payment for attendance during his last ill-

---

[1] Homans, Bk. ii.
[2] *Wills & Inv.*, i.224, where Copland is spelt 'Coplane'.

ness, which suggests, in the case of a man of such modest circumstances, that he died alone. Perhaps he was a newcomer to Witton Gilbert, and his own kin were in Northumberland, where his sown ridge of wheat lay. Like him, his sons had moved elsewhere, since their father could offer little to them at home. Probably Copland depended for help when it was needed more on his neighbours than his family. One of these, Peter Hird, with the parish priest and son John, witnessed his will. But the circle of neighbours also emerges in the list of debts he owed or which were owing to him, which in this setting were unlikely to have been usurious but represented rather exchanges of aid, trust, and obligation. Thus the dead man owed Robert Dobson of Shiplaw 8*s.*, and his son Thomas 5*s.*; Robert Watson and Robert Hall each owed him 1*s.*

This family was remarkably modern, in the sense that, like the typical family today, it was both nuclear (not much wider than the parent–child relationship) and probably also mobile. There is no awareness of the extended family of uncles, aunts, and cousins, both of the father's and mother's kin, which formed a strongly cohesive group, as will be seen, in some of the social contexts of the day. A good many other wills of the period from this social level echo the characteristics of John Copland's family,[1] and the mobility, for example, emerges clearly in the case of William Young, a smallholder at Sedgefield, who left all his goods (of much the same value as Copland's) 'unto my sonne Ralph Young, if he returne to Sedgefield anytime within the space of seven years'.[2] Such families, particularly if they were dispersed, could have had few surplus resources available to invest in the family visits and hospitality without which it was difficult to maintain the sense of unity of a wide group of kin. It is likely indeed that below this kind of level in the social scale family ties became increasingly relaxed, and that the really poor could hope for little from relatives in crises of want and sickness, and in old age. Many entries in parish registers attest to the loneliness and anonymity in which

[1] See e.g. Prob. MSS., Will of Thomas Arkyndal, 1499; Will of Lancelot Appleby, labourer, 1568; Will of Thomas Shafto, 1548 (*Wills & Inv.*, i.129); Will of John Hilton, 1566 (ibid., p. 263); Will of John Bancks, labouring man, 1542. See also *Ag. Hist.*, pp. 455–6.

[2] Prob. MSS., Will of William Young, 1613; *Wills & Inv.*, iv.80.

the really poor died, like the boy John 'a child from the [salt]
Pans, forsworne of his father, forsaken of his mother', who
was buried at Monkwearmouth on 13 December 1621; or
the unknown old man 'travellinge for his [poor] relief' who
was picked up dead in the street of Witton-le-Wear in April
1597.[1]

As we ascend the social scale to the husbandmen, richer
farmers, and yeomen, the same emphasis on the nuclear family
recurs, but with a number of differences. In the first place such
men were tenants or freeholders with a claim to a farm holding
and the land going with it, which could be transmitted to an
heir, even if this was no more than a claim on the good will of
a landlord for the renewal of a tenancy at will. The land in this
sense usually went to the eldest son, with the remainder of the
father's goods divided amongst all the children, daughters'
shares being regarded as their marriage portion. Thus the heir
probably enjoyed some advantage over his brothers, although
the latter might well receive enough by way of farm stock and
implements to set up in tenancies of their own. Rarely, however, at this social level, is the extended family given any part
in these arrangements, even as executors, witnesses, or supervisors of the will. Such legacies as are made to brothers,
nephews, or remoter relatives of the testator tend to be no more
than small tokens of affection and remembrance. It is the circle
of neighbours, rather than the kinship group, on whom
families of this sort tended to rely for external support when this
was needed, and from these a testator would choose two or
three often designated as 'trusty friends', 'good friends', or
'gossips'. These were appointed as 'supervisors' to see to the
implementation of the terms of the will, and to watch over the
interests of the wife and children.[2] Sometimes relationships of
this kind, based on neighbourhood and friendship, were supplemented by the spiritual kinship involved in god-parenthood.
Thus a prosperous husbandman of Norton, William Watson,
whose will was probably made in the 1560s, required 'my
trustie frendes Anthony Hoton John Robson and Roland
Goteard to be supervisors of this my will to see all my goods
and catalles bestowed as they thincke good for the upbringing

---

[1] *Chronicon*, pp. 88, 110.
[2] e.g. *Wills & Inv.*, i.127, 188, 189, 285; iv.116, 204.

3. *Raby Castle*: seat of the Nevilles

4. *Hylton Castle*: seat of the Hilton family

and welthe of my children'. He also left tokens to Simon Robson and William Goteard, perhaps sons of two of his supervisors, who were also his godsons.[1]

It seems as though families of this kind had sufficient resources to stand on their own feet, and that much investment in cultivating a wider kinship group than the nuclear family was not thought necessary, at least as long as a son survived to take over the management of the holding when the powers of the family head declined. The family resources were devoted to settling the children in callings or (in the case of daughters) marriages more or less on the same social level as that of the father; and in the majority of cases everything available was needed for this purpose, leaving little surplus to be disposed of elsewhere. Most families of this standing, moreover, were able to afford one or more servants, the number rising with the degree of prosperity enjoyed, and these provided a framework of support which poorer families could only hope to obtain from kin or neighbours. Servants were incorporated in the family, being housed, fed, and clothed, as well as paid wages, in return for their 'fidelity' and 'service'; and the developed Puritan (and Catholic) morality of the post-Reformation period required the householder to treat them as he would his children, and be responsible for their moral and spiritual, as well as material, welfare.[2] Thus servants also took their place in the structure of bequests made by testators, and sometimes received (in the case of the more prosperous families) substantial legacies amounting to half a year's wages, or perhaps a house or lease.[3] But such legacies were usually made conditional upon some such formula as 'provided he ... continue dutiful to my wife, and be my servante at my death', or 'if she staye with me till God call me', suggesting that in such cases the testator relied as much or more on servants than on children for care in the final stages of life, and for support for the bereaved widow.[4]

What has just been said about the families of smallholders, husbandmen, and substantial yeoman farmers relates to the Durham lowland, the countryside of the plain and coastal plateau, with their nucleated village communities. In the upland

---

[1] *Wills & Inv.*, i.189.   [2] See Hill, *Society*, ch. 13.
[3] e.g. *Wills & Inv.*, i.155, 176, 178, 228; ii.98, 293.
[4] *Wills & Inv.*, iv.200–1.

of Teesdale and Weardale, however, significant differences in family structure occur from the types so far encountered. One notices, for example, the many relatives, some of them distant, who as late as 1637 benefited from the will of Charles Bainbridge of Hardgill in the parish of Middleton-in-Teesdale.[1] His heir was his nephew, who succeeded to the holding. But there were substantial legacies to his brothers and sisters, to their children, and even to his great-nephews and great-nieces. In the same way Edmund Wilson of Loning Head in Teesdale bequeathed his land in 1600 to his grandson, but left money and stock not only to his daughter, but also to his nephews and nieces.[2] Weardale wills show a similar tendency for testators to leave a substantial part of their goods to a much wider group of kin than the nuclear family, even though the tenement usually (but not necessarily) went to a single heir.[3] It is notable too that in these upland families 'neighbours' seem to count for little, and only rarely do they appear in wills as legatees, executors, or supervisors; the latter were usually chosen from the family. Also in contrast to the lowland is the rarity with which servants appear in wills, and when they do, their names suggest that they were also relatives. Relatives too cared for the aged, if there were no children to do this. Robert Wilson of Middleton-in-Teesdale had his sister and nephew living with him when he made his will in 1623; and Edmund Bainbridge of the same place, some quarter of a century before, had given his goods and tenement to his son-in-law in return for maintenance for himself and his wife in their old age.[4]

These strong family ties in the upland, and the persisting cohesiveness of the extended kinship group, owed something to the extensive wastes and moors of Teesdale and Weardale. There younger sons could depasture their cattle and sheep, and also supplement their income from mining, so they did not need to emigrate. It was a frugal and precarious existence, but may have provided the compensation of a life spent in a community bound together by ties of familiarity, trust, and affection. As a result the kinship groups were not broken up by the mobility of their members, for although the able and ambitious might (and did) go away in search for advancement,

[1] Ibid., p. 273.   [2] *Wills & Inv.*, iii.179.
[3] e.g. *Wills & Inv.*, iv.45, 211; i.284.   [4] Ibid., iv.170; iii.183.

the majority were content to stay where they were. In other parts of the north upland communities of this kind, wealthy in wastes and commons which could sustain a large smallholder class, were characterized by partible forms of inheritance, under which the family land, as well as its goods, was divided amongst all the sons, instead of going only to the eldest. Partible inheritance was not the rule, during the sixteenth century or later, in Teesdale and Weardale, as it was further south in Swaledale, Garsdale, and Dentdale, and on the Border in Redesdale.[1] But the custom of the Forest of Weardale made provision for it as an alternative to primogeniture, for under this custom a younger son might succeed to the family holding or part of it; and the family farm could also be let as a whole or in part to 'under-settlers', or sub-tenants.[2] The way was open therefore for the land to be divided amongst the sons if there were enough of it, and also for the association of members of the family with the farm as under-settlers. Just as elsewhere in the Pennine upland too, so in Weardale the strength of the kinship bond made the heads of the prominent families the repositories of political authority in the dale; the Fetherstonhaughs, for example, establishing themselves in office under the Bishop (who was lord of Weardale) as keepers of Weardale Forest, the Emersons as bailiffs of Stanhope, and the Trotters as keepers of Stanhope Park. Similarly in Teesdale, Bainbridges of Middleton acted as keepers of Teesdale Forest.[3] Men of this sort mobilized and led their communities to confront any military threat from without, like the famous raid into Weardale in 1569 of Border reivers (celebrated in the ballad of 'Rookhope Ryde'); or to meet attempts by the lord or his agents to overthrow the 'custom' which guaranteed the rights of tenants in their holdings, and protected them against eviction or increased rents.

Family groupings of the upland kind therefore gave these communities a strength and unity which helped to protect them from external aggression, and enabled them to mobilize and strike back at external foes. Family solidarity however was valued not only in the geographical upland of the Durham

---

[1] See *Ag. Hist.*, pp. 9–10, 23–5; Cooper, *Muker.*, p. 17.
[2] Church Comm., Durh., MS. 277863, Survey of Stanhope, fo. 37.
[3] Ibid., fo. 10.

dales, but also in the social upland of the rich gentry. For in the competitive world of the governing class, family cohesion and family alliances were assets without which success in the scramble for office, privilege, and land was unlikely. In these circles too, even after the decline of the old-fashioned gregarious household routines, and the rise of the new emphasis on privacy, family visiting and hospitality were amongst the satisfactions of the gentry way of life, on which resources were freely lavished.[1] The extended family was therefore favoured by the rich, to an extent not possible for the poor, the husbandman, or those who were rising in the social scale. An example of such a family is that of Robert Claxton of Old Park, head of an ancient gentry house, who in his will made in 1587 remembered four grandchildren, two brothers-in-law, and nine cousins, as well as his three sons and six daughters.[2] The rich bachelor, Richard Bellasis of Morton, having no children of his own, made legacies to sixteen nephews and nieces, as well as to five cousins and a brother and sister.[3] Primogeniture was of course the rule in these gentry clans, for (in the words of a shrewd interpreter of the gentry way of life) 'If I shall leave my land and living equally divided amongst my children . . . then shall the dignity of my degree, the hope of my house, . . . be quite buried in the bottomles pit of Oblivion.'[4] To ensure the perpetuation of the wealth and prestige of his house the gentleman left the bulk of its resources concentrated in the hands of a single heir. But in the case of the rich there was enough in addition to provide daughters with appropriately sized marriage portions, and younger sons with annuities and leases enabling them to follow a style of life appropriate to their class. Families of this kind, united in loyalty to their 'name', usually (at least in the sixteenth century and as long as the values of the lineage society prevailed) acted together in politics, the wide ramification of their wealth, connections, and influence often making them a formidable force. The Nevilles all rose with the head of their house, the earl of Westmorland, in the 1569 Rising in the North, and shared his ruin. The Claxtons of Old Park, followers of the earl, brought a circle of their relatives by blood and marriage into the same rebellion,

---

[1] See above, p. 15.   [2] *Wills & Inv.*, ii.294.   [3] Ibid., p. 337.
[4] Markham, pp. 108–9.

as a result of which some of them lost their lives. Even when the family head remained in one political camp, and his heir in the other,[1] the impression of family division over political or religious issues is usually illusory, the object being to have a footing in both camps, and so protect family interests whichever side came uppermost. Politics at all levels were based on the family, and ideological causes could rarely prevail over the strong pull of dynastic interest. It was not until the seventeenth century, in the context of the 'civil society', that this began to be less the rule.[2]

By and large the family faced inward, not only as the circle of security and affection (or the area in which fathers and stepmothers tyrannized, and the jealousies of brothers and sisters were fought out) but also as a productive unit. For workshop, farm and even the landed estate were family enterprises, working communities of children, relatives, and servants under a master who was also a father. Work partook of the intimacy and inwardness of the domestic setting. The father, the patriarchal head, alone represented the family community in relation to the wider, formal structures of society and politics. But in order to exercise rights in these structures he had to possess claims to land, even if no more than a lease or a customary tenancy at will; and to exercise authority landed wealth was necessary. Poor husbandmen, labourers, copyholders, and artificers, as William Harrison pointed out in 1577, 'have neither voice nor authority in the commonwealth, but one to be ruled, and not to rule other'.[3] All the way up the social scale there rose a graduated ladder of dominance and subordination, tenants deferring to gentry, poor gentry to rich gentry, gentry to peers, and the latter to the Crown. The harshness liable to inform such relationships, however, might be softened and made more acceptable by the informal contacts which often developed between subordinate families in the scale and a patron

---

[1] There were many instances of such family 'divisions' in the Northern Rising of 1569. Cf. Sir Ralph Sadler's often-quoted comment of 30 Nov. 1569: 'The gentlemen of this country, do show themselves very willing and forwards in this service to the Queenes Majestie; but for all that . . . if the father come to us with x men, his son goeth to the rebels with xx; and therefore, gesse you what trust is to be reposed in such men' (*Memorials*, p. 83).

[2] On the terms 'lineage society' and 'civil society', see below p. 177 ff.

[3] Harrison, p. 118.

of superior social status who extended to the former protection, receiving in return trust, regard, and loyalty. One context in which this kind of relationship can be detected is when a testator appointed a social superior as supervisor of his will, invoking his intervention to assure the rights of wife and children after the death of the family head, and placing their welfare in his hands. Only a minority could appeal to the rich and powerful in this way, and supervisors of this sort were of varying kinds, according to the situation out of which the claims made on them arose.

For obvious reasons, for example, tenants liked to interest their landlord in their children, particularly to ensure that the family tenancy would pass smoothly to the heir.[1] But only the rich husbandman, or else the tenant who had got to know his landlord as a servant, could expect to strike up this special kind of relationship, and so be able to persuade the local squire to act as his supervisor. In the upland on the other hand protectors could be sought amongst the extended kindred, so that Ralph Fetherstonhaugh of Stanhope could call in the head of his family 'John Fetherstonhaugh esquire my kind friend' to see to the well-being of his daughter after his death.[2] The emigration to Newcastle of the able and energetic also provided some Weardale families with prosperous mercantile protectors. William Maddison of Aldergill, Stanhope, made his distant relative Lionel Maddison, a rich Newcastle merchant and alderman, his supervisor.[3] Connections of this kind could also be a useful source of loans, and two Weardale farmers from Brotherley, George Emerson and Richard Watson, benefited in this respect from their kinship with another wealthy Newcastle alderman, Robert Barker, mayor in 1577.[4] Gentlemen on the other hand looked to their masters (if in service), or to more wealthy and influential members of their own class, particularly if kinsmen, to protect the family and to provide sons with careers. Thus Robert Tunstall of Stockton 'gave' his 'boy' in his will to Richard Brackenbury, his wife's uncle, a courtier who was one of the Queen's gentlemen ushers, or else to his godfather Robert Conyers of Sockburn, head of a great

---

[1] e.g. Prob. MS., Will of Thomas Plumpton, 1562; *Wills & Inv.*, i.188, Will of William Watson.
[2] *Wills & Inv.*, iv.45.   [3] Ibid., iii.83.   [4] Ibid., ii.176.

family.[1] Similarly Francis Bainbridge of Wheatley Hill left his younger son Thomas a portion in kind of gold and silver plate and some military equipment, 'whom with his porcion I require my good lord the Busshop of Duresme to take, to whose godlie government I commit him'.[2] Noblemen, with many careers at their disposal in the administrative apparatus of their estates and households, were particularly liable to 'bequests' of this kind on the part of their dependants.[3] Such informal relationships contributed largely to the structure of the aristocratic 'connections' and 'affinities' of the region, and so to the loyalty and willing obedience which the upper gentry or magnates could command from their followers. They were probably more important in politics, for example, than the 'Pavlovian' devotion to their landlords which has been attributed to northern tenants.[4] Sometimes there may also have been the additional bond of godfatherhood, which by confessing spiritual paternity, brought the patron as close as was possible to a family relationship with the child for whom his protection was desired.[5]

THE SOCIAL STRUCTURE

The lack of any considerable town and the meagreness of the urban developments in the region have been matter for comment above. Urban communities were small and subordinate, overshadowed by landed interests; as Durham itself was, for example, by the clergy and lawyers of the cathedral and episcopal establishments. Consequently although there are instances of wealthy merchant-wholesalers at Durham, Darlington, and elsewhere,[6] no powerful and strongly organized urban interest existed which could compare, for example, with the rich and self-confident Newcastle bourgeoisie. But if Durham was not a county of great towns and rich merchants, it did

---

[1] Ibid., p. 104.   [2] Ibid., i.406.

[3] See e.g. ibid., p. 178, Will of Richard Thadye; ibid., p. 280, Will of Katherine, Lady Hedworth; ibid., p. 234, Will of John Hutton; ibid., p. 62, Will of Robert Lambton.

[4] See Stone, *Crisis*, p. 252.

[5] e.g. Robert Tunstall of Stockton, who desired Mr. Conyers of Sockburn 'to be a godfather' to his son after his own death; 'If my wife marie againe, . . . I give him frelie to his godfather'. *Wills & Inv.*, ii.104.

[6] See e.g. the inventory of John Farbeck of Durham, mercer, in *Wills & Inv.*, ii.281, and that of John Johnson of Darlington, ibid., p. 210.

contain well-endowed landed interests and exceptionally large landed estates. It is the persistence of these which accounts for many of the characteristic features of the Durham social structure both during the sixteenth century and later. In the structure of landownership the extensive Church holdings of land stand out with particular prominence. The biggest landowner in the region was the bishop of Durham. Even after Queen Elizabeth had seized considerable portions of the episcopal lands and assets for herself and her courtiers, the Bishop's estates still extended to about four score inhabited places— manors, boroughs, towns, and hamlets—with a rental of some £2,500[1] and a further large income from the fines levied when tenancies changed hands.

The Bishop's closest rival in landed wealth was his own Cathedral, a Benedictine monastery until the dissolution, and subsequently a corporation of canons presided over by a dean. The estates of the Cathedral Dean and Chapter, with lands scattered over more than a hundred places, brought in a rental of over £1,300,[2] not including fines. Next came the leading lay magnate of the region, the earl of Westmorland, whose lord-ships of Brancepeth, Raby, Eggleston, and Winlaton, with his Northumberland and Yorkshire lands, about equalled in in-come those of the Cathedral.[3] Lord Lumley, with just over £850 a year from his lordship of Lumley and manor of Hart in Durham and from Kylton in Yorkshire,[4] was by comparison a less impressive figure. His Durham rental of £600 a year probably puts him much on a par with such local families as the Bowes of Streatlam, the Eures of Witton, the Hiltons of Hylton, and the Conyers of Sockburn, with estates of six to a dozen manors, who together constituted the richest and most influential group in the Durham landed class.

The interests and contacts of these houses, and particularly

---

[1] Church Comm., Durh., MS., Survey of the Bishopric, 1588.

[2] In 1570 the rental of the Dean and Chapter lands in Durham amounted to £1,388; lands in Northumberland brought in a further £31, and tithes an ad-ditional £530. Out of this total the receiver paid in £1,659. See Durh. D. & Ch. MS., Receiver's Roll, 1570.

[3] P.R.O. E164/37, Hall and Humberstone's Survey, 1570. The Neville lands in Durham carried in 1570 a rental of £1,087 a year; the Northumberland estates brought in a further £183, and those in Yorkshire £280.

[4] See Milner, p. 338.

their marriage alliances, extended to Yorkshire, Northumberland, and other northern counties, making them members of the gentry society of the north, with wider horizons than those that Durham could provide.[1] A further half-dozen or so families belonged to the category of which the Claxtons, Tempests, Salvins, Blakistons, and Lambtons may be taken as typical instances.[2] Less wealthy and less widely connected than the Eures and their kind, these were nevertheless established and respected gentry stocks, solidly entrenched in Durham society, if less well known outside it. When it came to issues of politics and religion, however, they were most likely to be found in the role of followers, deferring particularly to the Nevilles, or else to the Bishop, or to the Eures or the Boweses, the two latter influential through their connections with the Court and the service of the Crown.[3] Finally there was the smaller parish gentry, a group which, practically non-existent as such at the beginning of the century, was in process of emerging from the ranks of the rich farmers, yeomen, and merchant-shopkeepers. This small gentry had its importance as the most volatile and mobile element in the society, some of its members building up great fortunes, others soon lapsing from their gentry status. A good instance of the type is William Smith of Esh, whose most valuable single asset was his manor of Stainton, which he farmed himself; less than half of the total income of nearly £100 received from his ancestral estate consisted of rents.[4]

Even that caustic Puritan critic of the nobility, Laurence Humphrey, had to admit that nobles (amongst whom he would have included the upper ranks of the gentry, like the Boweses, Hiltons, and their kind) 'bear the sway in all pryncely courtes, and in manner the pillar and staye of all common weales'.[5] The great families, particularly if like the Lumleys and Eures they held baronial titles, and still more such a great lord as the

---

[1] For these families, see Sur. *Hist. Durh.*, *passim*; Surtees, *Witton*; Foster, *passim*.
[2] See ibid.
[3] The Eures established themselves in the service of the Crown during the reign of Henry VIII, when Sir William Eure became warden of the East and Middle Marches and captain of Berwick, as well as a member of the Council in the North; he was raised to the peerage as Lord Eure of Witton in 1543. Sir Robert Bowes had a similar career during the same reign, becoming a member of the Council in the North as well as warden of the Middle March. The head of the family was steward of the Crown lordship of Barnard Castle.
[4] P.R.O., E137/38, fo. 235v.   [5] Humphrey, fo. 3.

earl of Westmorland, inherited the prescriptive right to rule and command which went with 'lordship'. They therefore enjoyed unquestioned deference both from the gentry and from those better-off strata of the tenantry and husbandmen whose way of life gave them some contact with their betters. Laurence Humphrey was probably right when he particularized the aspects of noble life which 'the common people' most venerated as hawking and the cult of the chase, the glamour of 'mighty power', aristocratic retinues with their 'traynes of horse and servants', and the prestige conferred by 'renowne and fame of auncestry'.[1] It is above all in this setting that we encounter the marks of the lineage society whose defining characteristics will be discussed in the Conclusion to this book. All who were close enough to this world to be aware of its apparent security and ease, its many-sidedness and colourfulness, so different from the monotonous routines and incessant toil which made up the lives of most, longed to identify themselves with it. One way in which this could be achieved was by becoming a servant in the household of a great family, and particularly by entering the ranks of that privileged group of servants known as 'officers', by means of whom the landed magnates managed their estates and collected their revenues.

The earl of Westmorland presided over just such a great household, with many 'offices' at its disposal. He appointed a receiver to collect his revenues, a constable to have charge of each of his castles, a bailiff for each of his lordships, stewards to preside over his courts, and keepers for his parks and forests.[2] Servants of this kind, holding office under a magnate as prestigious as the head of the house of Neville, by that very fact and irrespective of social origin, moved into the world of gentility and aristocratic values which prevailed in the earl's circle. Appointed sometimes for life, sometimes 'at the will' of their master, by letters patent which recited the earl's 'special trust and confidence' in them, such men participated in and exercised the latter's authority, while entering into a special relationship with him. On the earl's side this involved that he should support, protect, and reward his officers, showing towards them the 'magnanimity' which this aristocratic culture saw as the mark of a great lord, and 'good lordship', which was

[1] Ibid. [2] See P.R.O., E164/37, *passim*.

the traditional term for what the relationship implied. In return the officer gave his 'service', which should be characterized above all by 'faithfulness', and which required from him an unqualified and exclusive devotion to his master, and implicit obedience to his commands. Behind such concepts there was a tradition which went back to a remote heroic age in which great lords sustained, rewarded, and honoured a warlike following, in return for the latter's devoted service in battle. Even in the sixteenth century a close relationship persisted in the great households between lords and servants.[1] Henry, earl of Westmorland, who died in 1564,[2] remembered more of his officers and servants in his will than he did relatives. And when his son, Charles the last earl, embarked in 1569 on the desperate venture of the Northern Rising, many of his servants risked their lives and possessions with him.

Office had also its less idealistic side. It was a source of profit, and a ladder of social mobility for tenants to rise into the gentry. Officers were rewarded by the grant of lucrative and often under-rented leases of parks, demesnes, and mills. They handled large cash balances which remained in their hands for considerable periods of time. These might be used in their own business operations or let out on loan at interest. The favours they could offer tenants enabled them to sell their 'good will'.[3] Such were the means by which officers prospered and rose in society. The affluence which could result from an official career is attested by the will of William Lee, receiver-general to the last two earls of Westmorland, who left goods to the value of £433, and leases worth another £300.[4] John Swinburn the rebel, who was steward of the Neville lands in Northumberland, similarly founded a fortune, making extensive purchases of land, bought up mostly in small parcels in Durham, Yorkshire, and Northumberland.[5]

The profits to be made no doubt account for the attraction which office had for the more prosperous husbandmen and yeomen amongst the Neville tenantry, men like Henry Watson, bailiff of Langton, Michael Basse, bailiff of Eggleston, or

[1] For a discussion of these relationships, see James, pp. 6–9.
[2] See *Wills & Inv.*, ii.1.
[3] On this aspect of office, see James, p. 8; *Es. Accnts.*, p. xxxvi.
[4] *Wills & Inv.*, ii.43.
[5] P.R.O., E164/38, fo. 217, Estate of John Swinburn.

Bernard Natrass, bailiff of Staindrop.[1] Gentlemen who were the heads of leading families of the region were in fact comparatively rare amongst the Neville officers. But constables of castles and stewards were usually gentry, and in the 1560s these included representatives of two Durham landed families of first standing.[2] Gentry were more numerous amongst the wider circle of 'friends' who, although not officers, had a place in the counsels of the Neville family, some of them forming a part of the earl of Westmorland's 'following' and armed retinue when the military force of the Palatinate was mustered by the commissioners of array. These included representatives of such established houses as the Salvins of Croxdale, the Lilburnes, and the Claxtons; but also a significant group of 'new' families, still on the fringe of the landed establishment, represented by Richard Hodgson of Lanchester (of Newcastle merchant background), or William Smith of Esh (of yeoman stock, but who had made a lucky match with the heiress of an ancient family). Both were particularly close to the last earl of Westmorland, and played a prominent part in the Rising of 1569.[3]

In the matter of the armed force which the Neville connection could muster, and on which in the last resort the power of the family depended, it was not however solely the gentry who counted. For the support of the gentry 'friends' of the family was reinforced by that of the prosperous upper level of tenantry from which many of the Neville officers were recruited. It was only a small better-off group amongst the tenants which could afford the equipment of a light horseman, and so form part of the mobile well-armed cavalry force which provided a magnate with the most effective means of keeping order in his 'country' or, if necessary, of stirring up trouble for the government. Consequently well-off yeoman and leaseholding families like the Bainbridges, Watsons, and Newbies of Raby, the Wrens, Dowthwaites, and Jacksons of Brancepeth[4] were an essential

---

[1] P.R.O., E164/37.

[2] A Ratcliffe of Newton Hansard was constable of Raby castle, and Ralph Bowes steward of the Yorkshire lordship of Kirkby Moorside.

[3] For the Hodgsons and Smiths, see Sur. *Hist. Durh.*, ii.338, and 319. For the retinue of the earl of Westmorland at the musters of June 1569, see P.R.O., S.P.12/51/14.

[4] These were Neville tenants who appeared at the musters in the earl's retinue equipped as light horsemen.

element in the Neville 'affinity' or 'connection', which the earl of Westmorland exercised through his influence in the region. It is amongst this rural upper-middle class, many of its members well on the way to gentility, that we find most of the 'tenant loyalty' so often insisted on in connection with northern society, as well as regard for 'ancient blood'. These too were the 'substantial husbandmen', well armed and well horsed, who were the backbone, in the region, of the Rising of 1569.

A great aristocratic interest like that of the Nevilles therefore acted as a markedly cohesive and integrating factor over wide areas of the life of the region, bringing together significant gentry groups into the ambit of a common loyalty. It also provided the rural middle class (whose roots penetrated down into the world of the husbandmen and poor) with opportunities to rise in the social scale, and to involve themselves in the affairs of their betters, even in the latter's politics. At the same time the earl's standing at Court, as a prominent peer, linked the concerns of the Durham society to those of the kingdom at large.

From this point of view the Bishop's lands and his household and administrative apparatus were comparable to those of the Nevilles. But there are significant differences arising from the fact that the Bishop was an outsider; and as his office was not hereditary the element of continuity and the appeal of 'ancient blood' were lacking. Since episcopal offices too were usually granted for life, it was often difficult for the Bishop to exercise any effective control over them, particularly if, as was the case earlier in the sixteenth century, the holders were themselves prominent gentry or even peers. The tendency therefore was for the episcopal connection to be dominated and largely controlled by local factions in the region, and so simply to reflect the balance of power amongst the leading families. Strong bishops like Cardinal Wolsey in the reign of Henry VIII could temporarily reverse the trend.[1] But this became increasingly difficult for his successors, whose authority was shaken by the religious changes, and whose Protestantism after 1558 isolated them in a society which was long in developing a specifically Protestant orientation. As a result the Bishop was liable to be isolated in a narrow circle of followers recruited from his own

[1] See below, p. 41 ff.

family or brought in from London, with spasmodic and often ineffective support from some local families like the Tempests, Eures, and Boweses, who were connected with the service of the Crown.

The Bishop's power in the region was therefore less than the extent of his lands and wealth might suggest. In the two great crises of the Pilgrimage of Grace (1536) and the Northern Rising (1569) the then bishops, Tunstall and Pilkington respectively, proved completely unable to control events. They had to take refuge in flight, leaving their castles, lands, and cathedral in the hands of the rebels. Their reinstatement de-depended on the power of the Crown, and not on their own political resources.[1] On the other hand the administrative structure of the bishopric, including as it did the legal bureaucracy[2] of the Palatine courts as well as the estate officials, was much more elaborate and on a larger scale than that of the Nevilles. More opportunities were therefore provided for enrichment and local influence, even if in the Bishop's following there were fewer chances of participation in the excitements of high politics. As usual the superior and more dignified offices went to the upper ranks of the gentry, so that the sheriff, for example, was chosen from a restricted group of ancient families—the Lumleys, Hiltons, Tempests, Boweses, Conyers, and Eures. Earlier in the century gentry of this standing were also to be found amongst the Bishop's master foresters, his stewards, and even in the prosaic offices of coroner and escheator. But the tendency was for these local magnates to be increasingly displaced, except in the shrievalty, by professionals, and particularly by lawyers.[3] These were amongst the mobile elements gradually infiltrating the ranks of the gentry. A good example of the type, if an exceptional one, is Richard Bellasis, a man of modest, probably yeoman origins (in spite of the long pedigree subsequently provided for him). With the support of his London brother, a chancery clerk subsequently prominent in the service of Thomas Cromwell, he became Wolsey's agent in the bishopric and constable of

[1] See below, p. 48, 147.

[2] Apart from a chancellor and attorney-general, this included a clerk of assize, a clerk of the peace, and a clerk of chancery. There were a steward and sub-steward to preside over the Halmote court.

[3] See below, p. 44.

Durham castle. His fortune and that of his brother founded two wealthy landed families, and his great-grandson became a peer.[1] More typical were the sober and industrious lawyers and officers who after a lifetime of service in the Bishop's courts and offices of receipt, established their families in the lower or middle ranks of the gentry. Christopher Chaytor, registrar to Cardinal Wolsey (as bishop of Durham) and to Bishop Tunstall, founded the family which would remain long at Butterby.[2] A receiver-general, Christopher Maire, who served Bishop Pilkington, was ancestor of the Maires of Hunwick.[3] The Thomlinsons, bailiffs of Gateshead, were another family in the episcopal service which rose into the gentry.[4]

It is possible to exaggerate the extent to which the society of the region ought, in the turbulent sixteenth century, to be regarded as an 'armed' society. For when the men of the bishopric were mustered by the Bishop's commissioners in June 1569, a majority of those who attended, just over 4,000 out of the total number of 6,477 were without weapons of any kind.[5] Nevertheless arms defensive and offensive were widely disseminated. Only in the retinues of shire magnates like the earl of Westmorland or Sir George Bowes do we encounter well-equipped forces of the characteristic northern light horse. Bowes only brought 15 of these to the musters, and Westmorland 29, but a much larger number could be mobilized at need, as was to be seen a few months later, during the Rising. Bowes with his 25 arquebusiers and 15 pikemen plainly had the nucleus of an up-to-date force which contrasted with the traditional bowmen and billmen which constituted the great majority of the forces of the bishopric. Over 900 billmen appeared at the musters, with a further 500 who possessed some kind of armour as well as bills; there were nearly 1,000 archers, of whom almost half were armoured.[6] Most of this military equipment was either in the hands of husbandmen and yeomen rated as worth £5–10 a year, who were required both by statute[7] and the terms of their tenures to be armed, or was made available to their servants and tenants by the gentry,

---

[1] Sur. *Hist. Durh.*, i.203; Brydges, vi.23 ff.   [2] Foster, p. 69.
[3] Ibid., p. 226.   [4] Ibid., p. 302.
[5] P.R.O., S.P.12/51/14: Certificate of the General Muster of the inhabitants of the county palatine . . . taken 26 June 1569.
[6] Ibid.   [7] 4 & 5 Ph. & M., c. 2.

who often possessed considerable stores of arms.[1] The unarmed must have been made up of younger men not yet settled in tenancies, as well as the old, the poorer husbandmen, and labourers. Weapons at any rate were widely enough disseminated to make oppressive policies on the part of landlords unwise. If wide rifts had opened between classes, it would not have been easy for the gentry to keep order, particularly if the middling sort of husbandman had become disaffected.

The latter, involved mainly in the society of kin and neighbourhood, and in agrarian routine, usually had little concern with the gentry ethos and environment which often had a strong attraction for the yeomanry. Although there may have been a good deal of envy and dislike of the gentry in the ranks of the commons, there is no indication that the latter received any overt expression. The existing social order seems to have been accepted as natural and immutable, its patriarchal, property-orientated, and authoritarian character in fact harmonizing with much of the peasant's own experience in relation to his family and land-holding. It was in the relationship between landlord and tenant that the latter became most aware of and concerned with the world of the governing class. In this sensitive area the guiding rule, underwritten both by the Church and the Crown, was that landlords should so govern that 'the poor people be not oppressed, but that they may live after their sorts and qualities'.[2] Lords were entitled to the rents and services due to them, without which they could not live as their degree required. But tenants were not to be pressed to the point where their stability and continued existence as a class were threatened, public order endangered, and defence undermined because husbandmen no longer had the resources to meet their military obligations. Pressures of this kind on landlords, representing the considered responsible opinion of the governing class itself, mediated through the Crown and its courts and councils, were brought to bear with particular emphasis on the great Church and aristocratic landlords in Durham. These, as churchmen and noblemen, were particularly close to the Crown, and were expected to treat their tenants in an exemplary fashion. Their obligation to do

[1] As they were required to under 4 & 5 Ph. & M., c. 2.
[2] Instructions to the Council in the North, 1538; see Reid, *Council*, p. 158.

so was emphasized by the duty placed on tenants of the bishopric, from the reign of Henry VII onwards, as a condition on which their land was held, to serve the King against the Scots on the Border when required to do so, at their own costs and charges.[1] Those who oppressed tenants to the point at which the surplus of resources they needed to fulfil their military obligations became endangered, incurred social and governmental disapproval. It is not surprising then that copy-hold of inheritance should establish itself as the predominant, if not the only, tenure on the episcopal estates in the course of the century, with the tenants enjoying, in an inflationary period, stable rents and fines.[2] On the Neville estates, on the other hand, most tenants held by lease for term of years, with twenty-one years as the usual term. There was also a numerous cottager class holding simply 'at the lord's will'.[3] The earl of Westmorland seems to have been a benevolent landlord, however, and the government surveyor of his lands after the 1569 Rising noted of the lordship of Brancepeth, 'The lands . . . are very good . . . and not improved of long tyme past. The tenants hold all by Indenture for term of years, the fermes very good and the tenants wealthy and substantial . . . and have moche land for their rent. . . .'[4] Amongst the tenants of the great estates those of the Dean and Chapter seem to have been the most precariously placed, since most of them held by renewable leases, and had only a very dubious claim to the protection custom conferred, when, from the 1560s onwards, they began to be subjected to pressure to pay increased rents and fines.[5] Some of the Bishop's tenants, particularly in Weardale, were in the same position. Late in the century, as will be seen,[6] these uncertainties in the regime of custom were to lead to conflicts between the two great ecclesiastical landlords and their tenants. By and large, however, the latter benefited from the rule of the great estates, whether clerical or lay, and it is likely that harsh landlords were

---

[1] See *V.C.H. Durh.*, ii. p. 230.

[2] Of the 1,322 tenancies specified in the incomplete episcopal survey of 1588, 105 were freeholds, 156 tenancies by indenture for term of years, 116 tenancies at will for term of years, and 1,061 copyholds.

[3] In the lordship of Brancepeth for example, in 1570 there were 34 tenants by indenture, 63 tenants at will, and 101 tenants for term of years.

[4] P.R.O., E164/37.   [5] See *V.C.H., Durh.*, ii.226–8, 230 ff.

[6] Below, p. 79 ff.

2

POLITICS: BISHOP, CROWN, AND COUNTY COMMUNITY

THE continued existence, throughout the Tudor period, of the Regality of the bishops of Durham, whose core was the lands 'between Tyne and Tees' of the county of Durham and the wapentake of Sadberge,[1] commonly known as the bishopric,' left its mark on politics during these years. But the special tone imparted to the political arrangements of the region by its Palatine status can be over-stressed. There were other palatinates of course in the kingdom, but by the early sixteenth century Durham was the only one still surviving in the possession of a subject. The bishop of Durham was unique in his capacity to exercise, within 'the bishopric', powers which elsewhere were monopolized by the Crown. Throughout the Regality, until 1536, the King's writ did not run, and royal justice was excluded in favour of that dispensed by the Bishop's justices of assize and of the peace, and by his Chancery Court. Parliamentary statutes were obeyed in Durham, although their enforcement there was left to the Bishop; he also negotiated the assessment and collection of parliamentary subsidies within his franchise, although these taxes were not formally binding because Durham was not represented in the House of Commons.[2] The sixteenth century however saw extensive encroachments on the Palatinate's privileges by the Crown, and the Bishop's prerogatives were considerably diminished. But the changes made were more impressive in theory than in practice. The Act of 1536,[3] which transferred the Bishop's criminal jurisdiction to the Crown, with the appointment of justices of assize and of the peace, has

---

[1] The Regality also included the 'shires' of Bedlington and Norham in Northumberland, and the manor of Craik in Yorkshire. In the latter county the Bishop was also lord of Allertonshire and Howdenshire, but here his powers were not as extensive as in Durham and Northumberland.

[2] See Storey, ch. ii.; Lapsley, chs. v, vi, and vii.

[3] 27 Hen. VIII, c. 24; *Statutes*, iii.555.

often been represented as a typical assault by the centralizing Tudor monarchy on the 'feudal' liberties of the Palatinate, now an out-dated 'medieval' survival. But before the Act, as after it, the law which the Durham courts had applied had been the common law applicable to the whole kingdom; and the justices appointed to sit in them were often the judges of the King's Bench and Common Pleas who served the King.[1] There is little indication that Bishop Tunstall (1530–59), whatever second thoughts he may have had in the 1530s about Henry VIII's religious policies, was much concerned to defend his regalian rights. Like the other Tudor bishops of Durham, he was no feudal potentate, but a civil servant and intellectual eager to serve the Crown and reform the Church. He may well have felt himself more constricted by the pressures which could be brought to bear by his own subjects, the greater landowners of the bishopric, than by royal interference. Entrenched in the greater palatine offices, they could make things difficult for the Bishop and his little family and official circle, which was all on which he, as an outsider, could safely rely. The support of the Crown was essential if he was not to become the plaything of the local factions; the fact that after 1536 the royal justice and not merely that of the Bishop was immediately at hand may well have strengthened him.

The relatively narrow circle of rich upper gentry and lords which still in the early sixteenth century dominated the political scene was recruited from the famous lineages mentioned above: the Nevilles, Lumleys, Hiltons, Eures, Bowes, and their like, with roots far back in the medieval past, and bearing names already historic. The prominence of two leading members of the Durham landed class, the earl of Westmorland and Lord Lumley, ensured that both were appointed J.P.s and justices of assize, as well as commissioners of array to take the musters. In the latter function and as J.P.s they were assisted by the heads of the leading knightly families, but only the peers were put on the assize commission, membership of which was in any case largely honorary, most of the work being done by the professional judges. Palatine office was important for the prestige and power of the Durham magnates, whose landed and political resources, unless supplemented by those of the bishopric, were

[1] Pickthorn, i.53–4.

insufficient to enable them to claim more than a local significance. Even the earls of Westmorland had, since the partition of the family estates in the early fifteenth century, lost most of those lying outside the bishopric, in Yorkshire and elsewhere, which had once made them figures of the first importance, not only in Durham, but in the whole northern region.[1]

The Nevilles had a particular interest in the military resources of the bishopric.[2] One of the bitterest complaints of the family on the eve of the 1569 Rising was that it had been deprived by the Protestant Dean and Chapter of the 'conduction and leadinge' of the Cathedral tenants when the latter did their military service. This office (perhaps that of steward) had been held by the earl of Westmorland or one of his family, so it was claimed, for over a century. Probably the ideal from the Neville point of view was the state of affairs prevailing from the 1430s to the 1480s, when leading members of the family had also been stewards of the bishopric, and so had the 'conduction and leadinge' also of the Bishop's tenants.[3] It was as the captains of the bishopric, and not merely of their own following, that the Nevilles could make an important contribution to the defence of the Border, and so bring themselves to the notice of the Crown—or indeed raise a rebellion against it. The same was true of the Lumleys, who, as the Bishop's master foresters led the men of Weardale,[4] thus considerably augmenting the relatively modest forces which could be raised from their own estates.

Both the leading Durham families found it hard to come to

[1] The first earl of Westmorland had detached the lordships of Middleham and Sheriff Hutton in Yorkshire and the Honour of Penrith in Cumberland from the family inheritance for the benefit of his children by his second marriage; the second earl and his successors retained only the Durham lands, Kirkby Moorside in Yorkshire, and the barony of Bolbec in Northumberland.

[2] The importance of the house of Neville in the military leadership of the bishopric is instanced by Henry VII's appointment of Lord Neville in 1499 as captain of the Durham levies to serve on the Border, with power to appoint the inferior officers of the force in association with the Bishop (Lapsley, p. 308). Cf. the 4th earl of Westmorland's prominent part in mobilizing the Durham forces for the Scottish campaigns of 1522–3, when the Bishop's council met at his castle of Brancepeth to make the necessary arrangements (*L.P. Hen. VIII*, iii.2531).

[3] P.R.O., S.P.12/48/155 and 159. Under Bishops Neville (1438–57), Booth (1457–76), and Dudley (1476–83) the stewards of the bishopric had been successively William Neville, Lord Fauconberg, Sir Thomas Neville, and Ralph, Lord Neville. See Hutch., i.341, 360, 364.

[4] *L.P. Hen. VIII*, iii.2531.

terms with the Tudors. The third earl of Westmorland had tried to placate Henry VII by entering into a bond for his good conduct, and had given the King the 'kepying rule and maryage' of his eldest son and heir.[1] But perhaps the latter's subsequent marriage, when fourth earl, to a daughter of the traitor duke of Buckingham, whose ward he had been, contributed to a persistent distrust towards the Nevilles on the part of Henry VIII and his ministers. There may also have been unease on the Neville side because a large part of the family inheritance, since the fall of Warwick the King-Maker, had come into the hands of the Crown, and neither Henry VII nor Henry VIII showed any inclination to restore it.[2] Similarly the descent of the fifth Lord Lumley (1510–45) from a natural daughter of Edward IV, as well as the Yorkist traditions of the family, could scarcely have been in its favour. Both Lumleys and Nevilles may have come to be regarded in Court circles, particularly from the period of Wolsey's ascendancy onwards, as 'overmight subjects' in Fortescue's sense. If alternatives were available, the Tudors were often reluctant to entrust office on the Border to such families, in spite of the fact that the March offices had been their traditional perquisites. Moreover, at least from the later years of Bishop Ruthall's rule (1509–22) their leadership of the gentry had been increasingly brought into question, particularly during Wolsey's episcopate; and the situation in this respect hardly improved after Tunstall's accession. John, Lord Lumley, was involved in litigation with both Ruthall and Wolsey, and lost the offices of master forester and coroner of Chester ward which his family had enjoyed for nearly a century.[3] The connection of the Nevilles with the stewardship of the bishopric had lapsed with the accession of Bishop Sherwood as long ago as 1484. Subsequent attempts to bring the office back into the family in the person of Thomas, Lord Darcy, the fourth earl's step-father, or

[1] Gairdner, i.191, 196.

[2] A hint of this emerged during the Pilgrimage of Grace, when it was reported that the commons of Middleham (one of the Neville lordships which had come into the possession of the Crown) said during the rising that they would make new lords of Middleham, and restore divers who had been put from their offices by wrong (*L.P. Hen. VIII*, xii.1269).

[3] For the litigation in which Lumley was involved, see *Dep. Kpr., 36th Rep., App. I*, p. 105; Lord Lumley was replaced as master forester by Richard Pemberton in 1524 (Church Comm. MS., Durh., Receiver-General's Roll, 16 Hen. VIII). Sir William Eure was made coroner of Chester Ward in the same year (ibid.).

one of the latter's nominees, failed.[1] Instead the steward was now often a courtier, like Henry VII's unpopular minister Edmund Dudley, made chief steward by Bishop Bainbridge (1507–8), or Henry VII's natural son the duke of Richmond, appointed to the same office by Wolsey.[2] Particularly after the failure of the Pilgrimage of Grace there was a sharp decline in the Neville influence, and for the rest of the reign of Henry VIII the earl of Westmorland was very much overshadowed by Bishop Tunstall, who was made lord lieutenant of Durham in 1537, and who from 1537/8 was also president of the Council in the North.[3] It was during the rule of the great administrative bishops like Ruthall, Wolsey, and Tunstall, for whom the interest of the Crown came first, that an alliance established itself between the Bishop and those heads of Durham gentry houses who aspired to lead the region with the support and countenance of the Crown, and who saw prospects of advancement for themselves in the Crown service. Hence the rise of Sir Robert Bowes, Sir Thomas Tempest, and Sir William Eure referred to above.[4] By contrast with the favour which such men came to enjoy with Henry VIII, Westmorland was given only a brief period of office in the Marches in 1525–6,[5] and was made a privy councillor in the latter year. A little over a decade later he refused the wardenship of the East and Middle Marches in view of his failure to control his following and ensure the loyalty of his country during the Pilgrimage, and it was Eure who ruled the Marches in his place.[6]

Against this background the great northern rebellion of the Pilgrimage of Grace broke on the region. The great bishopric families, and particularly the Nevilles and Lumleys, were exasperated at slights received from the Tudor courtier-bishops. Perhaps there was uneasiness too at the growing influence imparted to the Court by the fund of landed wealth and offices

---

[1] *L.P. Hen. VIII*, i.290, v.77.   [2] Hutch., i.385; *L.P. Hen. VIII*, iv.1510.

[3] Reid, *Council*, pp. 151–2; Lapsley, p. 309.

[4] After holding office as sheriff in 1518, Eure was made escheator of the bishopric in 1523 by Wolsey, and was succeeded in this office by Bowes in 1532; Tempest first appears in the episcopal service as a deputy steward in 1510; he was to hold the stewardship until 1544 (Church Comm., MS., Durh., Receiver-General's Rolls).

[5] When he was deputy captain of Berwick and vice-warden of the East and Middle Marches under the duke of Richmond. See G.E.C., xii(2).554.

[6] *L.P. Hen. VIII*, xii(1).919, 222, 291. G.E.C., xii(2).554.

which the dissolution of the monasteries would place at its disposal; and distaste at the need for deferential approaches to Thomas Cromwell in the affairs of the bishopric.[1] And it may well be in these quarters that the Act of 1536 was seen with most unease as the harbinger of further interference from without. Once the Pilgrimage got under way, the earl of Westmorland cautiously stayed at home, but allowed his heir, Lord Neville, to play a prominent part in the movement, as also did the Neville Lord Latimer; and a letter of one of the rebel Lord Darcy's servants subsequently came into the hands of the government which stated that 'both he [Westmorland] and all his council are true' to the Pilgrimage, and that 'He thinks it in favour of the commons that the King should know it was past his power to resist them.'[2] Both Lord Lumley and his heir Roger were much more openly involved in the leadership, together with their relative Sir Thomas Hilton. More surprising however than the case of such obvious dissidents was that of the 'loyal' Sir Thomas Tempest and Sir Robert Bowes, who also joined, leaving Sir William Eure as the only Durham magnate who refused all truck with the Pilgrimage.

But a significantly different pattern of behaviour nevertheless characterized the two groups. The Lumleys and Hilton belonged to the extremist wing amongst the leaders of the Pilgrimage. They supported violent policies, and their distrust of Henry VIII made them ready for an appeal to force against him. Tempest and Bowes on the other hand joined the moderate majority party amongst the Pilgrims for whom the movement was more in the nature of a demonstration proceeding by appeal and petition on the part of oppressed subjects to the King than any incipient civil war. Their influence was used to advance policies of negotiation and pacification.[3] And it was the latter

---

[1] Both Westmorland and Lumley were suitors to Cromwell for favours on their own doorstep in 1534–6. See *L.P. Hen. VIII*, vii.1082; ix.401, 489; x.381; xi.178.

[2] *L.P. Hen. VIII.*, xi.945.

[3] According to Robert Aske, the grand captain of the Pilgrimage, it was on the advice of Sir Thomas Tempest (amongst others) that the Pilgrims decided, at their council at Pontefract in December 1536, to proceed to the redress of their grievances by parliamentary means, instead of seeking the 'reformation' of the statutes and policies against which they had risen by petition to the King, and then by 'sword and battle' if this were rejected. Tempest had probably already recommended this peaceful and constitutional course to Aske at Doncaster early in December in a letter brought by his 'cousin' Robert Bowes, who was one of the

which won. Although many thousands from the bishopric had marched behind the banner of Saint Cuthbert to join the Pilgrim host at York and Pontefract, they were not involved in any hostilities, but were induced to disband and return home peacefully on the promise of the King's pardon. Roger Lumley however became involved in Sir Francis Bigod's subsequent and abortive rising of January 1537, motivated by distrust of the King's promises, and it was this which gave Henry VIII the excuse for the violent suppression of the Pilgrims. In the bishopric the principal consequence was the execution of Roger Lumley for treason; and although his father was spared, the attainder of the heir put the whole future of the family title and inheritance in question. No punitive action, however, was taken against the Nevilles, who saved their lives and possessions at the cost of continued political eclipse and disfavour, which lasted into the next reign. There were reprisals too against humbler folk, although not it seems on a very large scale; thirteen prisoners were condemned to death in the city of Durham.[1]

Although in the region as a whole the Pilgrimage[2] partly reflected rivalries between leading local houses, the very wide measure of support which it received from the governing class suggests that it was also the reaction of a community accustomed to ordering its own affairs in its own way to interference from without, and to a threat to its traditional way of life. It is not surprising then that one of the Pilgrim demands should have been the restoration of the 'liberties' of the Palatinate.[3] It is likely too that the need to defend a regional identity lay in part behind the religious aspects of the Rising. The Ten Articles promulgated by Henry VIII in 1536 as Supreme Head of the

---

principal intermediaries between the Pilgrims, the duke of Norfolk, and the King. Their attitude contrasts with that of Lord Lumley, Sir Thomas Hilton, and the Neville, Lord Latimer. Latimer, at Pontefract, wished to secure a ruling from the clergy that if the demands of the Pilgrims were refused, 'it was lawful for them to fight . . . against their prince'. See *L.P. Hen. VIII*, xi.1211; xii(1).6 (p. 8), 901 (p. 404), 945 (p. 429). For Lumley's attitude, and his threat of another rising, see ibid., p. 8.

[1] *L.P. Hen. VIII*, xii(1).918.
[2] There is no study of the Pilgrimage of Grace in the Durham region. The standard work on the movement as a whole is Dodds.
[3] See Dodds, i.355.

Church, and the Royal Injunctions which followed, had brought into question the veneration of saints, images, and relics, and so also the cult of Saint Cuthbert on which rested the fame and sanctity of the great Church and monastic community at Durham. Monastic institutions themselves were in disfavour and endangered, although Durham as one of the larger monasteries had not yet been touched. As far as the religious affiliations of the great families were concerned, there are indications that the Nevilles had a connection of some closeness with the shrine of Saint Cuthbert and the Saint's banner;[1] the Lumleys, like others of their kind, had contacts with the cult of Saint George and with the militant crusading ideal which contributed significantly to the propaganda image which the Pilgrimage assumed.[2] The clergy were as conservative as their betters, and priests were active in raising parishes and spreading news. Even Bishop Tunstall's attitude is in some doubt, for instead of going south to join the loyalists he fled behind the enemy lines to his castle at Norham, and remained inactive, playing a waiting game until the movement collapsed.[3] The defeat of the Pilgrimage was in fact soon followed by the defeat of the regional cult it had sought to defend; in 1537 Saint Cuthbert's shrine was defaced, and by 1540 or 1541 the monastery at Durham had been dissolved.

After 1536 Tunstall, now installed as lord lieutenant, ruled without challenge in Durham for the rest of Henry's reign, in association with Eure, Bowes, and Tempest, the regime in some respects foreshadowing the kind of episcopal political predominance in the region which would emerge again under the Stuarts. But Tunstall's rule began to crumble when, in the reign of Edward VI, John Dudley, duke of Northumberland estab-

---

[1] The relationship finds expression for example in the Neville claim to 'lead' the tenants of the Cathedral church (mentioned above) on Border service. In the campaign of 1523 we find 'my lord of Westmorland with St. Cuthbert's banner, lying at Alnwick or thereabouts' (*L.P. Hen. VIII*, iii.3506). A prominent part had been played by Lord Neville in the battle of Neville's Cross, 1346, a victory over the Scots ascribed to the power of Saint Cuthbert, mediated through his relics.

[2] This aristocratic and martial ideal with religious overtones contributed to the furnishings of Lumley castle, where there was a tapestry of four pieces 'of the storie of St. George', a saint popular in England since the time of the early crusades because of his supposed assistance to the Crusaders at Antioch (1089). See Sur. *Hist. Durh.*, ii.161.

[3] Dodds, i.203.

lished himself as head of the government and began to look to the estates of the see of Durham as the landed base for his own connection and influence in the north. At the end of 1551 Tunstall was imprisoned in the Tower on a trumped-up charge, while the earl of Westmorland took his place as lord lieutenant, and was made chief steward of the bishopric. In the following year, after Tunstall's deprivation, the Durham see was divided into the two dioceses of Durham and Newcastle, and the Palatinate abolished. Northumberland was given the lordship of Barnard Castle and took Westmorland's place as steward. But these revolutionary plans collapsed with Edward's death, and upon Mary's accession in July 1553 Tunstall, the see, and the Palatinate were all restored. Now began a period of predominance for the Nevilles.[1] Mary endowed the earl of Westmorland with extensive grants of lands in Yorkshire and elsewhere which greatly increased his wealth,[2] and when in 1558 he was made lieutenant-general of the north, he emerged as the leading northern magnate.[3]

It was the sudden collapse of this pre-eminence after Elizabeth's accession[4] and the re-establishment of the Protestant order that followed which made the Neville connection such an intractable and unstable element in the region during the 1560s, with its hopes increasingly fastened on the new revolution which it was hoped would follow on the marriage of Mary Queen of Scots to the duke of Norfolk (who was brother-in-law to the sixth and last earl of Westmorland) and the ultimate succession of the former to the throne.[5] This was a policy supported by other

[1] For these events see Reid, 'Pol. Infl.'

[2] See in particular *C.P.R., Ph. & M., 1557–8*, pp. 39–40, for the earl's grant of the honour of Holderness in Yorkshire, and the manor of Torksey in Lincolnshire, valued at a yearly rental of £601.

[3] *A.P.C., 1556–8*, p. 250.

[4] The earl's commission as lieutenant-general was not renewed after Elizabeth's accession, and the Yorkshire and Lincolnshire lands granted him by Mary never came into his possession. His marriage in 1560 to his deceased wife's sister brought him into trouble with the Church, and on the Queen's instructions he was cited before the archbishop of York's court (see *C.S.P. Dom., 1547–80*, pp. 155, 183, 185, 187, 188; *C.P.R. Eliz., 1560–3*, pp. 336–7). His heir Charles, the sixth and last earl, who succeeded in 1564, had to alienate the manor of Cottingham to the Crown in part settlement of his father's debts (*C.P.R., Eliz., 1566–9*, p. 282). He inherited none of his father's offices beyond his membership of the Council in the North.

[5] See Williams, 1, chs. 8–10; MacCaffery., part v.

northern magnates, and particularly by Lord Lumley, whose family, like the Nevilles, had recovered from the disasters of the Pilgrimage of Grace. For during the reign of Edward VI the title and estates had been restored to Roger Lumley's heir. The new Lord Lumley, however, who would be enormously en-riched through his marriage to one of the co-heiresses of the earl of Arundel,[1] was more influential in London than he was in Durham. There he worked closely with Norfolk and other con-servative peers who favoured the duke's marriage to Mary. The Queen's veto of this marriage threw the group into such fear and disarray that in November 1569 Westmorland, with his fellow northern magnate the earl of Northumberland, an enthusiastic convert to Catholicism, embarked on an armed demonstration which soon assumed all the characteristics of an open rebellion. This received considerable support in the Palatinate,[2] but soon proved to be another disastrous failure. Like the Pilgrimage of Grace, it was in itself, if not in its consequence, a notably bloodless affair. The rebels occupied Durham and restored the Catholic Mass in the cathedral; Hartlepool was taken, together with Barnard Castle, after a siege causing only a few casualties, most of them accidental. An advance was also made into York-shire. Then came the retreat before enormously superior government forces into the Palatinate. At Durham, in December 1569, the earls disbanded their following and fled into Scotland. In a matter of weeks the movement had risen and collapsed, carrying away the Nevilles with it. The earl died in exile, his estates were confiscated by the Crown, and the family dis-appeared from the Durham scene. Sir George Bowes, on the Queen's behalf, executed perhaps a couple of hundred of the humbler supporters of the movement up and down the Palatinate.[3]

1569 was very different from 1536. The Pilgrimage had been a mass movement in which a wide spectrum of the governing class had been involved over the whole northern region. It had

---

[1] G.E.C., viii.277–8.

[2] The main source for the events of the Rising in the Palatinate is the corre-spondence of Sir George Bowes printed in *Memorials*.

[3] There were 320 persons 'appointed' by Bowes to be executed in the bishopric. But only an unknown proportion of these were actually put to death. In Darling-ton ward, where the number of executions is known, sentence was carried out in the case of only 24 persons out of 41 'appointed'. See McCall.

been careful, by and large, to keep up a show of respect for the law and constituted authority, including that of the Crown. The Northern Rising had been conceived as a similar broadly-based movement, but collapsed as such when the duke of Norfolk, Lumley, and other highly-placed allies of the northern dissidents controlling key-points in London and elsewhere submitted to the Queen. The two earls might have followed their example, but decided to try the arbitrament of a rising. It was a hopeless enterprise because it soon became clear that it had no effective backing amongst those close to the Queen, and so was supported regionally only by a rump of the duke of Norfolk's connection in the north. The movement therefore had a desperate character which accounts for its elements of extremism. The earls committed treason by the gesture of restoring the Mass at Durham; and by making religion their cause, as well as by their hopes of Spanish and papal aid, they invited the prospect of religious war and so put themselves outside the pale of practical politics. The solid peacefully inclined gentry, even if Catholic in sympathy, had too much to lose to contemplate such a course. The earls received much sympathy, covert support, and a measure of passive collusion, but otherwise were left to rush into catastrophe alone,[1] isolated and out-manoeuvred regionally, just as Sir William Cecil had isolated and out-manoeuvred Norfolk at Court. The result was the collapse of the traditional pattern of Durham politics, in which the Neville interest had competed with the Bishop for the leadership of the gentry community and the favour of the Crown. After 1569 political life wilted as single-faction government became the rule in the bishopric, just as it would be at Court in the later years of the Cecil dominance. The Bishop gradually emerged as the trusted agent of the Crown in the region, and the trend was set for the rise of a Church party which would monopolize political power.

[1] In Durham the rebellion was supported by only three houses of first consequence, the Claxtons of Old Park and Wynyard (traditional clients of the Nevilles), the Tempests of Holmside (who brought in their Trollope Lambert and Hebburn relatives) and the Salvins of Croxdale. Although members of other leading families are to be found in the ranks of the movement, these were younger sons with nothing to lose. The activists in the Rising tended to be 'new' gentry, like Swinburn, Hodgson, and Smith.

3

BELIEFS AND ATTITUDES

FOLK beliefs and rituals widespread in northern England during this period and surviving into modern times suggest a deep concern with an 'other world' lying beyond death, and with the fate of the deceased in that world. The desire is also present to ensure a separation between the world of the dead and the living, to ease the departure of the dying, and to prevent hauntings and any 'return' on the part of the deceased.[1] The folk rites of the dead involved the use of candle-flame, salt, and fire, and the best surviving comment on them is probably the 'Lyke-Wake Dirge', a funeral ballad or lament recorded as used in a death ritual in Cleveland, south of the Tees, from the Elizabethan period to the beginning of the nineteenth century.[2] An account of the 1580s states that 'when any dieth, certaine women sing a song to the dead body, receyting the journey that the partie must go'.[3] The other-world journey of the 'Lyke-Wake Dirge' involved pre-Christian elements, rooted mainly in Norse beliefs. There was a perilous and narrow bridge which the dead must pass, with a flaming gulf opening below it. Next, a great moor 'full of thornes and briars' had to be crossed barefoot, unless shoes were provided.[4] Here indeed a Christian conception particularly close to the teaching of the pre-Reformation Church appears, with the detail that, if the deceased has once in his life given a pair of shoes to a poor man, these are returned to him on the edge of the thorny moor.[5] With them he can 'go through thick and

---

[1] See Henderson, pp. 53 ff.; Blakeborough, pp. 116–25; *Examples*, pp. 101–3.

[2] *Minstrelsy*, iii.163 ff.; Blakeborough, pp. 122 ff.

[3] MS. Cott., Julius F.vi.459. The earliest version of the text of the 'Lyke-Wake Dirge' is in Aubrey, p. 31.

[4] For the other-world bridge and fire, Ellis, pp. 170 ff.; the journey over an other-world moor seems to be paralleled in Norse literature by a journey over the 'high fells' (ibid., p. 176).

[5] The idea however may be equally rooted in pagan tradition, shoes being amongst the grave-goods provided for the dead. See Ellis, pp. 62, 85.

thin without scratch or scalle'. Similarly when the 'Brig o'
Dread' had to be traversed:

> If ever thou gavest meat or drink
> Every nighte and alle
> The fire sall never make thee shrink
> Every nighte and alle.

In fact, in folk belief as well as in the teaching of the Church,
good works done in this life received their reward in the next.

Conceptions of this kind were easily related to the Church's
doctrines of Heaven, Hell, and (before the Reformation)
Purgatory. They were also relevant to the codification of 'good
works' and 'sins' in canon law, the body of regulations and
prescripts enforced by the Bishop's court, or at a lower level by
that of the archdeacon. In these courts a kind of generally
approved social morality was enforced, aiming particularly
at ensuring the stability of the patriarchal family and monogamous marriage, on which depended the orderly transmission
of values, skills, and property from one generation to the next.
The kind of litigation therefore which most often found its way
into the Church courts, after the Reformation as before it,
related to the marital bond and sexual morality, involving the
enforcement of the Church's law in such matters as adultery,
fornication, and incest. These offences (with slander, perjury,
and witchcraft, also within the jurisdiction of the ecclesiastical
courts) were most commonly punished by the public humilia-
tion involved in 'penance', and in the more serious cases, by
fine or imprisonment imposed by the secular magistracy.
Probably in fact for most, and in spite of the existence of other
and more 'inward' religious forms, 'religion' meant, first and
foremost, conformity to this body of moral and social regulation
backed by coercive sanctions, the ultimate of which was
'excommunication'. This implied exclusion from the body of
the Church and from the sacraments; and a person dying
excommunicate could not be buried in the consecrated ground
of a churchyard. In popular belief this condemned the deceased
to suffer eternally the torments of the damned. Thus although,
as far as the common man was concerned, 'religion' had a
strongly legalistic content, nevertheless the code which the
Church approved and enforced implied also a reference to an

'other world' beyond this life, and offences against the code involved the violation of a divine order transcending space and time. They therefore incurred eternal punishment, just as conformity earned eternal reward.

How effective excommunication was as a control making for social stability and conformity it is not easy to say. Excommunication carried with it straightforwardly secular, as well as religious sanctions; and the excommunicate might have to face a fine and imprisonment as well as the perils of the world to come.[1] The relative deterrent force of the secular and spiritual penalties involved in excommunication is anybody's guess. But there is at least some evidence to suggest that the exclusion from Christian rites which excommunication involved was taken seriously in unexpected quarters, so that such 'spiritual' penalties could become a significant reinforcement for secular authority. Thus before the Reformation the bishops of Durham used excommunication with some effect against Border raiders. Bishop Fox, for example, in 1498 was able to bring about the submission of fifteen prominent thieves of Tynedale and Redesdale, who upon the threat of excommunication surrendered themselves to him at Norham castle, and there made their peace with the Church, and received absolution.[2] No doubt other and more material pressures were also involved, but the testimony of Lord Dacre in 1524 on the power of the religious sanction is worth quoting. He urged Wolsey, then Bishop, to put the men of Tynedale, who had broken solemn engagements into which they had entered, to the excommunication, whereby (Dacre said) 'they, nor their wives nor children, shall not come within any church to hear the service of God, nor yet have anything administered to them that doth appertain to Christian men to have of the Church', as had been done in the time of Bishop Fox. This, he added, 'would be a fearful thing to them'.[3] When Dacre's advice was followed, however, Wolsey's resort to excommunication proved to be less effective than Fox's had been, but for a significant reason. This was that the Tynedale men were able to receive the sacrament at Easter as usual from Scottish priests who refused to obey Wolsey's ban.[4]

It seems therefore that in these primitive upland communities

[1] See Logan. [2] *Fox*, p. 80. [3] *L.P. Hen. VIII*, iv.10.
[4] Raine, p. xiii; *L.P. Hen. VIII*, iv.1289.

the approach to the 'power' and rites of the Church had a mechanical quasi-magical character, which made the efficacy of sacraments depend merely on their ritual performance. The rise of Protestantism, of course, was bound to undermine this attitude. Its teaching played down the objective power of the sacraments to ensure access to eternal life, and the extent to which the Church, through its priesthood, controlled this power. Instead faith and the subjective disposition of the believer were emphasized, so weakening the sanctions on which the force of excommunication had rested. Under Protestantism however, it was hoped that the deterrent force of eternal rewards and punishments would be made even more effective by means of the charismatic sermon. Thus during Elizabeth's reign the famous reformer and rector of Houghton-le-Spring Bernard Gilpin, as a result of his preaching tours amongst the raiding communities of Tynedale and Redesdale, came to be 'esteemed a very prophet, and little less than adored by that halfe barbarous and rustic people'. His repute was such that when his horses were stolen, the thief speedily returned them, humbly craved Gilpin's pardon, and 'protested that after it came to his knowledge that they were Mr. Gilpin's horses, he was afraid to be thrust downe quicke into hell . . .'[1] But preachers like Gilpin were few and far between, and the power of preaching was less easily brought to bear than the old-style excommunication.

Much of the mentality of the old religion soon to be displaced by the new Protestant order, its many-sidedness and different levels of appeal, found expression in the most impressive religious monument of the region, the great abbey church and cathedral at Durham, a description of whose pre-Reformation state, *The Rites of Durham*,[2] written by an unknown Elizabethan author, survives. Of the inner life of the community of Benedictine monks responsible for the daily round of liturgical prayer in the monastic church, we know little beyond that a tradition of solid learning persisted to the eve of the Reformation.[3] But if there were few 'abuses' of the kind revealed by royal or episcopal Visitations in other monasteries, there was

---

[1] Carleton, pp. 115–16. [2] *Durh. Rites.* See also Knowles, pp. 129–37.
[3] At the time of the dissolution out of the 66 monks at Durham or in one or other of its cells, 16 were D.D.s or B.D.s, and 2 M.A.s. See Greenslade.

also nothing of the mystical spirituality to be found at Mount-
grace in Yorkshire, a Carthusian abbey with a very different
tradition. The resources human and material of the Durham
community were used instead to project a religion of visual
images expressed through a gorgeous ritual and works of art
placed in a splendid decorative and architectural setting.[1] An
important aspect of this was the rites and beliefs connected
with Saint Cuthbert, the seventh-century monk and evangelist,
whose cult was a characteristic and major instance of the way in
which the old religion identified specific places and situations
with particular spiritual powers whose influence was benevolent
and protective. Thus Cuthbert (or rather 'God and Saint
Cuthbert') ruled and owned the lands between Tyne and Tees,
which were his 'patrimony', protected by him from any seeking
to invade and possess them. The Saint's power radiated from
his incorruptible body preserved in his shrine or 'feretory' in the
cathedral, and could be benevolent in relation to those whom he
favoured, expressing itself in miracles of healing (the last of
which occurred in 1502); or malevolent in relation to evil-
doers, particularly those who violated his possessions, church or
patrimony. Hence the disastrous defeat of King David of
Scotland in 1346 at the battle of Neville's Cross was still seen as
a formidable manifestation of the Saint's enmity, for David had
invaded the Palatinate in spite of a dream in which he had been
warned that 'in any wise he should not attempt to spoile or
violate the churche goods of St. Cuthbert or any thinge that
apperteyned unto that holie saint'.[2] Not surprisingly therefore,
when the men of the Palatinate went to war, they marched
behind the banner of Saint Cuthbert containing a relic of the
Saint sewn into it, which it seems was last displayed in 1536
during the Pilgrimage of Grace.[3] Nothing better expressed and
confirmed the 'power' of Saint Cuthbert than the splendour
and richness of his shrine, 'with most curious workmanship of
fine and costly marble all limned and gilted with gold . . . one
of the most sumptuous monuments in all England'.[4]

The sense of religion as a 'power' which could command all
the best which wealth could buy of the skills and materials of
the age was one of the lessons which the cathedral most

---

[1] Cf. Knowles, p. 136.   [2] *Durh. Rites*, p. 25.   [3] Dodds, i.205.
[4] *Durh. Rites*, p. 4.

obviously drove home. As he describes the images and pictures in the great church, the author of *The Rites* reverts again and again to such phrases as 'most richly and curiously set forth', 'most curiously and finely gilte', 'the rich jewells and ornaments . . . bestowed of that holie man St. Cuthbert'.[1] Riches and the ability to command rare skills went with sanctity. Those skills were nevertheless also used to evoke deeper trends in the religious sensibility of the time, as in the paintings of the Jesus Altar, which depicted the sufferings of the Passion, showing the Christ, 'as he was tormented and as he hung on the crosse, which was a most lamentable sight to beholde'.[2] But the cult of images might also express no more than an empty and puerile mechanical ingenuity, as in the peepshow piety of the image of 'Our Lady of Bolton', which opened 'from her breaste downward' to reveal in Passiontide an image of Christ holding a detachable crucifix, both removable on Good Friday; while on other principal feasts 'every mann might se pictured within her the father, the sonne, and the holie ghost, most curiously and finely gilted'.[3] The purpose which these works of art served was none the less a serious one. An image was to be 'so artificially wrought . . . with marvellous fyne colours and excellent gilt' that 'the more a man did looke on it the more was his affection to behold it'.[4] The sensibility was to be formed by means of the visual impressions created through contact with these objects. By contrast, the Protestant emphasis was on the Word, the internalized verbal image, resounding in the heart and soul. For the Protestant Bernard Gilpin, the fault of the old religion was that it sought Christ 'in our own inventions and devices'. To find Christ, the believer must enter no cathedral but rather 'the temple of his holy word', and 'faith cometh by hearing, and hearing by the word of God'.[5] Thus under the new religious dispensation the sermon became the decisive religious act without which even the sacraments lost their force. Charismatic preaching, the proclamation of the Word, displaced the Mass and the ritualized, visual effects of the old order.

As a result, the character of the religious environment depicted in *The Rites* was violently changed. Saint Cuthbert's shrine was destroyed in 1537, and the Saint's cult brought to an

---

[1] Ibid., pp. 33, 106.   [2] Ibid., p. 33.   [3] Ibid., p. 30.
[4] Ibid., p. 33.   [5] Collingwood, p. 51; Carleton, p. 139.

end when his body was reburied in a plain tomb in 1542.[1] At
the same time, the monastic community was dissolved and
converted into a cathedral chapter of twelve 'secular' canons
(assisted by twelve minor canons, and an establishment of clerks
and choristers) presided over by a dean. The element of continuity was at first strong; at least twenty of the Durham monks
were given positions in the new Cathedral foundation, and the
last prior became the first dean.[2] But following the royal Visitation of 1547, services began to be simplified. English was increasingly used instead of Latin, and a start was made with the re-
moval of images and stained glass windows.[4] These changes
were greatly speeded up when the duke of Northumberland
took the place of Somerset as Edward VI's chief minister, and
Tunstall was called up to London, disgraced and deprived. Durham now received (in 1551) its first Protestant dean, Horn, who
carried further the process of sweeping the cathedral bare of
such 'supersititious monuments' as still survived.[5] The Mass
was abolished, and the new English Book of Common Prayer
came into use. The reaction of Queen Mary's reign brought the
restoration of Catholic rites, although not at Durham of the
monastic community.[6] But the advent of Queen Elizabeth, and
the Acts of Supremacy and Conformity of 1559 were to mark the
final victory of Protestantism. In the Cathedral the rule of the
Calvinist Dean Whittingham during the 1560s completed the
process whereby traditional cultic objects and furniture were
destroyed. Whittingham's wife is credited with the gesture of
burning Saint Cuthbert's banner, which legend affirmed was
indestructible by fire. By the end of Whittingham's period of
office (1579) little remained of the traditional furnishings of the
cathedral except the stalls, and a suitably austere setting was
thus provided for the morning and evening prayer, the com-

---

[1] *Durh. Rites*, pp. 102–3, 284–7.

[2] But in spite of a measure of continuity in the personnel of the monastery and
the new Cathedral foundation, change was already implicit in the terms of the
letters patent of the new foundation in 1541. These emphasized the break with the
monastic past by changing the dedication of the Church, which now became to
'Christ and the Blessed Virgin', instead of to 'Saint Mary and Saint Cuthbert';
the object was now also to promote pure preaching of the Word and sacraments,
and to restore true religion, as well as to correct the irregularities into which
monastic life had fallen. See *Durh. Stats.*, p. xxxiv.

[3] See Wilson, 'Changes', i.118.   [4] Ibid., pp. 119–22.

[5] Ibid., pp. 122–3.   [6] Ibid., pp. 130–2.

munion, and the sermons of the new regime.[1] Similar changes were enforced at the same time throughout the parish churches, where altars were thrown down and replaced by communion tables; images and relics were destroyed, and the Mass was ousted by the new English service.[2]

There is little indication that these changes had much support in the rank and file of society. In the Durham region Protestantism established itself through the activity of an élite introduced into the ranks of the Cathedral clergy first in the reign of Edward VI, and then during the 1560s and later.[3] Their influence depended more on backing from the government in London than from local sentiment and opinion. The approach of these men, all of them university intellectuals, tended to be contemptuous of popular opinion. Bernard Gilpin, for example, lost the favour of Bishop Tunstall because 'the plebeians and ordinary people' were offended by his Protestant opinions. Gilpin was not perturbed by this, hoping in due course to gain their regard by his preaching, but 'otherwise I never desired the love of the vulgar'.[4] The break with the traditional religious practices and symbols produced tensions and conflicts. But the majority were accustomed to defer to their political and social superiors in matters of religion as in all else, and there was much less of a break in the structure of authority than there was in religious belief and practice. The Durham monastic community shaded off into that of the Dean and Chapter. Many of the persons who had ruled under the old régime were incorporated in the new, which itself only gradually assumed a clearly Protestant character. Tunstall refused to accept Queen Elizabeth's settlement of religion, and so had to be deprived in 1559; but the Protestant Pilkington (1561–73) took his place without any outward breach of continuity. He inherited most of the traditional deference which a bishop of Durham could command. Moreover the Reformation was the work of the Crown, to whose authority the laws of God and man required obedience.

---

[1] Ibid., pp. 146–8.   [2] Ibid., ch. vii.

[3] Amongst the Cathedral clergy, John Rudd had been Dean Horn's principal ally in the reign of Edward VI; in the 1560s the active Protestants were led by Bishop Pilkington and Dean Whittingham, supported on the Cathedral establishment by Rudd, John Pilkington, William Birch, Robert Swift, and Thomas Lever. See Wilson, 'Changes', p. 145.

[4] Carleton, p. 131.

Resistance therefore for most involved intense moral as well as
political difficulties.

The Northern Rising of 1569 is sometimes presented as the
explosion of a fervent popular Catholicism to which it gave
effective political expression. In fact the movement illustrates
how difficult it was for any body of opinion to assert itself outside the established structure of deference and authority. Some
of the leaders of the Rising, particularly the earl of Northumberland, were certainly convinced that an appeal to 'religion' (i.e.
Catholicism) would be the best way of securing popular support
for their cause. But this opinion was adopted largely as a result
of the 'persuasions' of one of the leading clerical instigators of
the rebellion, Dr. Morton, who affirmed 'that he had travelled
through the most parts of England, and did find the most part
of the common people inclined thereunto [i.e. to a return to the
old religion]; if so be that any should once begin to take the
enterprise in hand'.[1] It soon, however, became apparent that
mass support of the Rising depended much more on money
than on religion, and it melted as soon as pay proved to be in
short supply.[2] Religious change in 1569, as in the previous
religious revolutions, was the result less of any popular initiative,
than of action by 'authority'. Protestant symbols (Communion
tables, Bibles, and Prayer Books) were destroyed or removed
from the churches by the churchwardens acting on the orders of
the rebel earls, who claimed to represent the Crown, and whose
commands were backed by the threat of force. The typical
justification of these officials and others who had obeyed the
orders of the rebels relating to religion, was that this was done
'upon such commandements . . . receyved from Mr. Cuthbert
Nevill', 'upon payne of hanginge', or upon orders given 'in
the Quenes name and the earls'; or in one case, 'he would nott
have burnt them [the Bible and the Prayer Book] but for fear of
his lyfe'.[3] It is unlikely that these excuses were insincere, or that
the churchwardens, themselves respectable yeomen, shopkeepers, and professional men, but not of the ruling class, would
have taken any initiative in the dangerous field of religion
without the authorization of their betters. As far as the common
people were concerned, it was easy at Durham to assemble

---

[1] *Memorials*, p. 281.
[2] *Cal. S.P. Dom. Add. 1566–79*, xv.53 (p. 128); xv.73 (p. 134); xviii.35 (p. 276).
[3] *Durh. Depos.*, pp. 141, 167, 176, 188.

crowds in the cathedral to witness the illegal rebel Mass, and mobs to watch the churchwardens burn Protestant books. But this was not always the case, if we are to believe Sir George Bowes's report of the rebel Mass at Darlington, when John Swinburn 'with a staffe, drove before him the poor folks, to hasten them to hear the same'. At Sedgefield, however, a measure of popular religious participation showed itself. There 'the parish mett and consultyd' to set up a Catholic altar, and thirty parishioners helped to draw the altar-stone into the church.[1]

Thus any established form of religious belief and practice depended on countenance from 'authority', and it was the superior weight of this on the side of religious change which eased the way to the new world of Protestantism. At the same time the emergence of Protestantism confronted government with the problem of dissent, which in sixteenth-century Durham had mainly (if not wholly) a traditionalist Catholic character. But dissent was still very much a matter for the social and intellectual élites, giving expression to divisions in the ranks of the latter, rather than to any effective pressure of religious needs arising in more humble environments. Some of the dissenters of the 1560s were simple folk, who said they had attended rebel Mass in the cathedral and 'willingly used suche reverend gesture therunto', without giving any excuse for their action.[2] There may well have been many such, but both their numbers and influence on events are unknown. Very different is the case of the notable group of Durham cathedral clergy, among whom were Anthony Salvin, formerly Bishop Tunstall's vicar-general, and William Carter, late archdeacon of Northumberland. Deprived in 1559–60 for their refusal to accept the new religious order, they had their links with other Recusant circles centred on Richmond in Yorkshire, and also had contacts at Rome.[3] These able intellectuals had a wide influence on the northern nobility and gentry, particularly those out of favour with the Elizabethan régime. Among them the unheard-of idea had currency that rebellion was justifiable if it advanced the cause of true religion, and if by means of the device of papal excommunication it was authorized by Rome.

[1] *Memorials*, p. 45; *Durh. Depos.*, p. 187.   [2] *Durh. Depos.*, p. 164.
[3] On this group, see Aveling, pp. 36–41.

The influence of one of this group, the above-mentioned Dr. Nicholas Morton, an official of the papal court and ex-canon of Canterbury[1] who visited England in 1569, was an important factor in the decision taken by rebels to make the Rising one for 'religion' and the restoration of the Catholic order. It was he who revealed to the earl of Northumberland and the Nortons that Elizabeth was in danger of papal excommunication if steps were not taken to 'reform' religion in England to its previous state; in which case the souls of English Catholics would be endangered, and the country threatened by an invasion of Catholic princes. It was his assurance too, as noted above, which convinced Northumberland that the 'common people' favoured a Catholic rising.[2] In Durham such ideas were less enthusiastically received in the Neville family circle,[3] but caught on nevertheless amongst the activists in the Rising. One of these, William Smith of Esh, asserted that '. . . the Pope has summoned this land once [i.e. to appear before the papal court and answer to the charge of heresy], and if he summon it again, it is lawful to rise against the Queen, . . .; for the Pope is head of the church.'[4] The Rising in fact demonstrated how powerfully religious divisions promoted political instability, and how even authority itself—in its supreme manifestation the Crown—could be shaken if political discontents merged explosively with convictions which questioned the very nature and credentials of that authority. 'Religion' was moulded by powerful political and social forces, but was also the area within which men were liable to assert their freedom from them.

Protestantism in its Anglican variety was intended to be a 'reforming', but also a conservative force, with its emphasis on authority and the royal supremacy over the Church. As such it merged easily with the cult of the 'virgin queen' as this established itself during her reign. The point of view is expressed in the petition which the vicar and churchwardens of Saint Oswald's church, Durham, entered in their register book of

---

[1] On Morton, see *D.N.B.*   [2] *Memorials*, p. 281.

[3] The earl of Westmorland opposed a rising for 'religion' on the grounds that 'those that seeme to take that quarrel in other countreis are accompted as rebells . . .', and eventually only agreed because 'pressed and sore urged' by others. See *Memorials*, p. 196.

[4] *Cal. S.P. Dom. Add. 1566–79*, p. 100.

1580, that their 'doinges god directe to hys glory . . . and to the manteynynce of the quenes Magesties godly proceedinges, whome God preserve to regne over us to the abolyshment of popery, and strange and false religion, and to the mentenynge of the gospell'.[1] But the conservative role of the establishment was apt to be contradicted by the emphasis on the sermon and the proclamation of the 'Word'. Pressure was placed on the parish clergy, in view of their new preaching role, to become more articulate and better educated, Bishop Barnes (1577–87) playing an important part in the campaign for a more effective preaching clergy.[2] Protestantism and the need to read the Bible also stimulated the growth of literacy amongst the laity. It promoted a new interest in education, and towards the end of the century there was a marked increase in the number of bequests providing for the education of children.[3] Another related development was the foundation of new schools, so that those closed because of the dissolution of the monasteries were replaced and the total number increased.[4] The novel feature of post-Reformation schooling was the type of education provided.[5] Bernard Gilpin, who made a bequest to found a grammar school at Houghton-le-Spring, asserted: 'I may boldly affirm that whatsoever is given to a godly grammar school, it is given to the maintenance of Christ's holy gospel.' In the new schools the emphasis was not only on reading, writing, and grammar, but also on instruction in 'God's holy gospel'.[6] But the emphasis on literacy, and on an informed and articulate approach to religion provided the ground in which further dissension could arise within Protestantism itself. As early as 1567 the rector of Stanhope, William Birch, was deprived not for Catholicism, but because of his criticisms of Anglicanism from a radical Protestant point of view.[7] As a result, in spite of the defeat of Catholicism, the enforcement of religious 'uniformity' remained a problem, and with it the threat of political and social instability which religious disunity involved.

[1] *Chronicon*, p. 42.
[2] See *Durh. Eccles. Proc.*, *passim.*; Wilson, op. cit., p. 571.
[3] Wilson, p. 662.   [4] Ibid., p. 668.   [5] See below, p. 97 ff..
[6] Wilson, op. cit., p. 647. The school at Houghton was known as 'the Kepier school', the endowment consisting of lands formerly belonging to Kepier hospital.   [7] Ibid., p. 141.

PART II

Into the Seventeenth Century
1570–1640

4

SOCIETY: THE CHANGING CONFIGURATION

GENTRY OLD AND NEW

MORE than a dozen of the Durham gentry were attainted as a result of joining the Rising,[1] but there is no evidence that any of them were executed. Although three (Robert Lambert, Ralph Conyers, and Robert Claxton) barely escaped being 'stayed' for execution, in the outcome the sentences were not implemented.[2] But the physical survival of the rebel leaders contrasts with the accelerating process of social change which assailed their society after 1570. An environment gradually emerged to which the politics of the Rising, and the conditions which had produced it, were irrelevant. The structure of social prestige and political power which centred on the Neville family had collapsed, its fall bringing in its wake extensive changes in the disposition of landed property in the Palatinate, and in the character of the gentry. The last Neville earl of Westmorland died early in the seventeenth century,[3] an exile and pensioner of Spain. But the confiscated Neville estates did not continue for very long in the hands of the Crown. Once the Stuarts, with their chronic financial problem, had succeeded to the throne, Crown lands began to be sold on an increasingly large scale. Winlaton went to the coal-owning Newcastle Selbies, Hodgsons and Andersons; Brancepeth to the parvenu Gateshead Coles, whose wealth also came from collieries; Raby, just before the Civil War, became the property and seat of the courtier Vanes.[4] None of these new landlords could hope to recreate the role of the earl of Westmorland in the Durham scene. The attempt of James I to revive the influence formerly exercised by the Nevilles by making his favourite, Robert Carr, earl of Somerset, lord of Raby and Brancepeth, and in 1615

[1] See the list in *Memorials*, p. 263.
[2] Ibid., p. 228.   [3] Ibid., p. 304.
[4] Sur. *Hist. Dur.*, ii.272; Surtees., *Brancepeth*, p. 36; Sur. *Hist. Durh.*, iv.166.

lord lieutenant of Durham,[1] collapsed with the favourite's fall a few years later.

The fate of the properties of Westmorland's associates illustrates Durham's rapid evolution, from the later years of the sixteenth century, into one of those shire communities in which a traditional landed establishment was overwhelmed by a flood of newcomers. Both John Swinburn and Robert Tempest followed the earl into exile. The estates of the former passed to a Newcastle merchant family,[2] of the latter to the heirs of William Whittingham, the zealous Calvinist dean of Durham.[3] The Coatham estate of the Conyers family and the Hebburn property at Hardwick both went to courtiers.[4] Old Park, seat of a branch of the Claxton family who had been amongst the most devoted of Neville followers, was eventually bought by a professional man, John Wharton M.D.,[5] The Lamberts' Owton went to Richard Bellasis, a descendant of Wolsey's agent.[6] Some of the attainted rebels managed to hang on to their estates, as well as their lives—the Smiths of Esh being perhaps the most successful in this. The Smiths bought back their lands early in the seventeenth century, and subsequently retained them. In spite of their persistent Recusancy they secured a baronetcy from Charles II.[7] The Trollopes of Thornley did the same, but the result was to encumber their properties with loans and mortgages, besides the burden of Recusancy fines. Delinquency in the Civil War completed the ruin of an estate already fatally weakened, and the Trollopes disappeared from the Durham scene.[8]

This decline and fall of the rebel families of 1569 is symptomatic of a wider malaise afflicting many of the older Durham families as the seventeenth century got under way, which cannot be ascribed to any single cause. Sir William Gascoigne

---

[1] *C.S.P. Dom. Jas. I, 1611–18*, pp. 204, 211, 270; Sur. *Hist. Durh.*, iv.165. See below, p. 151 ff.

[2] The Swinburn estates at Chopwell were first granted to the government spy, Sir Robert Constable, and then sold by him to Ambrose Dudley, alderman of Newcastle. See Sur. *Hist. Durh.*, ii.277; *Memorials*, p. 33.

[3] Holmside passed to the Whittinghams from the courtier Sir Henry Gates, to whom it was first granted. See Sur. *Hist. Durh.*, ii.326, and *Memorials*, p. 33.

[4] Sur. *Hist. Durh.*, iii.218, 34.

[5] Ibid., iii.298. The first grant was to Sir George Freville, in 1569 clerk of the ordnance in the earl of Sussex's army.

[6] Ibid., iii.132.   [7] Ibid., ii.336, 338; *Memorials*, p. 265.

[8] Sur. *Hist. Durh.*, i.88 ff.; *Memorials*, p. 268.

parted with his great estate of the barony of Ravensworth to the coal-owning Liddells in 1607, in part no doubt to provide for his two co-heiresses. But this family too was burdened with Recusancy. The liquidation of its Durham properties, and Sir William's marriage to one of the parvenu Andersons, also coal-owners, suggests financial difficulties, perhaps arising out of mining ventures, and the overstrained credit which these involved.[1] Failure of male heirs brought the lands of the Claxtons of Wynyard to the mercantile Newcastle Jenisons.[2] The Davisons, another mercantile dynasty from Newcastle, supplanted the Blakistons of Blakiston as a result of the chuckle-headed extravagance of the courtier Sir Thomas Blakiston. Like Sir Bertram Bulmer of Tursdale, he was attracted to the Court of James I, but neither of these squires was able to seize on the opportunities of profit which Court life could afford. Instead both of them dissipated their family fortunes and had to sell their ancestral lands.[3] Quirks of character played their part in other instances of decline, as in the case of Henry Hilton of Hylton. He burdened his estate with eccentric annuities payable to the local parson and to the Corporation of London, so opening the way to a collapse which was completed by the Civil War.[4]

Many of these casualties no doubt simply manifested the process of decline and renewal in families characteristic of any land-owning group. What is remarkable about the Durham scene from the 1570s onwards is less the incidence of "decline" amongst the gentry than the sources from which new entrants into the class were recruited. Particularly striking is the large entry of Newcastle families of coal-owning background. Some dozen of these had settled on estates in Durham by the 1630s. Nowhere else in England, Northumberland included, were there so many landed fortunes founded on this kind of industrial basis, a result of the rise of the coal industry in the Tyne valley. This was particularly rapid and spectacular during the sixty years between 1565 and 1625, when coal shipments from Newcastle multiplied twelve-fold,[5] a rate of growth not again equalled until the eighteenth century.

[1] Aveling, pp. 173; Sur. *Hist. Durh.*, ii.211; Nef. ii.10–11.
[2] Sur. *Hist. Durh.*, iii.77.   [3] Ibid., iii.160; i.77n.   [4] Ibid., ii.21–2.
[5] Nef, i.25.

Thus a great industrial interest came into being centred on Newcastle, where a group of merchant families, members of the Merchant Adventurers' and Hostmens' Companies, built up great fortunes out of the development of collieries. They established themselves as a closed oligarchy, controlling the more important corporation offices.[1] The interests of the same circle of rich families was further advanced by the grant to Newcastle in 1600 of a royal charter. This conferred on the Hostmen's Company (which they controlled) a monopoly of all trade in coal from the Tyne, in return for a levy of a shilling on every chaldron of coal exported.[2] As far as Durham was concerned, their hold on the coal resources of the south side of the Tyne valley had been established by the conveyance in 1583 to Newcastle of the so-called 'Grand Lease' of Whickham and Gateshead. These were the principal coal-producing manors of the bishopric, which Queen Elizabeth had extracted from Bishop Barnes upon his appointment in 1577.[3] Subsequently, on the Durham side, Winlaton, Ryton, and Blaydon also emerged as important coal-producing districts, although Whickham, which was producing over 100,000 tons a year by the seventeenth century, still kept the lead.[4]

It was to be expected that the owners of the great Newcastle coal fortunes, eager for status and land, particularly if this overlay coal seams, should invade the Durham countryside. They were present in force by 1615, when ten coal-owning families, including the Liddells, Tempests, and Riddells, recorded their arms and descents at the herald's Visitation of that year.[5] In 1608 one of their number, Sir George Selby of Whitehouse, had become sheriff of the Palatinate.[6] The assimilation of these newcomers into the Durham landed establishment was helped by the involvement in mining and metallurgy of some of the older Durham families who were able and vigorous enough to seize new opportunities. The Bowes family of

---

[1] Ibid., ii.119 ff.   [2] Ibid., ii.268: for the charter, see Brand, ii.605.
[3] See Trevor-Roper.   [4] Nef, i.25–6, 150, 361.
[5] The Newcastle coal-owners registered in the 1615 Visitation were Sir Henry Anderson of Haswell Grange, Sir George Selby of Whitehouse, Sir Nicholas Tempest of Stella, Thomas Liddell of Ravensworth, Thomas Riddell of Gateshead, Robert Brandling of Felling, Robert Hodgson of Hebburn, Nicholas and Thomas Cole of Gateshead, William Jenison of Wynyard, and Christopher Mitford of Heulam. See Sur. *Hist. Durh.*, i.cliii, and Foster, *passim*.
[6] Hutch., i.481.

Streatlam and its cadet branch at Biddick was particularly active in this respect. Sir George Bowes, defender of Barnard Castle during the Rising, leased the lead mines of Teesdale and Weardale from the Crown and the Bishop, and became a principal lead supplier of the Newcastle Merchant Adventurers Company.[1] One of his sons, Robert Bowes, who settled at Biddick, owned in the 1590s salt pans at Sunderland and collieries at Offerton.[2] He was one of the pioneers of the Wear valley coal industry, which was to undergo a rapid development in the early seventeenth century, when Sunderland emerged as a significant rival to Newcastle as a coal-exporting port. Both the Lumleys and the Lambtons were similarly engaged in coal-mining activities. Their estates and those of the Hedworths of Harraton contained the most productive Wear valley collieries.[3] Another notable Wear coal-owning family were the Bellasises of Morton, closely linked by marriage with the Lambtons and the Newcastle Davisons.[4] The Durham gentry, if they possessed coal-owning interests, were gradually admitted into the circle of the Newcastle oligarchy, the members of which were in their turn assimilated into the upper level of the landed class if they held Durham estates. Thus, although strains and stresses between old and new gentry persisted, a composite and unified ruling group soon emerged, able by the weight of its wealth to dominate the Palatinate.

Below the level of the rich upper gentry, what is particularly striking in the half-century after 1570 is the increase in the number of families claiming gentry status. When the heralds held their Visitation of 1575, they recorded the pedigrees and coats-of-arms of fifty-six families; but at the Visitation of 1615 this number was almost doubled.[5] Already in 1575 the rich farmers, previously content with the traditional title of

---

[1] Raistrick, pp. 41–2.

[2] Galloway, p. 103. In the 1600s Robert's elder brother George was developing coalmining on the Biddick estate, and held a lease in the Lumley colliery; ibid., p. 104, and Sur. *Hist. Durh.*, i.200.

[3] In the years during and before the Civil War the Lumley colliery interests in the Wear valley appear to have been handled by Sir William Langley, brother-in-law to Richard, Viscount Lumley (*Roy. Comp. Pps.*, p. 262); for the coal interests of the Lambtons, see Nef, i.30; for the Hedworths, see ibid., p. 324.

[4] Apart from leasing coalmines at Morton from the bishop (Church Comm., Durh. MS., 190357) Bellasis was a partner in the Lambton colliery (*Roy. Comp. Pps.*, p. 280).   [5] Sur. *Hist. Durh.*, i.clii ff.

'yeoman', were eager to be called gentry. Amongst these early legatees of an agricultural prosperity which owed much to the growing market of Newcastle, there were the Hulls of Osterley, who (as Surtees put it) 'although but yeomanly folks appeared at the Visitation ... and were persuaded to indulge in coat armour'.[1] Similarly the Punshons of Herrington, granted the expressive coat of arms of 'a fesse embattled between three sheep's heads'.[2] There were more of these prosperous yeomen at the visitation of 1615.

Perhaps the most significant group of new recruits to the middle and lesser gentry at the latter date were the now married upper clergy. Throughout most of Elizabeth's reign these had few contacts with the landed class; but the tide was beginning to turn in the latter years of the Queen's lifetime. Intermarriage became increasingly frequent, and bishops, deans, and prebendaries were themselves founding landed families. Henry Ewbank, prebendary of the Twelfth Stall in the cathedral, established his son and heir on the manor of Snotterton, purchased from the Bainbridges, who before the Rising had held it from the earls of Westmorland.[3] Dean Whittingham's heir became the squire of Holmside.[4] Two other Durham prebendaries, Marmaduke Blakiston and John Hutton, founded landed families in the early seventeenth century; the former at Newton Hall near Durham, the latter at Houghton-le-Spring.[5] At the same time relatives of Bishop Barnes (1577–87)[6] and Bishop James (1606–17) established themselves as gentry and acquired estates.[7] These clerical families tended to ally with the lawyer fortunes of the Church establishment, the Calverleys of Littleburn for example (founded by Thomas Calverley, steward of the bishopric from 1576 to 1590) intermarrying with the Huttons and Whitinghams.[8] But by the early seventeenth century important gentry families like the Bellasises and the Boweses were also being brought by marriage into the clerical family grouping. As a result an influential and securely entrenched Church interest, emerged.[9] Those involved by an-

---

[1] Ibid., ii.331.   [2] Foster, pp. 264-5.   [3] Sur. *Hist. Durh.*, iv(1).141.
[4] Ibid., ii.327.   [5] Ibid., iii.163; i.149.   [6] Ibid., i.lxxxii; iii.355.
[7] Ibid., i.216.   [8] *Dugdale*, p. 61.
[9] The Bellasises intermarried with the episcopal Tunstall and James families (Sur. *Hist. Durh.*, i.203); the Bowes of Biddick with the Huttons (ibid., i.149). The Bowes of Streatlam also made several matches with church families (ibid., iv.107).

cestry and connection with the Church families were by no means necessarily political or religious conformists. The Huttons were Puritans and subsequently Parliamentarians in the Civil War; the clerical Blakistons produced a regicide.[1] Both these families, settled in the lower Wear valley, were brought by their marriage alliances close to the competitive, and socially mobile world of the Wear coal and salt entrepreneurs.[2] In this environment radical religious opinions, and oppositionist political attitudes tended to flourish.

In the activities of this numerous, varied, and many-tiered gentry group which was emerging in Durham out of the more conservative society of the earlier sixteenth century, agricultural and industrial enterprise went hand in hand. The coastal trade from Newcastle and Sunderland meant ships needed provisions, and the growing coalmining districts provided agriculture with a new, enlarged market making for more intensive production and increased specialization. At first this led, by the end of the sixteenth century, and in the coastal plain, to an emphasis on beef and mutton, at the expense of the more traditional arable products. It was not until later that more balanced forms of farming developed. One result of the concern with meat production was the rise of the wealthy gentleman grazier, the owner of large herds of cattle, and of balanced flocks of ewes, lambs, and wethers, yielding young sheep for sale to other farmers, as well as mutton for the butcher. Sir Cuthbert Collingwood, for instance, once constable of Alnwick Castle for the rebel earl of Northumberland, farmed Eppleton near Houghton-le-Spring in the 1590s, where he kept three sheep flocks totalling 958 sheep, and 143 cattle. He bred his stock at Eppleton, but fattened them at Dalton and Grindon on the coast.[3] Another gentleman farmer, Robert Widdrington, grew his crops on his farms at Monkwearmouth and Washington, but had his fatten-

---

[1] Robert Hutton, grandson of the Durham prebendary of the same name, became a captain of horse in Sir Arthur Haslerig's regiment (F. & D., i.239) and continued to support the Puritan interest after the Restoration (Sur. *Hist. Durh.*, i.147–8). John Blakiston, M.P. for Newcastle, who signed Charles I's death warrant, was a son of Marmaduke Blakiston of Newton Hall, another Durham prebendary.

[2] Both Blakistons and Huttons married into one such family, the Shadforths of Eppleton, of yeoman origin and parliamentary sympathies, whose 'rise' was based on an under-rented lease of the episcopal manor of Tunstall.

[3] *Ag. Hist.*, pp. 26–7.

ing land at Plessey and Cowpen in Northumberland; he also owned a salt-pan and a share in a coal keel.[1] Thomas Tempest in 1569 combined mercantile with agricultural enterprise, having a share (with the rebel Robert Tempest of Holmside) in a ship at Newcastle, as well as a flock of 600 wethers at Stanley.[2] Gentry of this kind, like their counterparts amongst the coal-owners and coal entrepreneurs, were not so much involved in the traditional relationship to a great household, involving dependence, service, or 'friendship', as in a relationship to a market. It was the market and the fluctuations of the coastal coal trade, particularly with London, rather than the vicissitudes of a regional aristocratic interest, like that of the fallen Nevilles, which increasingly determined what the region required of government and the Crown. Commercial influences left their mark on the emerging new styles in gentry politics and ways of living.

LANDLORDS AND TENANTS

The big gentleman farmers formed the top layer of the structure of landholding on the great estates, lay and ecclesiastical, in the early years of the seventeenth century. Amongst the most fortunate of them were the few lucky enough to occupy under-rented leases of episcopal granges, as the Bellasis family did at Morton Grange, held in the 1640s at a rent of £6 a year, but worth £90;[3] or the Shadforth family, which farmed the episcopal lands at Tunstall, valued in 1647 at £96 a year, at a rent of £10.[4] Sometimes, although rarely, a yeoman made his way into the exclusive circle of the big episcopal farmers, as did Ralph Allanson of Easington, who in 1647 leased Quarrington Grange, worth £138, at a rent of £22.[5] Allanson came from the substantial yeoman who formed the next level in the landholding structure below the gentlemen farmers. Few of these were as well-off as the farmer of Quarrington Grange, but most village communities included two or three tenants holding twice or three times as much land as their neighbours, and renting perhaps 100 or 150 acres. Next down the scale came the 'middling' farmers, with an average of 50 acres. They formed the

[1] Ibid., p. 27.   [2] *Wills & Inv.*, iii.48.
[3] Parl. Survey, 1647; Survey of Houghton-le-Spring lordship.   [4] Ibid.
[5] Ibid., survey of the manor of Easington.

majority of the peasantry, occupying modest farms mainly worked by family labour. The way of life of such working families would have been much the same in the seventeenth century as that described by Bailey at the beginning of the nineteenth: 'Enured to hard labour from their early youth, when they become farmers themselves, they continue still to work, but with increased exertion, anxiety and care.'[1] Toil and anxiety were very much the mark of the middling peasant's life, and in this milieu the support of the ties of kinship and neighbourhood must have been particularly important. The family farmers did not constitute the lowest or poorest level of the rural community. Below them came the half-dozen or so cottagers to be found in most of the lowland villages, renting a few acres, or making do with a garden and the right to pasture a few beasts on the moor.[2] In the special conditions of the coalmining communities however, and in the Teesdale and Weardale upland, such dwarf tenants were particularly numerous, and dominated the landholding structure.[3] Broadly speaking the pattern of landholding described by Bailey in 1812, as characteristic of Durham is already shaping itself in the early seventeenth century. A few large farms stand out of a preponderant mass of middling tenancies shading off into smallholdings.[4]

The increased scale of farming, the profitability of stock-raising, and the variety of crops raised had much to do with the trend towards enclosure which set in during these years, as well as with the exhaustion of the arable which was the usual reason given for it. A rotation which included long leys would, it was thought, increase yields. H. L. Gray noted from surveys of the lordship of Brancepeth in the early seventeenth century

[1] Bailey, p. 68.

[2] Typical instances of this kind of lowland structure of landholding may be found in the Parliamentary Survey cited above, e.g. the Surveys of Easington and Bishop Middleham. See also the rentals of the manors of Long Newton and Piercebridge in the lordship of Barnard Castle (Mickleton MS. 7[1]).

[3] For a typical coalmining community, see the survey of Whickham in the Parl. Survey and below, p. 96; ibid., Survey of Stanhope, and Durh. Pal. and Dip. Dept. MSS., Halmote Court Misc. Book M.64: 'The recept of George Emerson, particular receiver of the High Forest of Weardale', for dwarf tenancies in the Weardale upland. For the Teesdale upland, see the rental of Middleton-in-Teesdale (Mickleton MS. 7[1]) where of the 38 tenancies after improvement only 7 were rented at more than £1 a year.

[4] Op. cit., p. 67.

that there was a tendency for the proportion of arable in the open fields to decline in favour of parcels of meadow ground, and that this preference for meadow over arable strips also showed itself in manors of the lower Tees valley, downstream from Eggleston.[1] It seems that in several places in Durham the kind of farming procedures which had given the open fields their rationale was in decay. The obvious next step was consolidation of the open field strips and enclosure of the fields themselves. This was what took place, the common method followed being an agreement to enclose between the lord of the manor and the tenants, given legal force by a decree of the Palatine Chancery Court. The records of awards to enclose made by this Court are incomplete before 1633. But from then until 1700 twenty instances of townships enclosed by agreement are recorded, and a further eight of townships where the common pasture only was enclosed. Probably the rate at which enclosures were made by this procedure was just as high from 1580 to 1633, although the relevant decrees are missing. In addition there are many instances of agreements to enclose which were not confirmed in chancery, some of them relating to such large and important manors as Bishop Auckland and Chester-le-Street. It no longer seems possible (and would not perhaps be particularly helpful) to estimate the total acreage affected by enclosure. But it seems clear that the back of the open field system was broken in the Durham lowland during the seventeenth century. Relatively few open field villages were left to be dealt with by private Act of Parliament during the eighteenth century or later.[2]

By and large the change from open field to enclosed farming was carried out amicably and painlessly. There is certainly no basis for the picture of a catastrophic decline of arable farming painted by Dean James in 1597. The Dean asserted that 500 ploughs had been laid down in a few years, and that of 8,000 acres formerly under cultivation only 160 remained.[3] Possibly he may have been attributing to enclosure a disruption of agricultural routines which was really the result of the ravages of the plague during 1597–8, both bad years from this point of view. Nevertheless, agrarian change was not always painless.

[1] *Ag. Hist.*, p. 28; Gray, pp. 105–7.
[2] Leonard.   [3] *C.S.P. Eliz.*, *1595–7*, pp. 347, 420.

Depopulation did sometimes result particularly when landlords 'engrossed' holdings; and evicted tenants in order to
enlarge the home farms they worked themselves. The big
graziers and 'new' gentry tended to be well represented amongst
the engrossers and depopulators, sweeping their land free of
tenancies to make way for flocks and herds. Thus the returns
of the commissioners for the decay of military service in the
border counties made in 1584[1] show Sir Cuthbert Collingwood
as having converted three out of seven farmholds to grass in
Seaham, and Robert Widdrington as having decayed 'many'
tenants in Washington. In the parish of Stranton Sir Thomas
Gresham, the London financier and merchant, was returned
as having put out of their holdings thirteen of his fifteen tenants,
and three out of seven in Seaton Carew. Another notorious
engrosser was William Welbury, who had converted seven out of
sixteen ploughs to demesne at Castle Eden. The rich Newcastle
merchant William Lawson had similarly added four out of six
husbandlands at Thorpe Bulmer to his home farm. Sometimes
tenants were evicted to make way for the ornamental parks or
'domains' surrounding the new-style great houses, like Walworth. Complaints about clearances of this sort arose in the
1630s, an anonymous pamphleteer of 1634 asserting that Durham 'is nowe fruitfull of extortions and oppressions of this
nature, and it is verie easie to produce some townes as Walworth, Denton, Unaby, which (as the report is) are turned from
villages to domaines, and are depopulated by this meanes'.[2]

These instances confirm the point that practices like engross-
ment and depopulation, which were socially disapproved of
and intermittently subject to governmental prohibition, were
more likely to be found on small and medium-sized than large
estates. The big landlords were more in the limelight, and,
particularly if they were churchmen, required to set an example.
But even estates like those of the Bishop, in which enclosure by
agreement, was the rule, grievances could arise, the procedure
being liable to favour the wealthier and more powerful amongst
the tenants at the expense of the weaker. And abuses could

[1] P.R.O., S.P. 15/28: An Abstract of the Certificates of the tenancies and forces
decaied upon the borders . . . 1584.
[2] Hunter MS. 44(b) 'Certaine Observations Touching the estate of the commonwealth' (1634), fo. 31.

result from the profitable privileges conferred on estate officers, like the warrant granted Bishop Morton's steward in 1634 to improve land from the commons of half a dozen episcopal manors, and to let the improvements made, a concession which might easily lead to conflicts with the tenants.[1] Disputes of this sort may have been behind the petitions submitted to the House of Commons on the eve of the Civil War 'against the Bishop of Durham and others for their enclosures', and the serious disorders which followed. In 1641 companies three or four hundred strong assembled in several parts of the county 'in a warlike manner, upon pretence of pulling down enclosures'.[2] But the circumstances of these riots are obscure and the places where they took place are unknown; it is possible that the motivation was more political than agrarian.

The gentry who participated in the Rising of 1569 paid for the crime of rebellion with their property, not their lives. But this was not so in the case of the tenants and common people who rose with the earls and their adherents. The number of those set aside in county Durham for execution by martial law has been estimated at 320. But it is likely that only a proportion of these, probably less than half, were actually put to death.[3] Nevertheless there is evidence that the failure of the Rising, and the executions which followed it, made a deep impression. This was expressed in the two surviving ballads, 'The Rising in the North', and 'Northumberland betrayed by Douglas',[4] which are plainly the product of the society out of which the Rising arose. Both show an acquaintance with the events of the movement, and with the circle of the earls themselves. The verdict of this popular poetry on the Rising and its leadership indicates marked disillusion with the latter, although there is sympathy for the earls, and particularly for the tragic fate of the earl of Northumberland. As political leaders however both noblemen are presented as ineffective and irresponsible, proved such by the failure of their rebellion. 'The Rising in the North' comments bitterly on the flight of earls at the appearance of the

---

[1] A warrant of April 1634 authorized the steward to improve the commons of Lanchester, the Boldons, Bishop Auckland, Whitburn, Cleadon, and Sedgefield, and to grant out the improvements.

[2] *C.J.*, ii.471.   [3] See McCall.

[4] For 'The Rising in the North', see Child, Part VI, p. 404; for 'Northumberland betrayed by Douglas', see ibid., p. 411.

Queen's forces, abandoning their humble followers to the vengeance of the government. The Nortons, also involved in the rebel leadership, are said to have 'fledd away most cowardlye'. One verse contains a reference to the earls' promise of easy money, tempting the poor and ignorant into their treasonable and disastrous venture:

> Ladds with mony are counted men,
>   Men without mony are counted none;
> But hold your tounge why say you so?
>   Men wilbe men when mony is gone.

In 'Northumberland betrayed by Douglas' the consequences of political misjudgment and failure are put in the earl of Northumberland's own mouth:

> When I was at home in my [realm]
>   Amonge my tenants all trulye,
> In my time of losse, wherein my need stood,
>   They came to aid me honestlye.
>
> Therefore I left many a child fatherless,
>   And many a widdow to looke wanne;
> And therefore blame nothing ladye
>   But the woeful warres which I begann.

Sentiments of this kind, would not have been given ballad form if they had not been popular amongst the plebeian audiences which listened to ballad-singers in the ale-houses, and at fairs and markets. They suggest a *crise de confiance* in the traditional leadership which the great houses, and particularly the Nevilles, had provided. With the Nevilles gone, the Lumleys absentee, and the Newcastle men stepping into the place of the old families, ties of 'good lordship', 'faithfulness', and 'service' became increasingly meaningless. By the 1580s, on the Neville estates, the substantial husbandmen were no longer prepared to furnish themselves with the weapons and horses which had equipped Westmorland's armed and mounted retinue, although these were still required by their new lord, the Queen, for the defence of the Borders.[1] At the same time the trend, already apparent before the Rising, whereby landlord–tenant

---

[1] The commissioners of 1584 estimated that 100 horse which the earl of Westmorland had been able to raise to serve on the Border from the lordships of Brancepeth and Raby were 'decayed'. See P.R.O., S.P.15/28.

relationships were seen as contractual, rather than in terms of personal dependence, was strengthened; while the emphasis in estate administration came increasingly to be on what was 'most to the profit' of the landlord. There was a corresponding resistance on the part of tenants to increased rents, fines, and services, so that new conflicts and new forms of leadership emerged in the Durham countryside.

Underlying these landlord–tenant conflicts was the pressure of the sixteenth-century inflation. This resulted, over the country as a whole, in a fourfold price rise between 1500 and 1600, with a continued rise until a fivefold level was reached during the years between 1600 and 1630. There was pressure on landlords to raise rents because the real value of those paid progressively declined; but tenants stood to profit largely if rent payments remained stable while the prices of agricultural products rose. 'Custom' determined who would win out best, tenant or landlord. For it was the 'custom of the manor', as determined by the jury of the manorial court, which defined the tenant's obligations to the lord, the rents and fines he had to pay, the services he had to render. Custom traversed a spectrum of landlord–tenant relationships. On the one hand there was the fortunate 'copyholder by inheritance', his 'ancient' rent and fine specified in the 'copy' of the manorial court roll which was his title to the holding. 'Custom' effectively protected the copyholder by inheritance from any enhanced claims on the part of the landlord. At the other end of the spectrum there was the leaseholder, who in theory could not claim any protection from custom. Nor could custom ascribe any status at law to the lowly tenant at will, whose occupation of the soil was supposed to rest solely on the lord's tolerance of it. In the course of time, however, both these classes of tenant too had acquired a degree of protection; 'Customary' leases were renewed at 'the ancient rent' (i.e. without any enhancement) upon payment of a 'reasonable' fine, understood as three to five years of rent payments. Even the tenant at will might evolve into a 'tenant at will according to the custome of the manor', with a fixed rent and fine. And in the northern counties 'towards the Marches of Scotland', including Durham, tenants claimed a custom of 'tenant right' or 'Border service'. Their rents and fines were supposedly customary and they were bound to do service with horse and armour, at their own expense, against the Scots. But the status of customary tenants for years or lives (i.e. leaseholders) and customary tenants at will was unstable, liable to challenge by determined landlords willing to litigate with their tenants in the courts of common law. The status of 'tenant right' was similarly doubtful, particularly after the Union of the two Crowns of England and Scotland in the person of James I seemed to remove the likelihood of Border war. It was in these doubtful areas that conflict between lord and tenant was likely to arise.

On the lesser Durham estates tenants at will may well have been common.[1] But the great Church and lay landlords in the course of the sixteenth century had come to recognize customary rights as inhering in most of their tenancies. On the episcopal estates there was a numerous class of copyholders by inheritance, and the Weardale lands were a stronghold of 'tenant right'. There were also many leaseholds for lives or term of years, but these were granted for the most part 'according to custom', and so remained notoriously under-rented. Thus the manor of Easington in 1647 showed an 'improved' rental which was more than four times what the tenants actually paid; at Wolsingham the improvement was more than six times the rent.[2] There is less evidence about the rate at which the Bishop's officers levied fines on tenants. Those of the copyholders by inheritance were in some cases nominal, being less than a year's rent; but more substantial in others, as at Houghton-le-Spring, where fines were levied at three years' copyhold rent.[3] Fines on leaseholds conformed to the criterion of 'reasonableness', and ranged from as little as two, to as much as six years' rent.[4] The Neville estates were similarly under-rented on the eve of the Rising, and continued so subsequently as long as they remained in the hands of the Crown.[5] The Dean and Chapter were more reluctant to recognize the customary rights which their tenants claimed, but nevertheless rents remained remarkably stable on

[1] Above, p. 40 and n.   [2] Parl. Survey.
[3] Ibid.
[4] According to a note of leases to be renewed in 1601: Church Comm., Durh. MS., Misc. 221562.
[5] See above, p. 39. Dr D. S. Reid tells me that once the estates passed into the hands of Robert Carr, earl of Somerset, and then into those of the Vanes, rack-rents were progressively introduced.

this estate too, the £1,419 rent roll of 1541 having risen by little more than £100 almost a century later.[1]

Under the surface impression of calm and stability, however, the years between the Northern Rising and the Civil War saw recurring quarrels between landlords and tenants in Durham as elsewhere in the north. The former probed the weak points in the régime of custom in order to overthrow it and introduce enhanced fines and improved rents. The latter resisted this process. The conflicts which resulted were widespread, and broke out for example on the Neville estates while these were in the possession of the earl of Somerset during the second decade of the seventeenth century.[2] But Church estates were particularly prone to them; for Church landlords, with only a life interest in their lands, and needing to provide for heirs, daughters, and servants, were specially liable to be tempted by windfall gains and quick profits.[3] A common tactic followed to break custom was the grant of leases of customary tenancies to servants or agents of the landlord over the head of the customary heir. The lessee assumed the burdens and costs of establishing his title against the claimant by custom, and payed a correspondingly reduced sum for the lease. Thus in one of the earliest of the quarrels on the Church estates, between the Dean and Chapter and their tenants in the 1570s, the former tested the validity of custom by leasing customary tenements to 'strangers'.[4] Bishop Barnes in the 1580s assailed the tenures of Weardale by making leases of land supposedly held by custom to his

---

[1] Durh. D. & Ch. MSS., Receivers' Books.

[2] See Henry Sanderson's letter to Winwood of 12 Nov. 1615 (*C.S.P. Dom. Jas. I, 1611–18*, p. 328) commenting on the harsh treatment of the tenants of Brancepeth by Somerset's officers, and their desire 'to be the King's again'.

[3] Hence the Acts of 1571 and 1576 which forbade the letting out of Church lands on long leases in return for large fines; such lettings were restricted by these Acts to twenty-one years or three lives.

[4] According to the tenants' petition to the Council of 1575, the Dean and Chapter divided amongst themselves, by lottery, lands previously held 'in the right of their said church', in order that each prebend might hold his 'lottery' in severalty, 'so as everye of them might mak a singulre and private profett to them selves' (*Durh. Halm. Rolls*, p. xliii). The attack upon custom seems to have come from 'lottery leases' made by individual prebends (for instances of such leases see *Durh. Halm. Rolls*, p. 249) who 'for raiseing fines . . . lett leases to kinsfolk and servants, over the tenants' heads, menaced others, and by such like artifice, gott some [tenants] to submit to leases . . .' (Hutch., ii.163). Once leases had been introduced fines were gradually raised. For the circumstances in which the lottery system was introduced, see *Durh. Stat.*, App. p. 232.

servant Francis Conyers and others, who contested their leases with the customary tenants before the Council in the North.[1] Of a different kind was Bishop Neile's offensive against customary tenures in 1620, although this too was directed against Weardale. It was a much more direct, open, and uncompromising attack than in the past, the tenants being summoned to the Bishop's forest court under the title of 'Tenants at will', a designation which, if unchallenged would have effectively undermined the 'tenant right' status they claimed.[2] But Neile could expect the support of the Crown, James I having denounced 'the supposed custom of tenant right', with its requirement of Border service, as lapsed since the union of the Crowns. The King was at that time busily engaged on the overthrow of this same tenure on his own estates in Cumberland and Westmorland.[3] For the first time therefore the influence of the government did not underpin the customary régime.

The interest of these quarrels over tenure lies in the lively and novel forms of local initiative they produced, and the kind of political and social leadership they brought to the fore. The very possibility that the lord could be contested with in courts not his own over matters relating to rents, fines, and tenures involved a considerable readjustment of the traditional submissive posture characteristic of most Durham tenants in the early sixteenth century. Then, as the Dean and Chapter were to point out in 1662, the tenants of the Cathedral estates had held their lands 'onely for a terme of yeares, sometymes six, sometymes nine, but for the most parte but three, with condition to be obedient to the pryor and convent . . .'[4] Under the Tudors, however, fear of the agrarian disturbances which had accompanied the Pilgrimage of Grace, with the need to ensure that the peasantry should not be prevented by heavy rents and fines from equipping themselves for Border service, resulted in support for tenants from the Council in the North. In 1577 the Council conferred a custom of inheritance on the Cathedral tenants,[5] and in 1583 recognized the tenures of Weardale as customary.[6] These verdicts would not have been reached if the

[1] Weardale MSS., 93/1, 94/1, 96/1, 97/1; 99/1–29.   [2] Ibid., 109/5, 109/1.
[3] *C.S.P. Dom. Jas. I, 1619–23*, p. 430.   [4] Hutch., ii.165.
[5] *Durh. Halm. Rolls*, p. xxxvii.
[6] Weardale MSS., 93/2, 94/1–3, 96/1, 97/1–4, 113.

tenants had not organized themselves to present their case, and if a collective pressure had not been felt from 'combinations' of discontented peasants to obstruct the holding of manorial courts and prevent the collection of fines by the lord's agents. Determined leadership was present, this being most apparent in the Weardale dispute of 1620, when there was much complaint of the tenants' 'intemperate and disobedient behaviours', of the threat of 'some outrage against the officers', and of 'secrett combynations ... to resist all Authoritye'.[1] The kind of men who organized and led these movements came from much the same stratum of yeomen and substantial husbandmen which, earlier in the sixteenth century, had formed the background of the mounted retainers of the Nevilles and the other great houses. As bailiffs and the like they had held office under the great estates. John Robinson of Mid Merrington,[2] a leader of the Cathedral tenants in the disputes of the 1570s, belonged to this kind of background.[3] In the Weardale quarrels the leading role was played by the Emerson clan,[4] whose head traditionally held the bailliwick. This office, as late as 1569, when the last Border raid into Weardale was defeated by the bailiff and tenants, had its military implications.

Customary tenures may have been one of the issues involved in the Northern Rising, as well as in the Pilgrimage of Grace, for there was a tendency for dissident tenants to seek support from oppositional movements in the country at large. They continued to do so during the seventeenth century. In the Weardale dispute of 1620 the tenants drew up a petition to the House of Commons, appealing against decrees lately made in the Durham Chancery Court against their custom and in favour of the Bishop. They demanded a trial outside the county 'as the Bishop's prerogatives are so great, having jura regalia in the co. pal., ... they being 91 tenants and their families, and above 600 persons, who would all be turned abroad as beggars, if they lose their ancient estate ...'[5] There is no evidence that the petition was ever presented, or that the tenants were

---

[1] Ibid., 109/1.   [2] i.e. Middlestone.

[3] For the Robinsons, a substantial yeoman family, see Sur. *Hist. Durh.*, i.190, and *Durh. Halm. Rolls*, p. 237.

[4] Of the eight ringleaders in the Weardale dispute of 1620 against whom Bishop Neile instituted proceedings, four were Emersons.

[5] Weardale MS. 115.

granted their new trial outside the Bishop's jurisdiction. But it seems that they were not further molested. The agitation of the Dean and Chapter tenants in 1639 also had political implications, and stirred up a much more lively interest on the part of the government than the Weardale affair. For the tenants' petition to the Privy Council that the Dean and Chapter had violated their custom of tenant right by levying heavier fines than they were entitled to do by the decree of 1577 came at a time when Laud's régime of 'Thorough' had been shaken by the First Bishops' War. Writs had already been issued for elections to the Short Parliament, the first to meet for nine years. The movement of 1639 was the most elaborate and highly organized of its kind. As usual the leadership came from the prosperous middle class, in this case the rich Wear valley coal-owner George Grey of Southwick, a connection of the Hedworths and involved in the great Harraton colliery. His associate was Anthony Smith, a Durham lawyer. Both men would subsequently emerge as prominent Parliamentarians.

A member of the Chapter (probably Dean Balquanal) reported to Archbishop Laud on 10 March 1639 that the movement was a serious one. He described it as 'the great tumult in the country'. Grey and Smith assembled the tenants in 'tumultuous meetings' at which hundreds signed collective undertakings 'obliging themselves to one another to prosecute against their landlords before any judicatory these two should think fit'. They entered into a 'combination' and formed a 'public purse' with this end in view, to which £80 was subscribed.[1] Laud viewed the agitation with the utmost seriousness, asserting his conviction not only that 'it was a practice against the church', but also that 'he did believe there was some further design in the business'. The Dean and Chapter were urged to proceed against the tenants in Star Chamber, as well as 'never to renew their leases' either to themselves or to their children. Grey and Smith were imprisoned until they should reveal the names of the tenants who had subscribed to the fund. Both refused to obey, and remained in gaol until they were released upon the meeting of Parliament at the beginning of April.[2] The slogans and tactics followed, and the rituals used to express dissent were different. Nevertheless Grey and Smith had raised

[1] *C.S.P. Dom. Ch. I, 1639–40*, p. 538.   [2] Hutch., ii.157.

a countryside as effectively as Neville or Lumley had done in an earlier generation. They had done so, however, not by the appeal of inherited position and ancient blood but by the skill with which they had taken up and pursued an issue to which a large-scale popular response could be expected. A new style of regional leadership had made itself felt.

THE WORLD OF THE COAL INDUSTRY

As a result of the rapid expansion of the Tyne valley coal industry, by the early seventeenth century coal was being mined from a line of pits stretching upstream nearly eight miles from Newcastle, whose shafts, by using improved pumping machinery, penetrated more deeply into the seams than in the past.[1] As output mounted so the sinkings close to the river in the older coal-producing manors were becoming exhausted, and production was beginning to move inland. Already by 1635 collieries at Chopwell, Blackburn, and Ravensworth were producing for the export trade, instead of merely meeting a local demand.[2] From the 1630s however the rate of growth of the Tyne valley production began to decline. Expansion continued, but at a slower pace, although by 1659 the industry had recovered from the severe depression resulting from the parliamentary boycott of exports from royalist-controlled Newcastle. Shipments had doubled every fifteen years between 1565 and 1625; subsequently it was almost a century and a half before they doubled again.[3] By contrast the exploitation of the seams of the lower Wear valley began much later, but continued longer. It was not until the early seventeenth century, when demand in the south had already exhausted the more easily worked Tyne seams, that Wear coal shipped from Sunderland began to appear in the port books of Hull, King's Lynn, and Yarmouth. As a result by the 1630s Sunderland, incorporated as a borough by Bishop Morton, was already, after Newcastle, the most important coal-exporting port in the kingdom, shipments reaching 70,000 tons a year by 1634.[4] On the Wear however, unlike the Tyne trade, there was less of a fall-off in the growth rate after the first quarter of the seventeenth century. Shipments stood at 110,000 after the Restoration, and rose to 180,000 tons a year before

---

[1] Nef., i.26.   [2] Ibid., pp. 27–8.   [3] Ibid., pp. 25.   [4] Ibid., pp. 29–31.

---

5. *Antiquarianism:* (a) armorial shields at Lumley Castle, and (b) medievalized effigies of Lumley ancestors at Chester-le-Street ▶

1688. In 1609 Wear coal shipments had been only a twentieth of those of the Tyne, but by 1680 the ratio had risen to a third. Production on the Wear had originally centred on the Offerton colliery, sunk to supply the salt-pans of the Bowes family at Sunderland. But once the export trade got under way the lead was taken by the colliery at Harraton, which by the 1630s was contributing 6,000–8,000 tons a year to the shipments from Sunderland. By this time there were also important collieries at Lambton (probably with an annual output of 30,000 tons on the eve of the Civil War) and at Lumley. These with Harraton constituted the Wear equivalents of Whickham, Stella, and their like on the Tyne.[1]

The unrivalled concentration of resources and capital controlled by the Newcastle coal-owners, and the monopoly of the coastal coal trade from the Tyne put at the disposal of their Hostmen's Company by the charter of 1600, effectively prevented the rise in the Tyne industry of any independent Durham interest. Each partner in a Tyne colliery had to arrange for the sale of his share of the coal produced, but the Hostmen's Company forbade its members to deal in the coal of outsiders; with the result that it was no longer worthwhile for the latter, after 1600, to become partners in collieries. Consequently in the reign of James I to an increasing extent the Durham interests sold out to the Newcastle men, Durham mining entrepreneurs like Thomas Surtees, John Lyons, and George Downes disposing of their collieries in Whickham, Gateshead, and elsewhere to Hostmen.[2] By contrast Newcastle interests and names were almost wholly absent from the development of the Wear valley industry, which was undertaken partly by local men like John Sheperdson,[3] George Lilburne of Sunderland,[4] and Christopher Wharton of Offerton;[5] and partly by immigrant

---

[1] Ibid., p. 30.   [2] Ibid., ii.21–2.

[3] John Sheperdson and his family were involved in the partnership which exploited Harraton colliery, and also had extensive quarrying interests. See Nef, i.437; *Roy. Comp. Pps.*, pp. 395–6; *Sur. Hist. Durh.*, i.114; Parl. Survey, Survey of Houghton-le-Spring.

[4] For George Lilburne's colliery interests, see *Roy. Comp. Pps.*, pp. 275–80, and Robson, 'Lilburne', p. 92.

[5] The Whartons were Yorkshiremen by origin, but settled in the Wear valley in the sixteenth century, probably as a result of George Wharton's marriage to a sister of Bernard Gilpin, the famous rector of Houghton-le-Spring; Christopher Wharton was the latter's executor, another instance of contacts between the Church

---

◀ 6. *Stanhope Hall, Weardale:* seat of a family of upland squires, the Fetherstonhaughs

Yorkshiremen, like George Grey of Southwick or the Jacksons of Harraton.[1] Some of the capital was provided by London merchants, such as Richard Evans (in the case of the Lumley colliery) and Josiah Primatt, who financed Lilburne's ventures. But the Wear coal interest was never powerful or important enough to secure the monopolies and privileges granted to Newcastle. For in spite of recurring friction with the Newcastle coal-owners, it was government policy to concentrate the coal trade in their hands in order to ensure the effective collection of the levy on coal shipments.[2] This imposition was one cause of the tension which developed between the government and the Wear men, and of the latter's quarrel with the Newcastle oligarchy and their allies amongst the Durham gentry. The Sunderland coal-exporters resisted the attempts of the Hostmen to extend the 1s. levy on coal to shipments from Sunderland, until in 1610 this was denounced in the House of Commons and abandoned as far as the Wear trade was concerned. But its attempted reimposition in 1636 renewed the old resentments, and provided a solid economic basis for dislike of prerogative rule.[3] Nor was there any welcome on the Wear for the setting up, in 1635, of another government monopoly in favour of Newcastle, this time of the sea-salt manufacturing industry, which at Sunderland particularly was closely connected with the Wear coal interest. This was now to be controlled by a Society of Salt-makers consisting of the Tyne salt-pan owners and dominated by Hostmen.[4] The government also supported local landowners, in their quarrels with the Wear men, as in

---

and Wear entrepreneurial families. Christopher Wharton's coal interests appear to have been mainly in the Lumley colliery. See Nef, ii.35; Sur. *Hist. Durh.*, i.194; Foster, p. 322.

[1] Sur. *Hist. Durh.*, ii.19, 183. For George Grey, see also above, pp. 85–6.

[2] Hughes, pp. 93 ff.; Nef, ii.267 ff.

[3] *C.J.*, i.416, 428; Welford, iii.187–8; P.R.O. E126/4, fo. 244, 294.

[4] Hughes, loc. cit.; Carr, pp. lxxiii—lxxiv, 142–8, 167–72; Scott, i.209–10, 216, 219, 221–2; ii.468–70. The sea-salt industry on the Tyne at South Shields, where the Dean and Chapter were letting out 200 pans to 47 proprietors in 1635 (Durh. D. & Ch. MS., Prior's Kitchen, Receiver's Book, 1634/5), was on a much more extensive scale than that of Sunderland, where output was only about one-twelfth (the salt industry at Sunderland used 300 tens of coal in a year, as compared with 3,600 tens at South Shields; see *C.S.P. Dom. Ch. I, 1644–5*, pp. 98–9) of that of South Shields. But the Bowes colliery at Offerton had grown up in close association with Robert Bowes's sea-salt enterprises (see Galloway, p. 103). Most of the pans were on the Lambton estates. See also Pilbin.

the case of George Lilburne and Humphrey Wharton, who appealed in 1624 to the Council against Sir William Lambton and Sir Richard Lumley, for refusing passage for Wear coals over their lands, without which access to the river was barred. The response received was that the Council 'did not thinke fitt that the Board should be any further troubled with the foresaid question . . . untill the masters and owners of coales . . . to be vented at Sunderland . . . shall agree amongst themselves to allow the king such profitt upon theire said coales as upon the coales of Newcastle . . .'[1] The one ally of the Wear interests in government circles was Sir Robert Heath, chief justice of the Common Pleas, who had his own quarrel with the Newcastle men, and was a connection of a Durham family.[2] But Heath, suspected of sympathies with Puritanism and the opposition, was dismissed by Charles I in 1634.[3] It is not surprising then that Sunderland, under the leadership of its mayor, George Lilburne, should also have come under suspicion of oppositionist tendencies, religious and political. 'I confess', wrote one of Laud's informants early in 1640, 'it is an honour to the kingdom to have such towns as Sunderland was, to come up and flourish from small beginnings. But . . . I think . . . that the King's Majesty had better for awhile despise that honour and profit that accrues to him that way . . . than to suffer little towns to grow big and anti-monarchy to boot; for where are all these pestilent nests of Puritans hatched, but in corporations, where they swarm and breed like hornets . . .'[4]

The rise of the coal industry and of communities largely dependent on the collieries and the coal trade brought into being a novel kind of society whose way of life was not easy to harmonize with many of the traditional values and attitudes long accepted in the region. At the same time the coastal trade also brought a closer contact with London and with the restless political and ideological trends of the capital than had been the case in the past. The traditional way of life characteristic of the gentry was soon adopted by the 'adventurers' at the top of the industry, that is the entrepreneurs who provided the capital

---

[1] *A.P.C., 1623–5*, pp. 362, 487.
[2] Gardner, 1849 edn., pp. 86–9. Heath was a kinsman of the Heaths of Kepier, Durham.
[3] See *D.N.B.*   [4] *C.S.P. Dom. Ch. I, 1639–40*, p. 516.

to sink the pits, marketed the coal, and took the profits. In the case of the Newcastle men, as has been seen, these bought estates and country seats and sooner or later merged with the landed class. The Wear coal-owners by and large followed their example, although the smaller Wear fortunes made their ascent into the governing class less spectacular. But their contacts as managers and lessees of collieries with such established families as the Lambtons, Lumleys, Bellasises, and Hedworths of Harraton gave them the entry into gentry society, even if their relationship with the great landlords was not always a happy one. George Lilburne, George Grey,[1] and the Jacksons of Harraton all bought land and founded landed families, the Jacksons intermarrying with the Hedworths and settling themselves on a part of the latter's mortgaged estates.[2] At the same time, however, as has been seen, the Wear men remained a subordinate group, on the periphery of the ruling class, not securely within it, and sometimes unable to defend themselves against their Newcastle rivals and the latter's Durham associates.

A sense of grievance therefore helped to feed the radical and oppositionist attitudes which circulated amongst the group; and some of them emerged in due course as the natural agents of the Interregnum régimes in Durham, once the dominant families had been temporarily pushed into the background by defeat in the Civil War. The Lilburnes were the exemplary radicals, George Lilburne setting up in the 1630s as a patron of Puritans,[3] and his nephew Robert during the 1650s as protector of the emergent Baptist sect, while ruling Durham as one of Cromwell's major-generals.[4] In the democrat John Lilburne the family produced during the Interregnum a political and social theorist completely opposed to the dominant upper-class values of the age.[5] But the radicalism was inextricably entwined with other qualities: the ruthless opportunism and obsession

---

[1] George Lilburne bought lands at Offerton from the Wycliffes (1630) and the manor of Barmeston from the Hiltons (1669) (Summers, pp. 346–7). George Grey bought Hedworth lands in Southwick, and during the Interregnum purchased the fee simple of his Dean and Chapter leasehold there, as well as a Crown manor in Yorkshire; after the Restoration he lost heavily on the two latter purchases (Summers, p. 348; Sur. *Hist. Durh.*, ii.14–15).

[2] See Sur. *Hist. Durh.*, ii.179, 183.   [3] See below. p. 133 ff.

[4] See Douglas, pp. 32 and *D.N.B.*   [5] See Gibb; Gregg.

with gain of a rising and pushful entrepreneurial group. George Lilburne, in the course of a dispute whose rights and wrongs are not easy to sort out, fought a long and bitter battle with the Commonwealth grandee Sir Arthur Haslerig to secure possession of the rich Harraton colliery;[1] and Leveller John Lilburne was known in Durham as an oppressive and rack-renting landlord.[2] John Jackson was a political turncoat who was to profit from both sides in the Civil War, eventually securing a knighthood from Charles II.[3] Thomas Lilburne, having served Cromwell, in due course was to see himself as 'one of the instrumental persons in His Majesty's happy restoration'.[4]

It was the life of the pits themselves, and of those working them, which produced the most unfamiliar social structures and attitudes. In connection with these a new-style managerial hierarchy developed which had little about it of the overtones of service and dependence, or the legalistic background which characterized the traditional household and estate hierarchies of the region, like those of the Nevilles or the Bishop. In the smaller pits all that was needed was a foreman to oversee a few hewers. But in the big collieries a skilled manager was commonly employed, known variously as the 'viewer', 'banksman', or 'collier', who had expert knowledge of the whereabouts of coal and of the thickness and slope of the seams, as well as of drainage and pumping machinery.[5] Perhaps the most common background of such men was that of the substantial husbandman, usually from a coal-bearing manor, like Thomas Wakefield, a Whickham yeoman; but others claimed a higher status, like Thomas Surtees, 'a gentleman expert and skillfull in mineralls', who was paid £16 a week for pumping dry several of the Whickham collieries, and who was also a coal-owner himself.[6] 'Viewers' of this kind might act in a free-lance

---

[1] For the case for and against George Lilburne's behaviour over the Harraton affair, see Robson, 'Lilburne', and Sur. *Hist. Durh.*, i.258 and ii.178 ff.

[2] See *A true narrative concerning Sir Arthur Haslerigs possessing of Lieutenant-Colonel John Lilburnes estate in the County of Durham* (London, 1655), a petition to Parliament of the tenants of the Dean and Chapter lands granted Lilburne in Durham.

[3] See Sur. *Hist. Durh.*, ii.179, 183.

[4] Such was the inscription on his tomb. He had sat in the Parliament of 1656 and voted for Cromwell as King. See Summers, p. 347.

[5] Nef, i.418–20.   [6] Ibid., pp. 417, 422.

capacity, advising several coal-owners, and seeking to interest landlords or merchants (with capital available) in new mining ventures; or they might be permanently attached as managers to a specific colliery. In the latter case, not only did they decide on new sinkings, but also supervised all the coal-getting activities both on the surface and in the workings. They also hired and payed the work force and kept accounts of receipts and expenses. Where the pit had more than one shaft there was a surface foreman, the 'banksman' or 'overman', and another below ground, the 'underman'; the latter a skilled man who showed the hewers where to drive the 'headways', and how much coal to leave in pillars to support the roof of the workings. The sinking of shafts and driving of adits produced another kind of specialized and skilled foreman or overman, concerned solely with these activities.[1] There was therefore within the industry a graduated scale of posts and functions which (in spite of advancement by some 'adventurers' of relatives to managerial posts) encouraged a degree of social mobility, as in the case of Peter Pigg, overseer of Greenlaw colliery in 1627, who had been a workman there.[2] Viewers and their like however usually possessed at least some capital of their own, and often owned a share of the colliery they managed.

In the managerial hierarchy of the pits it was difficult to separate status from technical skill and the ability to apply this to maintain profitability, as well as to ensure the survival of the colliery enterprise and the pitmen working it. For the perils to be encountered in the harsh and dangerous underground world were still only partially known and charted.[3] Therefore, as one pit manager put it, ' . . . both the Officers and poor Miners, are in dayly Peril and Hazard of their Lives, for a poor Livelyhood, and . . . they may be easily destroyed by ignorant and unskilful Managers.'[4] The effective working of collieries depended on an empirical and pragmatic approach, and a willingness to learn from experience, attitudes which were characteristic of the men as well as the managers. Thus the colliers at the Lumley pit discovered a remedy for the dreaded explosive fire-damp by accidentally throwing lighted coals down the shaft, so igniting the gas; lighted coals were subse-

---

[1] Ibid., pp. 420–1.   [2] Ibid., p. 421.   [3] Ibid., ii.168 ff.
[4] *Compl Coll.*, pp. 45–6.

quently thrown down every morning before descending.[1] Members of the Royal Society were to learn much from colliers about the curious lore of their underground world. 'The colliers tell us', Dr. Henry Power told the Society in 1662, 'that if a pistol be shot off in a head remote from the eye of a pit, it will give but a little report . . . but if it be discharged at the eye of the pit in the bottom, it will make a greater noise than if shot off above . . .'[2] Similarly the fire-damp 'is observed to run along the roof of the pit, so that if the colliers have the fortune to see it issuing out, there is no way to secure themselves, but to lie flat into the seat of the pit, and do sometimes escape . . .'[3] Mr. Colepresse, imparting 'a Conjecture about the origins of wind' to the Society in 1667 used material declared to him by 'One John Gill, a man well experienced in minerall affairs . . . as a result of twenty years Experience and Observation of his own'.[4] In due course managers like Gill would be willing to generalize as well as observe, like one who asserted that all collieries had a 'rise', usually to the south or south-west, and a 'dip' in the opposing quarter, adding 'We can give no reason why this should be so, only I have myself fancied it may be by a magnetic sort of quality with respect to the Sun's noted ascent to the said South Points . . .'.[5]

The world of the collieries, whose perils increased as shafts were driven deeper, in which incompetence resulted in appalling accidents, and where fortunes were easily lost as won,[6] could not be easily related to the traditional concepts of gentility and hereditary status. Similarly there was a lack of contact with the dominant intellectual systems taught at the universities, whose abstract anti-empirical trend would have ruled out from the start any relevance to the preoccupations either of miners or their managers. Nor was it easy to incorporate the pit communities into the parish organization of the established Church. For miners were of 'the poor', who did not invest in the rented pews or 'places' (as they were called) which filled the parish churches;[7] and unlike the servant or journeyman, they had no master whose family pew they could share to partake of the parson's ministrations. Perhaps they might have responded to

---

[1] According to a paper given to the Royal Society in 1678. See Birch, iii.441.
[2] Ibid., i.134.   [3] Ibid.   [4] *Trans. Roy. Soc.*, vol. ii (1667), p. 481.
[5] *Compl. Coll.*, p. 40.   [6] Gray, p. 24.   [7] See below, p. 122 ff.

a 'preaching' of the vivid images of the Bible, but no preachers
seem to have appeared amongst them. In 1640, nevertheless,
the Tyne colliers, many of whom were Scots, were thought to
have convenanting and Puritan sympathies.[1] By and large the
setting required a practical and matter-of-fact kind of mentality,
with the emphasis on the quantitative and technological.
Tradition was irrelevant, and the connection with the past
already tenuous. There was most affinity therefore with the
scientists and 'experimental philosophers', a case in point being
that of Dr. Henry Power, an assiduous interrogator of colliers,
whose *Experimentall Philosophy* of 1663[2] included a section on
'Subterraneous Experiments, or, Observations About Coal
Mines'. In his book Power, in typical Baconian and Cartesian
fashion, denounced the metaphysical, 'peripatetick' preoccupations of academic intellectuals,[3] whom he contrasted with the
'experimentall and mechanical' philosophers, destined soon to
'lay a new foundation of a more magnificent Philosophy, never
to be overthrown: that will empirically and sensibly canvass the
Phenomena in Nature as we observe are producible by Art,
and the infallible demonstrations of Mechanicks . . .' The task
of the new-style philosopher was to unravel 'the management
of the great machine of the World', and his qualification was
to be that of an 'Artificer', 'well skilled in the wheelwork and
Internal Contrivance of such . . . Engines'. Power's 'experimental philsopher' was the manager writ large.[4]

The life of the pitmen also involved a break with the past in
that it lacked the family setting and the background of patriarchal dependence which formed the work-context of apprentice, journeyman, and farm-labourer. In the coal industry
labour was a commodity to be bought and sold, its price rising
and falling with the seasonal demand for it, wages being lower
in the winter when there was less work.[5] The coal-owners were
essentially employers, not masters, their remoteness from the
men increasing as the size of collieries grew. The relation-

---

[1] *C.S.P. Dom. Ch. I, 1640*, pp. 81–3.

[2] Power, a physician who practised at Halifax, was a naturalist with a particular
interest in 'microscopicall' studies, and a graduate of Christ's College, Cambridge;
he became a fellow of the Royal Society in 1663. He knew the Newcastle pits, and
also those of Leeds and Lancashire. For his career see *D.N.B.*

[3] Power, pp. 184 ff.   [4] Ibid., pp. 192–3.

[5] *Compl. Coll.*, p. 47, and Nef, ii.183 ff.

ship between them and the pitmen acquired an essentially 'economic' and quantitative character, which was underlined by the practice of paying hewers (although not other underground workers) by the piece.[1] Thus pit management came to be based on the number of 'corves' or baskets of coal cut daily by the hewers, which determined the wages each received. Carefully counted by the 'banksman' at the pithead, they were then entered in the colliery accounts.[2]

During the buoyant years of expansion in the Tyne industry between the 1560s and 1620s wages rose, and probably the doubling of miners' remuneration which took place between 1550 and 1700 happened for the most part at this time. Nevertheless it is unlikely that real wages kept pace with the mounting inflation; nor did the side-benefits spasmodically and to an uncertain extent available to pit-workers, like free coal, make much difference from this point of view.[3] Nevertheless what was most specifically characteristic of the pitman was less his poverty than his uneasy coexistence with the established social order. For he was a member of a despised and suspected group, recruited from the marginal and drop-out elements—the decayed husbandmen and wandering poor, immigrants from Scotland, or from the overpopulated Border dales whose half-savage inhabitants had a reputation for thieving and cattle raiding.[4] In the eyes of their Newcastle employers the colliers were an uncontrollable and potentially destructive force, liable in time of dearth 'to assemble themselves and make an uproar in the town', or 'if there be any troubles in the state, to make use of it to the damage of the town'.[5]

By the 1630s, with nearly 6,000 workers dependent on the Tyne coal industry, of whom nearly half worked underground, the size of the colliery community made it difficult to reabsorb such a large labour force back into agriculture during the slack periods.[6] Some miners, with cottages on the waste, like those illegally built towards the end of Elizabeth's reign near Chester-le-Street by one of the big Newcastle coal syndicates, could no doubt revert at need to the life of smallholders.[7] But the

[1] Nef, ii.181.   [2] For the procedure, see *Compl. Coll.*, pp. 36 ff.
[3] Nef, ii.180 ff.   [4] Ibid., pp. 146 ff.
[5] Welford, iii.348; *C.S.P. Dom. Ch. I, 1638–9*, p. 260.
[6] Ibid.; Nef, ii.138–9, 143.
[7] P.R.O., Durh. 2/1, Bill and Answers, Att. Gen. versus Gascoigne et al.

majority for whom no such alternative was available were increasingly accommodated in the new-style colliery communities which emerged, superimposed on villages whose traditional agrarian and manorial pattern they tended to disrupt. One of these was the manor of Whickham, a village which in the Parliamentary Survey of 1647 projected the outlines of a traditional order blurred and distorted by the impact of coal production. There were still seven substantial tenants with copyhold farms of forty to ninety acres scattered through the oxgangs and riggs of the open fields; and eleven more smallholders with twenty acres or less. But the majority of the holdings had been divided and sub-divided to form building-plots for the four score house owners and cottagers, many of whom were no doubt housing landlords, letting out rooms in their recently built messuages to poor families working in the pits. These studded the open fields and the town moor to the number of well over a hundred (there were seventy-nine in the Eastfield alone) with those near the banks of the Tyne already worked out and drowned. The traditional manorial jurisdiction and controls had broken down, partly no doubt because of the Civil War. Most of the householders and cottagers, although copyholders, had never attended the manorial court to take out their copies. The manorial mill, at which the tenants were supposed to grind their corn, was in ruins; and although the numerous quarries in the manor were the lord's, 'every one without controul diggeth what him listeth', without paying rent, impelled no doubt by the building boom. In Sunderland too, incorporated as a borough in 1634 with a list of aldermen which was a roll-call of the Wear coal-owning families, a similar quasi-urban landscape was growing up against a background of quarries and salt-pans. Here George Lilburne owned six housing and waterfront sites built over with a warren of messuages and tenements, with galleries, entries, ways, passages, and chambers, fronted by wharfs and ballast quays, and let to sub-tenants.[1]

FAMILY, HOUSEHOLD, AND SCHOOL

As the social order was thus subjected to the pressures and tensions of change, another influence asserted itself with greater

---

[1] Parl. Survey; Surveys of Whickham and Sunderland.

force and in a different direction than in the past. This was the influence of the school and of education. The interest of Protestantism in the 'godly grammar school' has been mentioned above.[1] For reformers like Bernard Gilpin, education implied above all the study of Scripture and the precepts of true religion. But the latter was from the first inseparable from the scheme of rhetorical education which in England owed most to Erasmus and Ludovicus Vives, and which had been incorporated in the statutes of St. Paul's School founded in London by Erasmus's friend John Colet in 1510,[2] the first establishment of its kind. The new-style instruction provided by 'grammar schools' of this sort based on the 'humanist' rhetoric of the Erasmians, was founded on the study of the classical languages and literature, beginning with Latin, and going on to Greek. The object was to inculcate a fluency in speech and writing, particularly in Latin, the literature being treated primarily as a source of terms, phrases, and expressions. These were to be learnt by the pupil for use in the various forms of literary and verbal expression sanctioned by classic usage, inherited from the rhetorical conventions of the ancient world.[3]

How this was done emerges from the course of instruction followed at Durham School, in accordance with orders laid down by Dean Matthew, in 1593.[4] Once the rules of Latin grammar had been mastered, the pupil went on to exercises in Latin prose composition, beginning with 'an epistle . . . according to the principles of Erasmus or Ludovicus Vives'. Next he was taught to make 'a theme according to the precepts of Apthonius'; and then learnt to 'frame and make an oration according to the precepts of rhetoric', with Cicero as his guide. Instruction in Latin verse, and in the rules of versifying and scansion, followed. Lastly Greek was to be learnt, and the rhetorical forms of epistle, oration, and theme, followed by versification, were to be mastered in this language as well. The new-style instruction was much more literary in its emphasis than that usually given in schools of comparable status before the Reformation, and had less of a vocational content. The more traditional kind of teaching had also been based on Latin, but with less reference to classical literature and style, and more

[1] See above, p. 63.   [2] See Simon, pp. 73–80.
[3] Simon, pp. 102–23; Watson, pp. 5–8.   [4] *V.C.H. Durh.*, i.377–8.

to the mechanical inculcation of grammatical rules with the Latin liturgy as the main text used. Priority had also been given to the use of Latin as an instrument of dialectic, which played a large part in the study of theology as taught at the universities, rather than of rhetoric. The vocational bias therefore was clerical; instruction was geared first and foremost to the needs of the Church.[1]

The emphasis on fluency in the humanist grammar school by contrast had no specific vocational bent, but had a relevance to all callings, secular as well as clerical. The training provided had two aspects. In the first place the grammatical structure and literary forms of classical culture had to be mastered, but the pupil was not intended merely to imitate what he had learnt. Instead he was taught to select passages and phrases which interested him, entering these in notebooks and commonplace books. They were then adapted and used in his own compositions. The grammar school thus imparted the experience first of assimilating, and then of manipulating and using, a generalized system of cultural standards and values, that of humanist rhetoric. Access to this was by means of the Latin Grammar composed by William Lily, whose use after 1540 was made obligatory in the schools by royal proclamation. At the same time the religious and moral instruction which all grammar schools provided was based on the use of a Latin and Greek catechism, and on the treatment of the sermon as a form of rhetorical exercise, to be memorized and repeated. This helped to relate educated lay opinion to the established religious system. In the grammar school this had to be assimilated with a thoroughness previously thought unnecessary except on the part of the professionally religious, i.e. the educated clergy.

The humanist school established itself in the region after the Reformation, the model in this respect being the grammar school at Durham, where a master, under-master, and eighteen scholars had been maintained by the abbey before the dissolution. This establishment was refounded in 1541 at the same time as the monastery was converted into a Dean and Chapter of secular canons. The first clear indication that an Erasmian and humanist style of instruction had become the rule is to be found in the Cathedral Statutes of 1555, which

[1] Simon, pp. 48–50; Watson, pp. 3, 5.

provided that the pupils were to be taught to speak and write Latin, as well as the traditional grammar. The master was also required to know Greek and 'to train in piety and to adorn with sound letters' the pupils of the school. He provided the religious inculcation and moral example which were also part of the Erasmian educational schema.[1] With such an influential figure as Dean Whittingham interesting himself in the school and teaching in it in the 1560s,[2] the way opened for its development into the fully fledged grammar school of Dean Matthew's 'Orders'. Subsequently the rise of such establishments owed as much to lay as clerical initiative, an exception in this respect being Bernard Gilpin's school. This was notable for a particularly emphatic religious bent, the statutes affirming that the first duty of the master was to see 'his schollers frequent divine service on holy dayes, with godly bookes to looke on'. But the provision that 'he shall read them the catechismus Greek and Latin appointed for all scholes', and that the usher was to spend his spare time talking to the pupils of 'books, commentaries, poets' fables, hard places and grammar rules' shows that the instruction here too was essentially humanist, and that there was provision for learning Greek.[3]

This was certainly intended to be so in the case of another clerical foundation, the grammar school set up by the widow of Robert Swift, late chancellor of Durham, at Bishop Auckland in 1605, as in the similar school at Heighington founded by the Jenisons of Walworth four years previously. The statutes of both made provision for instruction in grammar (at Heighington Lily's book is prescribed) and in Greek as well as Latin.[4] More modest in scope were the schools established at Darlington in 1563, the result of local initiative backed by Bishop Pilkington; and by William Grimwell (a London Merchant Taylor who was presumably a local boy made good) at Wolsingham in 1612. In both instruction in Latin only seems to have been contemplated. Finally there were two foundations which although just outside the boundary of the region had many connections with it. One was the grammar school at Hexham, to whose endowments the Durham Lawsons of Usworth contributed, which received a royal charter in 1599. This taught

---

[1] *Durh. Stats.*, p. 145.   [2] Strype, *Parker*, i.268.   [3] *V.C.H. Durh.*, i.393.
[4] Ibid., pp. 396, 399.

an elaborate humanist syllabus, including Greek, which probably owed much to the arrangements at Durham School. The other was the grammar school at Newcastle, founded in the 1540s by a local alderman, but which received a royal charter in 1600. In the course of the next four decades many of the Durham gentry would attend this school.[1]

During the half-century or thereabouts before the Civil War a significant development was the progressive replacement of the family and household by the School as the setting in which the gentry and rural middle class were educated. The Durham episcopal *familia* still exceptionally survived as late as the 1630s as a place of educational resort on the part of the well-born. Bishop Morton (according to Spearman) had 'young gentlemen of good families in his household whom he educated and preferred'.[2] But since the fall of the Nevilles, the departure of the Percys and the Lumleys, and the extinction of the Latimers (to mention only some of the casualties amongst the great households) the opportunities for this kind of education had become few and far between, with the disappearance of the aristocratic 'affinities' which had sustained it.[3] In addition the traditional styles and values of the 'noble' culture disseminated by the household establishments had become superfluous and outdated, or subjected to persistent criticism by the same humanist intellectuals who were behind the new educational forms. The rituals of waiting and the serving of ceremonial meals taught in the houses of the great were now increasingly dispensed with or relegated to menials. The acquisition of military skills and the arts of the chase were no longer regarded as primary in the education of a gentleman, which now acquired an essentially literary core. To this such activities were peripheral, and could be harmful if they distracted overmuch from grammar and its associated disciplines.[4] A recurrent theme too of the humanist culture, given a wider dissemination

[1] Ibid., pp. 368 ff., 399. For the Hexham school, see *N.C.H.*, iii.211 ff.; for Newcastle, Laws, *passim*, and Tuck.

[2] Spearman, p. 43.   [3] See above.

[4] Cf. Starkey, 'Fyrste, loke what an idle route our nobul men kepe and nurysch in theyr housys, which do no thyng els but cary dyschys to the table and eate them when they have downe; and after, gyving themselfe to huntynge, haukynge, dysyng, cardyng, and other idul pastymes and vayne ...' Erasmus popularised the humanist tradition which denigrated military pursuits in comparison with literary activities.

than in the past through the set texts which circulated in the schools, required that such basic aristocratic values as 'honour' and 'lineage' should be confronted by those of 'reason' and 'virtue'. These were presented as the basis of a 'true nobility' which excelled that of blood and descent, and which was more consonant too with Christian teaching. Erasmus, in one of his books for children, trenchantly set the values of the school against the trappings of lineage, exhorting the children: 'Let others have painted on their escutcheons lions, eagles, bulls, leopards; those people possess more real nobility who in place of all the quarterings on their shields can produce as their ensigns the proofs of so many liberal arts.' It was Erasmus who had put the same point in religious terms which would also establish themselves as grammar school commonplace: 'Let it not move thee one whit when thou hearest the wise men of this world . . . so earnestly disputing of the degrees of their genealogy or lineage . . . thou, laughing at the error of these men after the fashion of Democritus, shalt count . . . that the only most perfect nobleness is to be regenerate in Christ.'[1] These ideas were not new but had long been commonplace amongst university intellectuals. The grammar schools however gave them a wider circulation.

Attitudes of this kind tended to be reinforced by the specialized environment which the schools provided, now increasingly emerging as a feature of the childhood experience of the gentry and better-off in the region. The schoolmaster, in the humanist educational schema, was no mere imparter of knowledge and skills, but a quasi-charismatic figure, by his example and teaching the source of morals and religion, and standing *in loco parentis* in relation to his pupils. The requirement made in the statutes of such grammar schools as Durham, Newcastle, and Hexham, that the master should 'cultivate religion and adorn learning', that he should be 'discreet, sober, and of godly conversation', had such a role in view. Office and man were more than adequately matched in the case of the formidable Puritan Peter Smart, appointed master of Durham School in 1597, or such markedly successful Newcastle headmasters as Robert Fowberry (1607–23), that 'learned and painful man to indoctrinate Latin and Greek', and Amor Oxley (1635–45);

[1] Erasmus, *De Civ.* and *Enchiridion Militis Christiani*, quoted Simon, pp. 68–9.

or Henry Smelt at Durham in the 1630s. In the school environment the master, as the authoritative representative of the system of morals, values, and religion which the school inculcated, now shared with the father the educative role which in the family and household setting the latter had monopolized as the patriarchal family head.[1] Family traditions, values, and skills were irrelevant to the requirements of the school, where standing depended on excellence in performance of the tests and tasks set by the master, and where success was rewarded by the latter's approbation. Thus at Hexham grammar school, because 'Socrates saith the love and comendacion of praises are a great spur to a scholler to stir him up to virtue', every quarter all exercises prepared by the boys, both in Latin and Greek, were submitted to the master, who after 'due examining, perusing and reading, shall place that scholler who hath the best epistle etc. in the chiefest or best seat of that form in the which he remayneth, without anie favour or respect of persons whatsoever'.[2] This hierarchy of meritocratic preeminence had already been described with approbation by Erasmus as applied at St. Paul's early in the sixteenth century. There the boys were not only divided into forms, but each form had its 'head or captain' who 'has a little kind of desk by preeminence'. The system was general in the humanist schools,[3] and its pressures and requirements were at the very least different from those of the household community of relatives and servants which had previously formed the educative background of most children of the upper class.

The developing layout of gentry houses suggests, however,[4] that the household was itself evolving and changing, the emphasis being increasingly on a specialized private setting for the

[1] *V.C.H. Durh.*, i.378; Laws, pp. 65–74, 85–95; Tuck. pp. 264–5. A more complete picture of the ideal godly/humanist schoolmaster is given in the statutes of the Free Grammar School of Wakefield. The master was required not only to be an M.A. but also 'withal well reported for his knowledge, religion and life, . . . a lover and forward imbracer of God's truth, a man . . . diligent and painful in his own studies, of a sober and amiable carriage towards all men, able to maintain the place of a schoolmaster with dignity and gravity, given to diligent reading of God's word'. His first charge was to instruct his scholars in 'the ground of religion', next 'in the plainest and most familiar sort teach them grammar, and the Latin and Greek tongues', and finally to inform them 'in good nurture and manners which are of themselves an ornament to religion and good learning'. See Simon, op. cit., pp. 329–30, and Peacock, pp. 62–3, 65–6.

[2] *N.C.H.*, iii.215.   [3] Carlisle, ii.82.   [4] See above, p. 13ff.

7. *Humanism becomes visible:* (a) a renaissance fireplace at Lumley Castle; (b) the entrance to Walworth Castle ▶

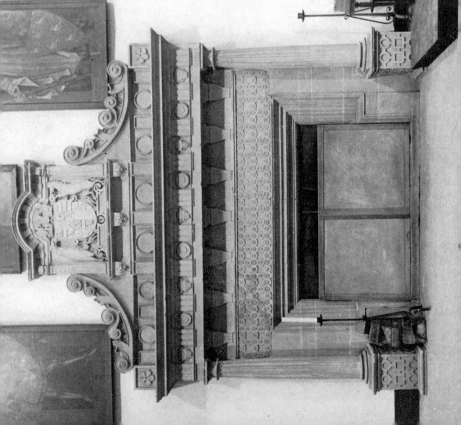

8. *New-style gentry housing:* Horden Hall

9. *The past romanticized:* castellated effects at Walworth

family adults, another for servants, and a nursery for children. As the nuclear family of parents, children, and close relatives withdrew into the privacy of their apartments, a decline took place in the socializing function of the household, the school becoming the latter's natural complement in this respect. The school also increasingly monopolized the equipment and contacts needed for entrance to the universities and the Inns of Court, places where the foundations were laid for a successful career. The household style of education continued to enjoy prestige in Court circles until the end of Elizabeth's reign, Burghley's household school being notable in this respect;[1] but this had already ceased to present itself as a practical educational alternative for the provincial gentry, including that of the north-east. Educational opinion increasingly pointed (as for example did Richard Mulcaster in 1581)[2] to the school as the only appropriate setting in which the children of the gentry would make contact, on terms of equality, with classes other than their own, and so acquire a sense of the total polity over which they would subsequently rule. There is little to surprise therefore in the mounting influx into Durham School, from the 1590s onwards, of the offspring of leading Durham families, beginning with John Bowes, son of Sir George, of Streatlam, who in 1591 matriculated at Saint John's College, Cambridge, from this school. Subsequently until the Civil War there was a flow to Cambridge, from the same source, of Salvins, Blakistons, Lambtons, and others.[3] Bernard Gilpin's school was the resort of the gentry, yeomen, and entrepreneurs of the lower Wear valley, and from there Shadforths, Shepardsons, Huttons, and members of the influential Bellasis family found their way to the university (all to Cambridge) and to the Inns of Court.[4] Most of the great Tyne coal-owners of Newcastle origin who had settled on Durham estates continued to patronize the grammar school of their native town, the Newcastle school however being also attended by some members of older Durham stocks connected with the north of the county and with coal, like the Lilburnes and the Blakistons of Gibside; also by some representatives of Church families, like the Blakistons of Newton Hall, the Cradocks, Comyns, and Ewbanks. Amongst the

---

[1] Simon, pp. 344–6.   [2] Mulcaster.
[3] *Alumn. Cantab.*, i.191, 161–2; iii.38.   [4] Ibid., i.130; ii.442; iv.60.

Durham coal-owning squires who sent their children to Cambridge from Newcastle were the Andersons of Haswell, the Liddells of Ravensworth, and the Davisons.[1] Recusants of course were thinly represented in the schools (although several Salvins attended Durham); and although Riddells of Gateshead and Tempests of Stella attended the universities, the rule in these Romanist families was probably instruction in the household by a tutor.[2]

It is difficult not to connect this closer involvement of the governing class with school, university, and Inns of Court, with the increasingly ideological cast which politics assumed during these years. For by assimilating the articulated cultural, religious, and legal systems which these institutions disseminated those effectively thus equipped became inclined to express their grievances, conflicts of interest, and convictions in generalized constitutional, religious, or philosophical terms. Moreover, although the full breadth of the new educational system was only available to the relatively well-off, and to the small élite of poor boys who were given free places in the grammar schools or scholarships at the universities, literacy (although to an unknown extent) was spreading downwards, largely as a result of the Protestant concern that all should have access to the written Word of Scripture. To what extent Bishop Barnes's injunction to his clergy in 1577 to 'duly, painfully, and freely teach the children of their several parishes and cures to read and write' cannot be known.[3] But the impulse to educate the poor persisted, and found expression in some of the new school foundations. The Heighington school for example aimed primarily at providing cheap instruction for parish children of humble origin; and in Bernard Gilpin's school the usher was required 'to help the meaner scholars to write cipher and understand figures'.[4] Similarly the schools at Wolsingham and Darlington, and the foundation of Robert Swift at Sedgefield, seem to have developed primarily as reading and writing schools for local boys of modest background.[5]

---

[1] Laws, pp. 65–95; *Alumn. Cantab.*, i.28–9; ii.18; iii.83, 456. The Andersons were also well represented at Oxford; *Alumn. Oxon.*, i.23.

[2] *Alumn. Oxon.*, pp. 1256, 1465.   [3] *Durh. Eccles. Proc.*, p. 19.

[4] *V.C.H. Durh.*, i.395, 399–400.

[5] Ibid., pp. 387–8, 399; Sur. *Hist. Durh.*, iii.419.

Something can be learnt about the diffusion of literacy, and its incidence at the various social levels from the depositions made by lay witnesses before the Durham Consistory Court, which were either signed, or else validated by mark, in the case of deponents who could not write. For the years 1565–73, of the total number of deponents appearing before the court, nearly four-fifths could only make a mark.[1] Of the remainder, the gentry constituted a relatively literate group, 70 per cent of them being able to write, as compared with less than half of the yeomen, or substantial farmers, ranking next to the gentry in the rural social scale. In the case of both yeomen and gentry an interesting contrast emerges between the older and younger generations: illiteracy was most prevalent amongst the former.[2] If the relatively small sample which is all the deposition books make available can be trusted, merchants and shopkeepers were another highly literate group, the equals of the gentry in this respect, over two-thirds of them being able to sign their names.[3] But then begins the non-literate world of the lower classes. Less than one-fifth of the blacksmiths, weavers, shoemakers, and others who followed craft occupations could write.[4] Illiteracy was still more prevalent amongst the peasantry. Of the 119 'husbandmen' or small farmers who made depositions before the court, only nine could write their names; of the still more humble 'labourers', mostly farmworkers, 37 out of 39 were illiterate.[5]

But by the 1620s an appreciable decline has taken place in the rate of illiteracy. Gentlemen no longer appear at all amongst   ✓

---

[1] Cons. Ct. Bks., V/2, 1565–73. Of the 645 depositions recorded during these years, 472 (73·18%) were marked, and 173 signed. 40 clergy made depositions, and the exclusion of these reduces the number of signatures from 173 (26·82%) to 133 (20·06%).

[2] Out of 36 gentlemen, 25 (69·5%) signed their depositions; out of 63 yeomen, 28 (44·5%) signed. Amongst the gentlemen illiterates were James Elmeden aged 80, James Shafto aged 60, John Rackett aged 54, Nicholas Porter aged 40. John Lilburne, aged 31, grandfather of the Leveller, is however a case of a relatively young gentleman illiterate. A characteristic if extreme case of the contrast between two yeoman generations is that of the illiterate Robert Smith, yeoman, aged 87, and his son William, aged only 16, who wrote a good, flowing signature.

[3] Only 13 merchants and shopkeepers appear amongst the deponents, 4 of them being illiterate. The latter are again of the older generation, like Thomas Whitfield, aged 58, and Thomas Fewter, aged 50.

[4] Out of 65 deponents in various craft occupations, 55 (84·6%) were illiterate.

[5] i.e. 92.4% of the husbandmen were illiterate, and 94·8% of the labourers.

the deponents unable to sign their names. More important, the proportion of illiterates amongst witnesses of all classes has fallen from the near four-fifths of 1565–73, to just above two-thirds for the years 1626–31.[1] In what social milieu the improvement was most apparent is, however, unclear, since the books for these latter years do not specify the occupations of deponents. It would be surprising if this development had no connection with the many-sided educational activity described above, and if the result of the latter had not been to carry literacy more deeply into the world of the middling husbandman, in which it had been notably rare in the previous generation.

This trend towards an increasingly literate society suggests a connection with the tendency, present even in remote Durham, for local conflicts, like those over tenant right and religion, to place a premium on informed and instructed leadership, able to formulate grievances in general terms. It is significant that John Lilburne, a seventeenth-century exemplar of this kind of leadership, should have claimed as his credentials for the role not only the traditional ones of gentility, in the sense that 'I am the sonne of a gentleman, and my friends are of rank and quality in the Countrie where they live . . . My father wore a gold chain as the badge and livery of a very Illustrious and Noble Earl . . . My mother was a Courtier bred . . .',[2] but also those of the educated man, being 'brought up well nigh ten yeares together, in the best schools in the North, namely at Auckland and Newcastle' where 'beside my knowledge in the Latin tongue, I was a little entered into the Greek also'.[3] Here the ceremonious world of the great houses, with its badges, liveries and gold chains, already mythologized and presented through a romantic haze,[4] is neatly juxtaposed with that of the common-

---

[1] Cons. Ct. Bks., V/12, 1626–31. Out of 489 deponents, 25 were clergy; of the remainder, 157 signed (32·1%) and 305 (67·9%) made a mark. If the clergy are included amongst the literates, the percentages become 47·21% literates to 52·89% illiterates.

[2] Lilburne, 'Letter'.   [3] Lilburne, *Innocency*.

[4] The Lilburnes had been followers of the Nevilles before the fall of that family, but there is no evidence of any subsequent connection with a great house, or that Richard Lilburne, John's father, ever held office under any earl, including the earl of Northumberland, his most probable patron. The fact that the peer in question is not named, and that Lilburne had been content the year before merely to claim 'I am the sonne of a Gentleman, and my friends are of rank and quality

place books, exercises, overpowering pedagogues and 'desks of preeminence' which were the marks of the very different environment of the school.

---

in the Countrie where they live' (Lilburne, *A Work*) suggests that he was probably romancing about his father's office and gold chain, in much the same fashion as Father William Palmes, in *Lawson*, romanced about the ancestors of Mrs. Dorothy Lawson. See below, p. 137 ff.

5

PATTERNS OF BELIEFS AND IDEAS

ANTIQUARIANS, ARMINIANS, AND PURITANS

As THE pace of change, economic, social, and political, within the region quickened, so a renewed interest in the Durham past emerged. In part this can be connected with the rapid turnover which, after 1570, was increasingly apparent in the gentry class, and with the need which therefore arose to constitute newcomers as gentry, but in ways which emphasized the persistence and continuity of the traditional gentry norms and values. Heraldic Visitations played an increasingly important role as the means whereby newcomers were admitted, with the seal of social approval, to be gentry. These were inquisitions, authorized by royal commission, at which families claiming gentry status were required to attend the visiting herald and submit the symbols of gentility, pedigree, and coat of arms, for his approval (he also provided both, at a price, for those without). Their popularity, and the effectiveness of their procedures, grew with the appetite for gentry status. For whereas 56 families appeared before the heralds at the Visitation of 1575, and 102 in 1615,[1] in 1530, before the enlargement and renewal of the gentry class had got under way, only some half-dozen families took the trouble to enroll at the Visitation.[2] The obsession with pedigree and 'ancient blood', which was quite as strong amongst the 'new' and 'rising' gentry as amongst the old, led to an interest in the past, the result of a sharpened concern to re-establish the historical continuity of a region so many of whose social and religious traditions had been undermined or destroyed. Significantly enough one of the earliest sixteenth-century Durham antiquarians was a Recusant gentleman and late follower of the fallen earl of Westmorland,

[1] Above, p. 71 ff. For the background and procedure of the Visitations see Wagner, pp. 55 ff.

[2] Tonge. But if the practice of visiting the gentry at their homes, instead of requiring them to attend the herald at a designated centre, was still prevalent in 1530 (Wagner, p. 56) this would be a factor in the restricted scope of this Visitation.

William Claxton of Wynyard, who in the 1570s collected materials for a history of Durham, and corresponded with Camden and Stowe. The connection between the cult of antiquity and that of pedigree and 'ancient blood' is suggested by the hospitality and assistance Claxton extended to the heralds Flower and Glover when they made the Durham Visitation of 1575. Nearly a third of the pedigrees then registered seem to have been recorded during Glover's stay at Wynyard.[1]

The high priest of the same cult however was Durham's sole surviving peer and leading (though absentee) lay magnate, John, 6th Lord Lumley (1533–1609), a cultured nobleman who built up a great library, and belonged to Elizabeth's Society of Antiquaries. Camden described him as 'a person of entire virtue, integrity and innocence, and now in his old age a complete pattern of nobility.[2] In the course of his career Lumley had been closely involved with the decline at Court of the influence of the 'ancient' nobility to which he belonged, and had witnessed the triumph of Cecil and other courtier 'upstarts' whose influence he had opposed as a supporter of Norfolk and his faction during the first decade of the reign; just before the outbreak of the Northern Rising he had been arrested on suspicion of treason, subsequently spending fourteen years in the Tower. Through his wife he eventually secured for his family the greater part of the property of the wealthy earl of Arundel, but nevertheless died childless, and alienated from his heirs. No doubt the difficulties and failures which Lumley had undergone in the course of his own career played their part in turning his mind towards the past, and the former glories of his family. At any rate the gathering together of the family records was a principal preoccupation of his old age; and he set up in Chester-le-Street parish church a long line of mostly spurious funeral effigies, commemorating each generation of Lumleys from the founder, the Saxon Liulph, to his own father, with a Latin genealogy composed by himself.[3] He also made the hall of

[1] See Sur. *Hist. Durh.*, i.5.

[2] See G.E.C., viii.276, *D.N.B.*, and *Lum. Libr.*, pp. 7 ff.

[3] See the description in Sur. *Hist. Durh.*, ii.139–42 and 159; see also Pevsner, pp. 66–7, 'The majority of the monuments are Elizabethan, but in imitation of the medieval style, an extremely interesting case of early, self-conscious, medievalism.' Camden says they were 'either gotten together out of monasteries that were subverted or caused to be made anew' (*Britannia*, p. 742).

Lumley castle a family shrine, hung with fifteen specially painted portraits of ancestors, with 'a pillar' of his pedigree in marble, and an equestrian statue of Liulph in full armour.[1] Inscriptions on the walls drew on conventionally pessimistic themes of the late medieval culture relating to the transience of the world, of honour, fame, and nobility before the onslaught of time, which creates but also destroys empires and honours. Finally there was the pious exhortation: 'The world passes away, Christ does not pass away; worship not that which passes away.'[2]

This sense of transience, nourished by religious, political, and social change, stimulated the sense of history, the past seeming the more poignant by contrast with the 'decay' of traditional values, which some could perceive around them, and the supposed stable permanence which antiquity had achieved. Thus the author of *Certaine Observations Touchinge the Estate of the Common-wealthe*,[3] written in 1634 'principally for the benefit of the county of Durham', pointed to the ruin of castles, the decline of martial skill, and 'Depopulation of the Commonwealth, by the hard, unnatural, uncharitable and unchristian dealing of the landlords' as symptoms of a state of social disarray which he hinted was a punishment for the 'sins of the past', including in particular the overthrow of the old religion and the monasteries. But for others this same sense involved a reaching back over the gulf of the Reformation, and the break which this had brought about in the religion, institutions, and attitudes of the region. Thus there was a search for the continuities, particularly in matters relating to the Church, which might help to close the gap. As early as 1574 Christopher Watson had begun to write at Cambridge an *Ecclesiastical History of Durham*, and an *Abstract of the Lives of the Bishops*, although his work remained in manuscript.[4] The same themes were developed in the reign of Charles I by the Oxford don Robert Hegg, a native of the city of Dur-

---

[1] See Sur. *Hist. Durh.*, ii.154–5; The display of eighteen shields on the wall above the entrance to the courtyard of Lumley castle is another instance of Lord Lumley's consciously 'medievalizing' tendencies; see Pevsner, p. 182.

[2] A contemporary account of Lumley castle and the inscriptions which the 6th lord had painted on its walls exists amongst the Lumley papers at Sandbeck Park; portions of this, with English translations of parts of the inscriptions, are included in Milner, App. pp. 322–7. See also *Lumley Inventories*.

[3] Hunter MS. 44(6).   [4] Sur. *Hist. Durh.*, i.5.

ham, who in 1626 wrote an account of *The Legend of Saint Cuth-bert*,[1] in order to fulfil 'this duty I owe to that Countrey, where I had my cradle, to renew the decayed Epitaphs upon the Tomb-stones of her Antiquities', for 'this is all our sublunary Eternity, if att the Funerall of things, Historie become the Epitaph, and rescue their memories from the Grave that entombs their Ashes . . .'[2] Hegg presented the marvels attributed to Saint Cuthbert from a sceptical and Protestant point of view, but also showed a nostalgia for and near-belief in the same monkish superstitions which he denounced; for example he reproduced without comment or refutation the report of the Catholic Harpsfield, that when Cuthbert's tomb was opened by Henry VIII's commissioners, the Saint's body was found to be still in-corrupt.[3] These were attitudes which, by the 1620s, found a sympathetic response amongst some of the Cathedral clergy.

Hegg concluded his *Legend* with a significant reference to the then Bishop, Richard Neile (1617–27), under whom (he said) not only had Durham castle been repaired and renovated, but also 'the Church of Durham seems to renew her age, and take a new Lease of Eternity; whose internal beauty (for her Cathe-dral Musick and Majesty of the high Altar, and sacred Laver) may challenge her Sister Churches for Priority'.[4] It was during Neile's episcopate that Durham cathedral, in some aspects of its worship and outward appearance, began to revert to the reli-gion of rite, sacrament, and the visual image with which a break had been made at the Reformation. A new stone altar was set up in the choir to take the place of the uncompromisingly Pro-testant wooden Communion table, and candlesticks placed on it revived the imagery of light characteristic of the traditional Catholic rituals. There was a new emphasis on the use of splen-did vestments, some of these, inherited from the monastic com-munity, bearing representations of the Trinity and God the Father, so arousing the indignation of Protestants as idolatrous. The ritual followed in the daily services became more cere-monious and elaborate, with much bowing to the altar (the

---

[1] Hegg. Cf. a Catholic work of a similar kind by 'T.R.', translated into English by John Hall of Consett in 1603 (reprinted Darlington, 1779) entitled *The Origin and succession of the Bishops of Durham*, undertaken 'in regard it is much to be feared, that many of the ancient records have perished in these late troublesome and rebellious time . . .'

[2] Hegg, p. 2.   [3] Ibid., pp. 74–5.   [4] Ibid., p. 92.

very use of this term seemed to involve a revival of the Catholic 'sacrifice of the Mass', abolished by the Reformation); while sermons, so beloved by Protestants, were played down in favour of increasingly liturgical, musical forms of worship. The appearance of the church was changed in several relatively small but significant ways. The font was restored to its pre-Reformation position at the west end, and decorated with an elaborate cover which incorporated a carved dove (symbolizing the Holy Spirit) and statues of the four Evangelists; after 1633 the seating provided in the quire for the members of the City Corporation and other privileged persons was removed, so that this part of the church was reserved, as in pre-Reformation days, for the clergy, and a clearer view of the altar made available. These tendencies were also apparent in some of the parish churches like Brancepeth, Sedgefield and Bishop Wearmouth, where the cures were in the hands of Cathedral clergy. Here too altars were set up, a more elaborate ceremonial introduced; and the churches were refurnished in a style, which, already in the 1630s, prefigured the remarkable blend of gothic and baroque architectural themes which would reach its full development after the Restoration, giving effective expression to the sense of tradition, of grandeur, and emphasis on hierarchical authority which this sophisticated new-style Durham clergy saw as being the essence of their Church.[1]

The new trends were the work of the dependents and followers of Bishop Neile, whom he introduced as prebends into the Cathedral Chapter, particularly five who had been his chaplains: Augustine Lindsell, Eleazar Duncan, Gabriel Clark, Francis Burgoyne, and John Cosin.[2] All were university dons, and exponents of the 'Arminian' theology of Overall and Lancelot Andrewes, playing down Calvinist predestination, and stressing instead the importance of free-will and 'good works', so showing affinities with the Roman teaching on these matters; and with this went a reaction against the Calvinist emphasis on preaching and 'the Word' in favour of sacraments and rites.

---

[1] We know about these changes mainly from the records of the quarrel they caused in 1628 between the Puritan Peter Smart and his fellow prebendaries, particularly John Cosin. See Cosin, *Corres.*, pp. 161–200; *Durh. High Comm.*, pp. 197–250.

[2] For details of the careers of these men, see Hutch., i.532, ii.171,176, 188, 201, and *D.N.B.*; also *Alum. Cantab.* and *Alum. Oxon.*

With the theology there went a stronger reference to history and tradition, the latter, as conceived by Archbishop Parker in the reign of Queen Elizabeth, having roots in a supposed autonomous 'British' Church subsequently perverted by 'Popish' influences which the Reformation had eradicated, but with the continuity of its life and institutions otherwise preserved.[1] In this way it became possible to challenge the Catholic claim to a monopoly of tradition, and to reply to the Catholic apologists who asked 'Where was your Church before Luther?'; or who insisted that 'it is propre to the heretikes to appeal to the scriptures onely, because they are quickly condemned by tradition, custom and manner'.[2] The sense of the antiquity of the Roman Church was one of the assets which helped to make Recusancy attractive, vying in this respect, particularly as far as the 'new' gentry were concerned, with the prospect of alliances with 'ancient' Recusant families. The Arminians countered with an Anglicanism which was decorous, traditional, and ceremonious, as well fitted as Romanism to provide a religious setting for a gentry way of life, and as well adapted to the life of courts as the baroque Catholicism of the European monarchies, if more restrained in its modes of expression. In Durham the seal was placed on the Arminian claim that their Church stood for continuity and antiquity when in 1633 King Charles I, on his way to Scotland, paid his respects to the Cathedral. He also visited the tombs of Saint Cuthbert and the Venerable Bede, whose relics were thus given official recognition for the first time since the Reformation.[3]

From a wider point of view, however, it becomes apparent that the appearance of this talented and energetic group of clergy under the leadership of a bishop like Neile, a practised courtier who enjoyed the favour of King James,[4] contributed in important ways to a build-up of tension. There was a widening of the gap between the different religious and political points of view which divided society. Socially speaking, this same educated clergy constituted one of the 'rising' social groups, comparable with the big yeoman farmers, the Wear coal-owners, and the Newcastle men; all mobile social elements, aggressive

[1] For Archbishop Parker's role in this respect, see Levy, pp. 114–23.
[2] Rastell.   [3] See the Latin account of the visit in Cosin, *Corres.*, p. 212.
[4] For his career, see *D.N.B.*

and pushful, concerned to stake out for themselves and their children a secure place in the upper levels of the traditional social hierarchy. Neile and his associates were almost without exception of humble or modest social origin, the Bishop himself being the son of a tallow-chandler, Cosin of a Norwich tradesman, Gabriel Clark of a yeoman.[1] Exceptional talent, persistence, and determination were necessary if men of this background were to join those who ruled and governed. For others of the sort a ladder of social ascent became available through the legal profession, the coal industry, or farming. But for these the Church, through its graduated hierarchy of offices and benefices was the catalyst of social mobility. For the structure of the Church eased the able clergy upwards by way of university posts, cathedral and episcopal offices, or chaplaincies in the households of the great, to the deaneries or bishoprics which made men who had started as poor students the equals of the upper gentry and the peerage.

The great Anglican apologist Richard Hooker in the 1590s expounded the structure of the English Church. He justified its basis in the forms of landed property which sustained it, by pointing to the close interconnection of the secular with the ecclesiastical social structure. This made it difficult to dismantle the traditional order in the Church without also threatening the stability of the State. Those who turned against the honours and privileges enjoyed by the clergy and the episcopate were also liable to reject the dignities and marks of respect accorded to nobles and magistrates.[2] And since the lands of the Church, in addition to being a divinely sanctioned form of propriety conferred by God, were also enjoyed by as good a secular title as those of the laity, the one could not be overthrown without the other being called into question.[3] In the same way, if the marks of privilege and honour which went with the exercise of episcopal authority were challenged, the structure of honour and

---

[1] Of the Durham prebendaries of the Jacobean and Caroline period, only Marmaduke Blakiston and his sons and (more doubtfully) William James came of established gentry background. None of the seventeenth-century bishops of Durham before Crewe were gentry. In this respect Durham followed the national trend, only one of the clergy raised to bishoprics between 1625 and 1641 having any connection with the gentry or nobility (Kenyon, p. 151). For the political and cultural implications of the social status of the clergy, see Hill, *Econ. Prob.*, pp. 200–223, and Kearney, pp. 91 ff.

[2] Hooker, iii.141–2.   [3] Ibid., p. 322.

deference which prevailed in the secular society was equally endangered.[1] For Hooker, in fact, the emergence of a dissonance between the organization and the property basis of the religious society and the secular society involved a threat to both, at least as long as religion retained a central place in men's personal and social preoccupation. The Puritan offensive therefore, in so far as it involved a radical critique of the hierarchical structure of the Church, by implication brought all subjection to established powers into question.[2]

Hooker's ideas were echoed amongst the Durham men, and particularly in the writings of John Cosin. 'Jerusalem stands not here for the city and the state alone' he said of his text in one of his sermons 'nor for the temple and the Church alone, but for both together; and our care, our love, to be shewed unto them both . . .' And again[3] 'I told you before that Sion would be found to be both the house of God and the house of David, that is, both the religion of the temple and the government of the kingdom; Church and State both . . . kings are taken into so near a conjunction with God in Sion, that the league is so firm, and the knot so strait between them, as one cannot have ill will to the one, but he must have it to the other also.'[4] The privileges and rights of the Church must therefore be firmly established as a necessary condition for the stability of society. Thus Cosin was diligent to 'search and study the Rights and Antiquities of the Church of Duresme', and set its records in order.[5] There were still in Durham, he was to point out after the Restoration, those who like the Puritan party before the Civil War 'would humble the bishop and his courts, together with all his clergy, especially those of his cathedral church', which 'may prove to be of very dangerous consequence against both church and state of this kingdom . . .'[6] If then the Church was seen in this close involvement with secular society, the preoccupation of the Arminian clergy with the hunt for preferment, rich benefices, and office secular as well as ecclesiastical becomes more

---

[1] Ibid., p. 266.
[2] See Hooker's critique of the Puritan discipline in his Preface, particularly ibid., i.173–94.
[3] Cosin, *Works*, vol. i, Sermon VII, p. 109.
[4] Ibid., Sermon XIV, pp. 198, 201.
[5] According to Basire, *Sermon*.
[6] Ibid., Hutch., i.545.

understandable, whatever part straightforward greed and self-interest may have played in it. In their own terms the game could be played with a good conscience, for a rich, powerful, and authoritative Church interest was necessary for maintaining those social and political continuities which a period of rapid change seemed to endanger.

Those same 'continuities' were most typically represented amongst Neile's supporters on the Cathedral Chapter by a younger son of a prestigious and ancient Durham family, Marmaduke Blakiston, who had become a prebend under Bishop James in 1601.[1] Unlike Neile's 'young men', most of them imported into Durham from Cambridge, Blakiston, although an Oxford M.A. was not remarkable as a scholar. It is likely that his continued prosperity under James's successor reflects Neile's regard for 'the ancient houses'[2] of the Palatinate, and his desire to maintain the Church interest amongst the gentry. Of all this rich and privileged Cathedral clergy, Blakiston amassed the most impressive accumulation of benefices and offices. A prebendary of York as well as Durham, and archdeacon of two Yorkshire Ridings, he was also the incumbent of three Durham livings, including the rich rectory of Sedgefield.[3] Not only did he found a landed family, but also placed two of his sons in prebendships, so ensuring a share of the wealth of the Church for his descendants.[4] The Blakistons,[5] like such other clerical dynasties as the Huttons, Jameses, Bunnys, and Whittinghams, almost certainly adhered to the Puritan and Erastian Cathedral tradition of the pre-Neile era. But the favour which Bishop Neile enjoyed with King James, as well as the disgrace into which the Puritan Bishop James had fallen by the end of his

[1] Ibid., ii.196.

[2] Blakiston matriculated at Trinity College, Oxford, in 1579, and subsequently proceeded to M.A. See *Alum. Oxon.* Neile's solicitude for the older and more decayed Palatine families appears for example in his concern to spare 'the ancient names' whose fortunes had declined the burden of the forced loan of 1625 (*C.S.P. Dom. Ch. I, 1625–6*, p. 122), and his unwillingness to disarm a Recusant of the 'degree' of Lord Eure (ibid., p. 134).

[3] Hutch., ii.196.

[4] Blakiston resigned both his rectory of Sedgefield and his prebendship in favour of his son Robert in 1631 (Hutch., ii.197). Another son, Thomas, succeeded his father in the latter's prebendship of Wistow in York Minster.

[5] There is no hint that the clerical Blakistons ever showed any sympathy to Catholicism, in spite of the fact that the senior branch of the family, the Blakistons of Blakiston, were Recusants.

life,[1] must have seemed sufficient indication that the future lay with the 'Arminians', as Neile's followers came to be called. At any rate an alliance established itself between Neile's men and some of the more prominent of the conservative prebends, this receiving expression in the marriage contract concluded in 1626 between Cosin and Blakiston's daughter Frances. Blakiston resigned his archdeaconry of the East Riding to his new son-in-law shortly before the match took place, Cosin also receiving (at the instance of Laud and Buckingham) the rich rectory of Brancepeth.[2] The appointment of Bishop James's nephew William as a prebend in 1620, with the addition of the vicarage of Merrington in 1629 to the rectory of Ryton which he already possessed, was another manoeuvre to divide and neutralize the conservatives.[3] At the same time the appointment of two Neile chaplains to the archdeaconries, Gabriel Clark to Durham and Francis Burgoyne to Northumberland, ensured Arminian control of key-points in the diocesan administrative system. With a large Arminian majority on the Chapter, and Cosin as its treasurer, the way was prepared for the innovations of Neile's episcopate.[4]

The effect of the rule of Bishop Neile, however, with the predominance of the Arminian clergy which it involved, was to divide the Church interest; the animosity of powerful elements in the ruling class was also aroused. Tensions and resentments resulted, initially suppressed, but subsequently reasserting themselves once the Civil War got under way. Part of the trouble lay in the arrogance and over-confidence shown by Neile and his associates in Durham affairs. This arose partly from their assurance of support from such great men as Buckingham and Laud at Court, and partly from the need of this newly risen plebeian élite to justify by quick and tangible results the large possessions and powers which had been conferred upon them.[5] Neile's attempts, as lord lieutenant of Durham, to

[1] James, a former chaplain to Elizabeth's favourite, the earl of Leicester, must have shared the Puritan sympathies of his patron. Unlike Bishop Neile, he was no favourite of James I, and a rebuke delivered by the latter while on a visit to Durham in 1617 is said to have hastened the Bishop's death, which took place four days later. See *D.N.B.*

[2] Cosin, *Corres.*, pp. xvi–xvii.

[3] Hutch., ii.215.   [4] Ibid., pp. 171, 201, 221, 225.

[5] The theoretical difficulties involved in entrusting wealth and power to a low-born clerical meritocracy were cogently stated by the Puritan peer Lord

enlarge the trained bands and improve their efficiency, to persuade the county to pay purveyance and contribute to the forced loan of 1626, while at the same time opposing its representation in the House of Commons; his assaults on tenant right, and the over-bearing manner in which he overrode opposition, are sufficient explanation for the antagonism which developed to his rule.[1]

This, led by the Newcastle oligarch Sir Henry Anderson, was inevitably Puritan, Anderson being a great enemy of bishops, and an opponent even of Bishop James; for him and his friends 'Arminian' became the blanket term of invective for a general assault on the Church establishment.[2] Amongst the churchmen and their allies on the other hand the monopoly of preferment by Neile's men caused resentment; while their accumulation of offices and benefices roused indignation and fomented division, leading to collaboration between dissident clergy and lay anti-clericals. 'As for you, Marmaduke Blakiston,' wrote a clerical critic of the leading Cathedral pluralist, 'you have had 6 goodly preferments and dignities, and although you have bargained away 4 of them, yet you keep 2 in your hands, worth 600 li. a yere, at neyther of which you have preached or said service, as much as once in seven years, being a non-resident from both.'[3] The writer was Peter Smart, a Durham prebend who had been a rising man under Bishop James, but an outsider to the counsels of the Arminians under Neile.[4] His main ally was Robert Hutton, brother of Bishop Hutton (1589–94), rector of Houghton-le-Spring, and like Smart a prebend. It was Hutton who

---

Brooke in his *Discourse touching the nature of Episcopacy* (1641). Brooke believed that 'high place causes a swimming in the braine' and that 'Those horses which are designed to a lofty aire must be of a noble race'. Intellectuals were not fitted to wield power since 'long active and dangerous observations are the only way to create a wise statesman'. Hence for 'such a low-born man to be exalted high . . . all at once, as oft it is, . . . must needs create as great a chasm in politiques, as suche leapes do in naturals'. See Haller, ii.47–53 and Kearney, p. 92.

[1] See above p. 83, and below p. 166.   [2] See below, p. 164 ff.

[3] Cosin, *Corres.*, p. 185.

[4] Originally master of Durham School, Smart was made his chaplain by Bishop James in 1609, and collated to a prebendship in the Cathedral; he also became rector of Boldon, and in 1612 master of Gateshead Hospital. James also made him one of the high commissioners of the Northern Province. This meteoric rise came to an end however with the advent of Bishop Neile, when Smart, although senior prebend, received no further preferment, and was excluded from the inner ring of the new Bishop's chaplains. Hutch., ii.183.

fired off the first shot against the Arminians in a sermon preached at the cathedral for which he was cited before the High Commission in 1620 because it reflected 'on the king, the bishop, the church and its ceremonies'. Nothing came of Hutton's boldness, and he died in 1623.[1]

More effective was Peter Smart's better-known sermon of July 1628,[2] which initiated a comprehensive attack on the innovations made in the furnishings and services of the cathedral, and particularly on Cosin, Lindsell, and Burgoyne as the clergy mainly responsible.[3] The latter reacted with characteristic precipitancy and violence. Smart was immediately summoned before the Durham High Commission Court, suspended from his prebendship, and excluded from the cathedral.[4] But unlike Hutton, Smart had powerful allies in Charles I's third Parliament, which had met in the previous March. His charges were taken up in the House of Commons by the oppositionist members, who brought a charge of treason against Cosin on the basis of statements of his made in Durham, which were interpreted as a denial of the Royal Supremacy over the Church.[5] At the same time Smart sought the help of the courts of common law, citing Cosin and his associates before two successive sessions of the Durham assizes, the first before Judge Whitlock, the second before Judge Yelverton. The former dismissed Smart's charges as groundless, while the latter first supported him, but then turned against him.[6] It was the dissolution of Parliament in March 1629, however, which saved Cosin and made Smart's case hopeless. In 1630 the York High Commission Court deprived him of all his preferments and he was fined £500. When he refused to pay he was put into prison, there to remain until he was released by the Long Parliament in November 1640.[7]

---

[1] Ibid., ii.180.

[2] *The Vanitie or Downe-fall of Superstitious Popish Ceremonies, or, a sermon preached in the Cathedral Church of Durham . . . Containing not only an historicall relation of all those severall Popish Ceremonies and practises which Mr. J. Cosins hath lately brought into the said Cathedrall Church; but likewise a punctuall confutation of them etc.* (Edinburgh, 1628; Durham Cathedral Library).

[3] See Cosin, *Corres.*, p. 162.   [4] *Durh. High Comm.*, p. 197.

[5] Gard. *Hist. Eng.*, vii.44–9; Cosin, *Corres.*, pp. 147–52; *Durh. High Comm.*, App. A, pp. 199–201.

[6] Cosin, *Corres.*, pp. 145–6, 155–60.   [7] *Durh. High Comm.*, pp. 204 ff.

These quarrels within the clerical establishment left a lasting mark. The attempts at compromise with a view to rebuilding a united clerical front, initiated by Dean Hunt and Neile's successor Bishop Howson (1628–32), were resisted by Neile's men, led by Cosin and Lindsell and supported in London by Neile (now bishop of Winchester) and by Archbishop Laud. In 1631 the latter secured a letter from the King forbidding Howson to meddle further with the affairs of the Cathedral clergy 'till wee shall appoint some other to be joyned with you . . .'[1] Subsequently for a few years the disputes did subside, helped perhaps by Lindsell's departure to be bishop of Peterborough in 1632, Cosin's to be Master of Peterhouse, Cambridge, in 1634, and by Burgoyne's death in 1633. Bishop Morton (1632–59) tried to advance the process of reconciliation, bringing Puritan preachers into the diocese, and taking a studiously moderate view of his prerogatives both as bishop and as Count Palatine.[2] But the scars remained, and account in part for the extensive representation of Church and Cathedral families in the ranks of the Parliamentary party in Durham during the Civil War, as well as on the County Committees between 1642 and 1660. Amongst those associated with the Church interest who defected to the other side were John Smart, Robert Hutton, Sir Timothy Whittingham, George Bunny, John Blakiston, and Francis Wren.[3] The impact of the Arminian meritocracy on the conservative Durham Church establishment, which had already evolved a tradition, liturgical and doctrinal, of its own,[4] and whose material interests in the matter of Church preferments were only

---

[1] Cosin, *Corres.*, pp. 200–10; for the King's letter, see p. 207n.

[2] See below, pp. 169 ff.

[3] For Hutton, Whittingham, and Blakiston, see above, pp. 72–3; Smart was a relative (probably the son) of Peter Smart, who bought an estate at Snotterton from the Ewbank family before 1661 (Sur. *Hist. Durh.*, iv.142); George Bunny was the brother of a prebendary and former archdeacon of Northumberland who settled his family on the manor of Newsham (Sur. *Hist. Durh.*, iv.40); Francis Wren's brother Sir Charles had been a friend of Bishop James, and constable of Durham castle (Hutch., i.481; *Diaries II*, pp. 8, 12, 205); the family held leases of church lands. All these men sat on the Durham county committees under the Interregnum régimes.

[4] Cf. Peter Smart '. . . you have so removed, translated and transformed . . . that now scarce *vestigium* remaynes of things and fashions amongst us in Bisshopp James his tyme. . . . If there be no church nor service, without these comly gestures and ceremonies, as you tearme them, then there was no church in Bisshopp James his tyme' (Cosin, *Corres.*, pp. 192, 193).

partly reconciled with those of Neile's new men, proved to be
disruptive and divisive. So far from fitting the Church for a
stabilizing social role which would reinforce the accepted structure of authority and obedience, the movement weakened the
Church itself.

Smart asserted, in his charges against Cosin and his associates, that the new Arminian style of ceremonial religion had
established itself much more widely than the sophisticated
clerical circle connected with the Cathedral; 'all which your
abominations,' he thundered 'both towne and country begin to
imitate, to the shame of our church, and the complaynt of all
well affected people . . .'[1] But while Cosin and Burgoyne may
have been able to set up their altars at Brancepeth and Wearmouth it is likely that in the region as a whole there was not
much demand or enthusiasm for the Laudian sacraments and
rites for which the Arminians stood. The Erastian conservatism
of Smart and his kind, flavoured with sermons and Calvinist
overtones, was probably closer to the religious recipe accepted
by the majority within the established Church. Cosin insisted
that the Church of England should make provision for daily
celebrations of the Holy Communion, and that ideally the
people ought to participate in the service weekly.[2] But Bishop
Barnes, in the 1570s, had failed, except for a brief period, to
make even monthly Communions the rule.[3] In practice, subsequently, the Communion service was used only three or four
times a year, and attendance was enforced by the Church
courts only once, at Easter. The neglect may have been in part
due to the increased cost of the Protestant sacrament, since all
the people (and not the priest only as in the Catholic Mass) now
received the consecrated wine as well as the bread. The need to
provide the former in quantity raised the problem of a sufficient
supply, and involved parishes in a larger financial burden than
some were willing to meet.[4]

Thus the services of Morning and Evening Prayer came to
constitute the staple content of the Church's public ministrations. These assumed a special character as a result of the system

---

[1] Ibid., p. 165.
[2] Cosin, *Works*, v.16, 104, 124, 480. But Cosin recognized that attendance at
Communion was obligatory for the people (as distinct from the clergy) only three
times a year.
[3] *Durh. Eccles. Proc.*, p. 13.   [4] See *Durh. Ch. Accnts.*, pp. 6–7.

of appropriating seats or 'places' in churches to individuals or families whose occupation of these came to constitute a form of ownership. Sometimes this was based on faculties granted by the Church courts, but might also be able to claim the protection of the courts of common law.[1] The usual practice, which seems to have established itself in Durham parishes from the 1580s onwards, was for parishioners to be assigned 'places' for life in return for a payment, usually quite small, to the churchwardens. After the death of the first occupant, the latter's representatives could usually renew their right upon a further small payment. A place, however, sufficed only for one person, so that it was usual for the head of a household to hire enough room to accommodate his whole family, with his servants if he had any; and he then built, and subsequently kept in repair, a 'stall' or pew in which he and his dependants sat through the common prayers and the lengthy sermons.[2]

The placing and size of the pews thus occupied, in Durham as elsewhere, soon came to project visibly the social structure of the parish, marking out those who enjoyed deference and authority within the community;[3] a process helped forward by the rise of the practice of buying and selling places. The gentry were commonly placed in the front of the church, in an order which reflected the pre-eminence which particular families enjoyed. Their large households, with their many servants, occupied extensive pew accommodation, and their tenants sat near them. Next came the yeomen and substantial husbandmen, often occupying pews allocated to specific farmholds. The smaller farmers, cottagers, and tradesmen (in urban parishes)

---

[1] On this practice see Hill, *Econ. Prob.*, pp. 175–87.

[2] *Durh. Ch. Accnts.*, pp. viii–xi, 3.

[3] Thus at Pittington Sir Henry Anderson, the farmer of the manor, was allocated the front pew, and seating was provided for his tenants near him (*Durh. Ch. Accnts.*, p. 13). At Norton in 1635 Squire Blakiston was allocated the seat 'next unto the chauncell', with his servants in the porch called 'the Blakiston porch' (Robson, 'Furniture', p. 7). At Saint Oswald's, Durham, it was provided in 1608 that no journeyman, apprentice, or maidservant shall 'presume in the quire', or sit above the 'cross-alley' (*Durh. Ch. Accnts.*, p. 214). At Gateshead in 1634 the vestry distributed seating to the parishioners 'according to our discretions and their several qualities' (Robson, op. cit., p. 6); and at Easington the seats were reallocated to provide places proportionate to the dignity of Sir William Bellasis and Sir Alexander Hall (ibid., p. 5).

On the significance of church seating arrangements as a projection of the social gradations in parish communities, see Thomas, *Religion*, p. 152.

seem to have shared pews, usually towards the back of the church. But even in these more humble quarters it seems there was competition for status, some places or 'rooms' in a 'stall' commanding more prestige than others.[1] Thus from one point of view, appearance at church fulfilled an essentially secular function, by providing an occasion on which parishioners could assert a claim to status in the parish society, while giving visible expression to the validity of that claim. The emphasis in this kind of church furnishing was on the provision not, as in pre-Reformation churches, of 'kneeling' places from which the altar could be observed, but on 'seating' from which long didactic services with little ritual content could be sat out.[2] Pews were frequently elaborate enough and high enough to hide the Communion table at the east end of the chancel. Only the pulpit, with the reading-desk well below it from which the Common Prayer was read, rose above the seating, and imposed the sermon as the dominant feature of the proceedings, eagerly awaited as most likely to enliven the monotony of the set prayers of the liturgy. Preaching was popular.

It was precisely in this relation between church attendance and social structure that effective expression was given, at the grassroots parish level, to that mutual interdependence of Church and State, religion and the secular, of Hooker's ideal. At the same time, the alliance between the Church and the dominant elements in these local societies was sealed by the rise of self-perpetuating oligarchies of the more substantial householders to the rule of each parish—the so-called 'Select Vestry', whose emergence in Durham dates back to the generation after 1570. The exclusion from the churches of the poor and those who could not pay pew rents (or had no master able to pay these on their behalf) had the same effect.[3] Many of the Arminian preoccupations, however, tended to disrupt this wholly spontaneous and natural alliance of the ecclesiastical and secular powers in the parish. For them the haphazard cluttering of churches with pews obscured the ritual purpose of the building by hiding the altar, or by encroaching on chancel or quire, areas reserved in the Arminian scheme of things for the clergy and for ceremony and rite. Pews, for the Arminian, were to be 'driven out of the Temple, with the buyers and sellers . . .' and

---

[1] *Durh. Ch. Accnts.*, p. 3.   [2] Ibid., p. xi.   [3] Ibid., pp. 2–4.

more appropriate seating provided.[1] Cosin found Durham
cathedral unsuited for the kind of services he wished to introduce, which required that the congregation should face east,
towards the altar, and he apparently altered the pew arrange-
ment of the quire, including the Dean's stall, so that it faced in
the required direction; and 'he sends the vergers about the
church to remove all those, strangers and others, which sit with
their backs to the east', a posture which the seating at any rate
in the aisles evidently still permitted.[2] In 1633 the seats for the
mayor and corporation and for the prebends' wives and other
'women of quality' in the quire were removed in preparation
for the visit of Charles I. A royal letter was subsequently received commanding that they were not to be replaced, and that
alternative accommodation was to be provided of such a sort
that 'the Quire may ever remaine in its auntient beawtie'.[3]

Whether vested interests were similarly brushed aside in the
parish churches refurnished to conform to the requirements of
Cosin and his friends[4] is unknown; but there is some evidence
that here more caution was displayed. James at Ryton and
Blakiston at Sedgefield, apparently only altered the chancels.[5]
Cosin at Brancepeth made provision for large family pews
which could have been occupied by the wealthier parishioners.[6]
Nevertheless, the case of Easington, where difficulties arose over
the provision of seating in the refurnished church to the satisfac-
tion of the rival parish magnates, Sir William Bellasis and Sir
Alexander Hall, suggests the tensions liable to arise.[7] The appeal of the innovations on the other hand does not seem to have
extended beyond a small cultured élite, represented by the
courtier Sir William Webb, who was inclined to go over to
Rome until he had 'been with Dr. Cosin at Brancepeth' where
he 'received the blessed sacrament most reverently here ad-

[1] *C.S.P. Dom. Ch. I, 1633–4*, p. 83.   [2] Cosin, *Corres.*, p. 174, and footnote.
[3] Ibid., pp. 215–16. The Mayor and Corporation were given new seating in the
quire stalls, but women were excluded altogether. Prebends' wives were given
special alternative seating, but 'other women of quality' would have to be content with temporary seating. It was the sense of clerical initiative and control
which was liable to make these arrangements rankle, particularly since, although
imposed under the King's name, they were in fact dictated by Laud, and so must
have enhanced the importance and prestige of his dependents in the Chapter.
[4] See Robson, 'Furniture', pp. 1–12.
[5] Op. cit., p. 7; Pevsner, pp. 198, 207.   [6] Pevsner, pp. 60–1.
[7] Robson, 'Furniture', pp. 4–5.

ministered, intending to continue in the communion of the Church of England as long as he shall live . . .'[1] But in the parish it was the financial aspect of the new furnishings which made most impression, and the 'offering money' needed to complete the work came in but slowly, as Cosin's curate informed him in 1638.[2] There was little demand from the rank and file for such changes, which reflected the preoccupations of the educated clergy, which were often remote from those of the farmers, artisans, and squires who filled the pews in the churches.

Ritualism undoubtedly had its place in the amorphous, unsystematic, but nevertheless tough and persistent structure of popular belief. But the spells, charms, and petitions resorted to at this level had little relevance to the rationalized ecclesiastical 'beauty of holiness' which the Arminians had in mind. Rather these simple and archaic rites gave access to the kind of 'power' which Saint Cuthbert had exercised, protective and reassuring, effectual against those dark forces which might erupt into human life at any point or at any time.[3] It is possible that a sub-Catholic religious culture long persisted in the region. Its presence had been noted in Northumberland at the end of the sixteenth century when it was reported that most of the people 'dye and cannot saie the Lordes Prayer . . . They are fytt for any religion and old tradicion called Papistrye fytteth them best',[4] while in 1628 Sir Benjamin Rudyerd similarly 'exampled . . . the utmost skirts of the North where the prayers of the common people were more like spells and charms than devotions'.[5] The strength of Catholicism had been its hierarchy of benevolent spiritual powers, adapted to and available at all the varied regions, places, and situations where their help was needed. Such, as Cosin shrewdly observed, was 'the practice of Popery' in which 'for every region, city, and family, for every man, every state and profession of men; for every fruit of the earth, every beast of the field, every disease of the body, they have appointed a peculiar saint, to whom they pray as devoutly, and from whom they expect help as securely, as from God himself.'[7] Protestantism however, as much in its Arminian as in its

---

[1] *C.S.P. Dom. Ch. I, 1633–4*, p. 154.   [2] Cosin, *Corres.*, p. 222.
[3] cf. Thomas, *Religion*, ch. 2.   [4] *C.B.P.*, vol. 2, pp. 494–5.
[5] Rudyerd, pp. 135–6.   [7] Cosin, *Works*, vol. i, sermon X, p. 146.

Puritan version, was uncompromisingly monotheistic. Cosin's advice to his parishioners, 'if any grief or sickness befalls them, if they happen to have any loss of children, or corn, or cattle . . .'[1] was to resort to God, and to God alone. They were to pray, fast, give alms, reform their lives, and 'if this means succeed not', each was told to 'submit himself under the mighty hand of God . . .'[2] Many were not content so to submit however, and had recourse to less respectable spiritual powers, 'exclaiming and crying out that they are bewitched, that such a woman had done them harm, that such another can do them good . . .' or 'run to a wizard, that they may ask the devil counsel for us . . .'[3] It was in this twilit, underground affective zone that the organization of Catholic Recusancy could make direct contact with the common people in ways not possible for the clergy of the established Church. The annual letter to Rome of the Residence of Saint John at Durham, the headquarters of the Jesuit mission in the north-east, reported thirty-seven conversions in 1637, and eighty in 1638, several of these involving the successful exercise of the Church's power of exorcism. One case was of a woman tormented with witchcraft, and who had applied in vain to Protestant ministers for help; but after instruction by one of the Jesuit Fathers, followed by penance and exorcism, she was cured.[4] In general, miraculous cures, visions, and divine interventions played a considerable role in the Recusant piety of the region.

Puritan critics bundled such 'Popish' and popular 'superstitions' into the same category, ascribing both to ignorance, the result of a scarcity of 'preaching ministers' and the prevalence of 'dumb dogs' amongst the Durham clergy. Substance is given to the Puritan critique by Bishop Morton's complaint in 1636 that he could hardly procure enough competent ministers to provide sermons in the market towns, let alone the countryside. But Morton may merely have been justifying to the government his patronage of such radical Puritan preachers as Anthony Lapthorne.[5] In fact it is likely that the educational level of the clergy gradually improved after the 1570s, and that some at any rate of the improved supply of university graduates available to the Church by the early seventeenth century

---

[1] Ibid., p. 149.   [2] Ibid., p. 150.   [3] Ibid., p. 149.
[4] Foley, iii.122–3.   [5] *C.S.P. Dom. Ch. I, 1636–7*, p. 410.

reached Durham.[1] Indeed, by the time of the Civil War, if we are to judge from the cases of the Anglican clergy then ejected from their livings by the victorious Parliamentarians, a majority were graduates, and so qualified to preach.[2] Whether they did so is another matter, one factor tending to ensure that they did not being the practice whereby some clergymen held two or more livings 'in plurality', residing on one, but rarely visiting the others. Some of the Cathedral clergy, particularly Blakiston, Cosin, and Burgoyne, were accused by Peter Smart of thus accumulating benefices to the neglect of the duties of their charge.[3] Most of the Durham prebends were in fact pluralists. This however did not always mean that the interests of the parishioners were neglected by their non-resident parson, or merely served by some ill-paid and therefore ill-qualified 'stipendiary priest' put in as curate. William Milburn, whom Cosin put in charge of Brancepeth when he became Master of Peterhouse, Cambridge, was a man of considerable attainments, and no inarticulate 'dumb dog'.[4] Nevertheless, by and large absenteeism did tend to undermine the ideal of a preaching clergy.

Another feature of the structure of ecclesiastical income and property thought to have had the same effect, because it impoverished the clergy, was the system of 'impropriations'. The tithe income of an 'impropriate' rectory ceased to belong to the parson, and became the property either of some corporate body (a monastery in pre-Reformation days, or a cathedral dean and chapter) or person (a bishop, or after the dissolution a layman who had bought up monastic impropriations). The impropriator put in a vicar (who lived on the 'lesser tithes' levied on livestock), or else a 'stipendiary priest' who was paid a wage, usually a very small one. The Durham Dean and Chapter were as much involved in this 'abuse' as in that of pluralism and absenteeism, since the tithes of nine Durham rectories, worth nearly £300 a year in the 1630s, were impropriate to the Cathedral.[5] However, in the case of impropriations, as in that of pluralities, the effects were by no means as straightforwardly

[1] Curtis, p. 184.
[2] Of the 58 clergy ejected, 34 had degrees (*Walker Rev.*, pp. 139–44).
[3] Cosin, *Corres.*, p. 185.   [4] Ibid., pp. 221–3.
[5] Durham Dean and Chapter MS., Receiver's Book, 1634.

depressive of clerical standards as the critics tended to maintain. For the eight vicars whom the Chapter appointed were, with one exception, amongst the better-paid clergy, their incomes ranging from £40 a year (in the case of the vicar of Dalton) to £80 (in the case of the vicar of Pittington). The vicar of Saint Oswald's, Durham, had a legitimate complaint against impropriations, since the tithes of his parish brought in £45 a year, while his vicarage was worth only £20; but the stipendiary priest of Jarrow might well praise it, since the tithes of the parish were worth only £5 a year, but the Cathedral paid him a stipend of £26. 13s. 4d.[1] The likelihood seems to be that in the Durham lowland there was sufficient wealth, and the revenues annexed to benefices large enough, for such abuses as impropriations, and even pluralism, to be carried without the functioning of the Church's organization being seriously impaired.

It was the setting in which such 'abuses' operated which seems to have been the decisive factor. There were environments, physical and social, which in their very nature were unfavourable to the established Church, highlighting the weaknesses of its organization. One such was the Durham upland. Here the parishes were large, and the population dispersed in hamlets and farmsteads, instead of being gathered into nuclear villages as in the lowland, clustered around church and manor house, and so accessible to the authority of parson and landlord. Here a network of kinship and neighbourhood groupings spread over remote and inaccessible countrysides. In Weardale there was only one church and one chapel,[2] as in Teesdale,[3] and for many of the inhabitants of both dales, attendance at church services must have been rare. In the upland areas of Derwentdale and the Browney valley there were more churches, and Lanchester parish, for example, had three chapels to supplement the parish church. But here the livings were poor, no vicarage being worth no more than £23 a year; and since the dissolution of the college of prebends at Lanchester in

---

[1] The stipends are taken from Barnes's 'Clavis Ecclesiastica', in *Durh. Eccles. Proc.*, pp. 1–10, where their value about the middle of the seventeenth century has been inserted in brackets in a later hand. The value of the tithes is taken from the Dean and Chapter Receiver's Book referred to above.

[2] At Stanhope and Saint John's Chapel; at the foot of the dale, where it opened out into the lowland there was also the church at Wolsingham.

[3] The parish church of Teesdale was at Middleton, with its chapel at Eggleston.

1547 the tithes of the parish had passed into the hands of lay impropriators, who paid the priests serving the chapelries stipends of just over £13.[1] The parsons who had to make do with these small incomes were not easily distinguishable from the poor peasantry amongst whom they lived, had not attended any university, and did not care for preaching. Bishop Barnes found them particularly impervious to his zeal to raise the educational level of his clergy. The vicars of Hunstanworth and Muggleswick had to be threatened with excommunication for their complete neglect of the educative tasks their bishop had set them; the curates of Lanchester and Medomsley had performed those tasks only imperfectly, while the curate of Tanfield pleaded illness.[2] Things were no better on the eve of the Civil War, when his parishioners described the vicar of Muggleswick as 'the most debased amongst the sons of men', who 'will neither preach himself, nor yet permit others'.[3] In Teesdale and Weardale the clergy were remote; in Derwentdale and the uplands above the Browney valley they could not lead or command respect.

As has been seen, charismatic preaching, the proclamation of the Word, was at the heart of Protestantism, displacing the ritualized, visual, and didactic effects of the old religious order. Preaching of this sort was not primarily intended to instruct, but rather to explode in the hearer's heart, setting on course an inner transformation whose outcome none could see. It was the explosive quality of this style of sermon, the problem of control which it raised, and the unpredictability of its results, which aroused the concern of the judicious Hooker, as he contemplated the dictum of the Cambridge Puritan Thomas Cartwright, 'this is given to the preaching ... for that it is the excellentest and most ordinary means to work in the heart of hearers'.[4] For preaching could become the vehicle of contention in Church and State. For this reason Hooker emphasized its didactic rather than charismatic function, while placing 'reading' on an equality with it in the Church's worship, i.e. the public reading

---

[1] *Durh. Eccles. Proc.*, pp. 1–10; the impropriators in the seventeenth century were the Recusant Hodgsons of Hebburn and Lanchester.

[2] Ibid., p. 73.

[3] *A most lamentable Information of Part of the Grievances of Muggleswick ...*, Lond., 1641.

[4] Quoted Hooker, ii.90, n. 18.

of Scripture, without comment, and of a set public liturgy, that of the Book of Common Prayer.[1] In this he was followed by his Arminian disciples. 'If men be left to themselves,' wrote John Cosin on the matter of permitting free, spontaneous forms of public prayer 'whatsoever opinion in religion, whatsoever debate between neighbours, whatsoever public matter in church or kingdom a man pleases to make his interest, he may make the subject of prayer for the congregation . . .'[2] From the point of view of order in Church and State there was much to be said for the plain reading from the pulpit of the authorized *Book of Homilies*, which any clergyman, educated or uneducated, could do as long as he was literate. 'Preaching' in its Puritan sense, particularly on the part of the unlicenced and unauthorized, was 'subject to passion and affection' and liable to be 'misapplied by the people'. It was not without reason that Cosin placed pulpit and reading-desk side by side in the refurnished parish church at Brancepeth, to emphasize that preaching had no special or superior status in relation to the reading of set liturgical and scriptural texts; and prebendary William James informed the parishioners of Muggleswick, when they asked the Dean and Chapter to provide them with a preaching minister 'that if he could reade the prayer booke, and an homily, it was nothing [to them] what kind of a man he was'.[3]

Nothing better expressed the disruptive effect of the 'spiritual' preaching of the Puritans on the established order of deference and authority than the case of the parishioners of Muggleswick with which James was thus confronted in 1640. The insistence of this poor peasantry of a remote upland region on its need for a preaching minister was the result of the work of Anthony Lapthorne, a Puritan of some distinction (he had been a chaplain to James I) who had been deprived of his vicarage of Tretire in Herefordshire for heterodox opinions.[4] Lapthorne's speciality was the evangelization of the rough impoverished population of 'barbarous' upland areas whose traditional culture was one of ritualistic 'superstition'. His qualities in this respect had first been brought to the attention of Bishop Morton when he was bishop of Lichfield, Lapthorne having been a marked success in that diocese as a preacher

---

[1] Ibid., pp. 88–115.   [2] Cosin, *Works*, v.403.   [3] *A most.*
[4] *Alumn. Oxon.*, iii.882; Thomas, *Religion*, p. 486, n. 2.

amongst the miners, iron workers, and small farmers of Cannock Chase. Morton had brought him to Durham in 1636, and had placed him as minister of Ovingham, just over the Northumberland border. From there his influence spread widely in Hexhamshire and into the Durham upland of Derwentdale and the adjoining areas.[1]

Lapthorne's preaching inculcated a bleak Calvinist moralism founded on the fear of Hell confronting those who failed to respond to the preacher's demand that they 'repent' and experience a 'choice' by God to be of his Elect, and so saved from damnation. Paradoxically, however, Lapthorne's gloomy sermons, with their obsessive sabbatarianism, and insistence that even though the penitents were provisionally saved, yet 'if they fall into those sinnes againe, are utterly damned',[2] brought to his audiences (which were large) positive experiences previously unknown. A new sense of being presented with choice, for example, in matters which had previously involved no more than conformity to authority and tradition. A new sense too of individuality, of the working and tensions of the inner self, the key to which was to be found in Scripture, and so in the hearing, reading, and meditation upon, a book. The response therefore to Lapthorne's exhortations involved the emergence of a new-style peasant culture in which pressure was brought on humble folk to order their inner experience, to relate it coherently to what the Bible was thought to teach, and so to discuss and read. Puritanism thus induced a heightened sense of the freedom and breadth of the self. But it also involved a threat to authority and social order in that Lapthorne was bound to challenge the unpreaching clergy. For it was only through the preaching that men could be confronted with the choice of repentance. Hence, 'Away with theis dumbe dogges and blind guides, they being blind, lead the blind, and soe both shall fall into the ditch of Hell.'[3]

It is not surprising therefore that such views should have led to Lapthorne's citation before the Durham High Commission in 1638, with the local clergy testifying to his attacks on their authority. And it was thus too that the parishioners of Muggleswick were brought into conflict with their landlord and

---

[1] *C.S.P. Dom. Ch. I, 1638–9*, p. 434.
[2] See *Durh. High Comm.*, pp. 190–1. [3] Ibid.

impropriate rector, the Dean and Chapter of Durham Cathedral, who appointed the vicar of Muggleswick, but who had consistently put in men who were merely 'readers' (and again did so in 1640). For the parishioners, in the light of Lapthorne preaching, such appointments were no longer tolerable, since they made the parish 'void of the meanes of salvation', 'to our soules great griefe and dreadfull hazard of destruction'.[1] As a result the transition was made from an act of religious to an act of political assertion and choice, when the parishioners refused to submit to the unpreaching appointee of the Chapter, and chose their own minister. There followed a battle for possession of the church between the Chapter's new vicar and the nominee of the parishioners; while the latters' defiance of the law led to their being cited before the Quarter Sessions.[2] Eventually there was a petition to the Long Parliament, which in 1642 vindicated the parish against the impropriator. The Chapter's vicar was summoned up to London to answer before a Commons' committee as a delinquent; and he was ordered to give a lecturer appointed by the House access to his church to provide the preaching he would not give himself.[3] There could be no better example of the threat which this same 'preaching' presented to the stable, mutually interdependent social and religious order which was the Arminian ideal. Lapthorne's evangelizing activities no doubt prepared the way for the formation in the area, during the 1650s, of a breakaway Baptist congregation, which had the support and patronage of the military radicals Robert Lilburne and Colonel Paul Hobson.[4] If only temporarily, the traditional order had been broken by a radicalism which, like its conservative Arminian counterpart, had mutually supporting religious and political aspects.

Whatever the strength of the tensions in the social and mental world of the Derwentdale peasantry,[5] leading them to flock in

---

[1] 'How many of your for elders, thinke yow, are gone to hell through ignorance and want of the word preached?' Lapthorne asked. The doctrine that preaching was essential to salvation was Cartwright's; see Hooker, ii.101, n. 47; also *A most*.
[2] *A most*.   [3] *C.J.*, ii.77, 449.   [4] See Douglas, pp. 32 ff.
[5] More research than can be attempted here would help to define more clearly the conditions out of which this upland sectarian movement emerged. As far as the psychological background is concerned, an incident of interest is the case of demonic possession at Edmondbyers which occurred in November 1641, related in *Most Fearefull and Strange Newes from the Bishoppricke of Durham* (Lond., 1641). The person concerned was the wife of an Edmondbyers farmer 'who was most

crowds to Lapthorne's preaching, and eventually to assume a stance of religious dissidence and secular disobedience in relation to their traditional superiors, without help from outside the movement would not have had the degree of success which came its way, powerful though its own inner impetus may have been. In the event, however, the resources in money, in political know-how, in access to those in power which the Derwentdale men lacked were made available to them by George Lilburne, the mayor of Sunderland, already encountered as a leading figure in the world of the Wear coal industry. It was Lilburne who sent up the petition of the Muggleswick parishioners to London for submission to the House of Commons, while at the same time bringing some of the signatories at his own expense to Newcastle, ready to be summoned to London to give evidence before the Commons' Grand Committee.[1] From one point of view this was another instance of the emergence of a new-style regional leadership like that developed by George Grey and Anthony Smith in relation to the grievances of the Dean and Chapter tenants over tenant right; a kind of leadership, that is, which was not based on a traditional and established role which in the nature of things commanded deference, but on a response to needs, religious or social, rising from below, which required to be given political expression. Thus the affluent coal-owner George Lilburne became the prototype of the Whig magnates of a later generation whose patronage of Protestant dissent would give them the allegiance of nonconforming urban communities and countrysides.

Sunderland, where Lilburne 'rules both the wealth and religion of the town',[2] was a far cry from Muggleswick, yet here too was one of those environments in which the difficulties involved in the Church's structure and its commitment to traditional social forms were particularly evident. The parish church

---

fearfully possessed and tormented with the Devill', but was eventually relieved by the prayers of her husband and brother-in-law, Stephen and John Hooper, the latter one of Lapthorne's followers who 'did charge the Devill in the name of the Father, the Sonne, and the Holy Ghost, to depart from her . . . then they laid hands on her, and prayed to the Lord, to helpe them in their great neede.' The exorcism was successful. Evidence of ability to confront and control the demonic forces which played such a large part in the popular mental world may have increased the prestige of the local religious radicals.

[1] *C.J.*, ii.77.   [2] *C.S.P. Dom. Ch. I, 1639–40*, p. 515.

of Sunderland was that of Bishop Wearmouth, whose rector was also lord of the manor,[1] and the most important figure in the neighbourhood until the rise of the raw, Sunderland port community in the early seventeenth century. Sunderland was incorporated as a borough by Bishop Morton in 1634, and had George Lilburne as one of its founding aldermen, and subsequently its mayor.[2] The situation was one which invited tension between the rector and Lilburne, his most prominent parishioner.[3] This was the more likely to arise in view of the Arminian tradition of the parish, rector Francis Burgoyne having set up an altar there before which, so Smart told him, 'you bow downe . . . so profoundly, that you dash sometime your nose to the ground, til you make it bleed . . .'[4] Burgoyne's brand of religion was not likely to be congenial to the Puritan Lilburne, who at the end of the 1630s was to be imprisoned by the High Commission for his attacks on the 'superstitious prayers' of one of the Durham prebends, and summoned before the Council because of his disrespect for bishops, as well as for his failure to pay Ship Money.[5] Lilburne and his associates developed the neighbouring parish church at Monk Wearmouth as a rival centre for Puritan preachings, the sermons being provided (with the tolerance of the vicar, who was Lilburne's father-in-law) by itinerant Puritan ministers who (according to an opponent) preferred to 'go abroad seeking out knots of Puritans, and be a preacher at large, receiving present pay'[6] rather than settle in any living, where they would be subject to episcopal control. Puritanism could establish itself in this way largely because of the divisive effect of Arminianism on the Church interest in the region. Bishop Morton, like Bishop Howson, did not find the Arminians on his Cathedral Chapter congenial; nor could he approve of the direct approaches made by Arminian zealots amongst his clergy (like Thomas Triplet, the rector of Whitburn) to Archbishop Laud, to the exclusion of his

---

[1] Hutch., ii.513.

[2] For the charter, see Summers, p. 335; Robson, 'Lilburne', p. 97.

[3] Lilburne's importance is reflected in the seating arrangements in the church. He was placed in the first pew in the north aisle, side by side with a local squire, William Wycliffe of Offerton, from whom he had bought land. Other Sunderland notabilities were seated behind him. See Robson, 'Lilburne', p. 99.

[4] Cosin, *Corres.*, p. 175.   [5] *Roy. Comp. Pps.*, p. 276.

[6] *C.S.P. Dom. Ch. I, 1639–40*, p. 519.

own authority. Morton's incorporation of Sunderland, his tolerance of Puritan lecturers like Lapthorne, his lack of enthusiasm in pursuit of Lilburne and the Sunderland Puritans, suggest attitudes which were soon to subject him to the distrust and disapproval of the government.[1]

Little is known about the content of this Sunderland Puritanism, but one comment of Lilburne's on a well-worn Puritan theme is worth recording. In controversy with John Johnson, Burgoyne's successor as rector of Bishop Wearmouth, he remarked, 'Prove it out of Scripture, or you say nothing.' Puritanism,[2] by its appeal to Scripture, and Scripture alone, threw overboard the synthesis of Christian beliefs, Aristotelian metaphysics, and tradition which Hooker had brought together into a single all-embracing world outlook which extended from the nature of the universe and its laws, and the place of religion within it, to the rules of political life and the structure of Church and State. Hooker's achievement was an impressive one, but its very scale and universality also gave it a claustrophobic quality; it was difficult to break out of Hooker's world, or to incorporate in it new experience, whether of the natural world, of religion, or of political life. Scripture on the other hand was a body of knowledge both more simple and more open. It spoke only of the encounter between man and God and of the rules which ought to govern this; the world of nature and of politics was otherwise left free to be reinterpreted in terms of that encounter. As a result the Puritan was not saddled, for example, with the sense of history as inevitable decline and 'decay' encountered in the attitudes of men like Robert Hegg or John, Lord Lumley, which were basic to the Aristotelian tradition out of which Hooker spoke. That same tradition made the Arminians see authority in Church and State, and obedience to this, as the defence of a world in which 'order', as they understood it, was the only alternative to collapse; and which itself stood constantly under assault from the inherent tendency in things to 'decay'. From their point of view the calamities of the Civil War and the Puritan Revolution were to prove the correctness of their insights.

But for the Puritan historical events were not particular instances of the general principle that all sublunary things were threatened by decay; but rather the theatre in which God encountered men with judgements on sinners, and with blessings on those who repented. In the calamities with which men were liable to be overwhelmed the negative side of the encounter with God expressed itself in divine anger and judgement. 'May God in his mercy,' said the Newcastle Puritan Sir Lionel Maddison in February 1645, as he contemplated a Durham wrecked by military occupation and civil war, 'turn away his judgements of the sword and pestilence, and keep from us the great judgement of famine . . .'[1] But all historical events were included in God's overriding purpose and design, and if approached with prayer and repentance manifested themselves positively, as blessing. Those who were compelled by their circumstances to move out of the shelter of traditional religious, social, and political forms were sustained in the unfamiliar territory through which they moved by the encounter (as John Blakiston the Durham regicide put it) with 'the great God with whom we have to do in this business, as well as with men', so that 'The disasters . . . at this conjuncture of affairs, call us upon knees for to ask assistance and direction . . .' Similarly the mining manager and entrepreneur Robert Bowes of Biddick, whose brother had met his death in the Keswick mines in 1606, could testify that it was precisely in the darkness and uncharted perils of the miner's world that the divine benevolence was to be encountered. 'By former experience', he asserted, 'in such mynerall actions, I have tasted of God his miraculous delyverance.'[2] It is not surprising that the dynamic, rapidly changing society of the lower Wear valley, which contained so much of what was novel and radical in the life of the region, and which had been accustomed until recently only to 'the simplicity of obedience in these parts, that, before Lilburne grew great, knew not what it was to confront royal authority' should have centred on Sunderland, one of those corporations 'where . . . all these pestilent nests of Puritans are hatched . . . where they swarm and breed like hornets in a horses head'.[3] It was the mark of Puritanism that it could both challenge established religious institutions and intellectual structures, and also sustain a

---

[1] *C.S.P. Dom. Ch. I, 1644*, p. 255.
[2] *C.S.P. Dom. Ch. I, 1645–7*, p. 124; Sur. *Hist. Durh.*, i.200.
[3] *C.S.P. Dom. Ch. I, 1639–40*, p. 516.

state of mind in which movement beyond them, into new territory, was facilitated.

In this connection, it is worth noting in conclusion 'the
senseless opinion' reported by Thomas Triplet to Laud 'which
those of Sunderland have got out of Peter Martyr ... viz. ...
equality of glory in the Saints'. This not only led Lilburne to
assert 'that all such as used to give thanks for the Blessed Virgin,
did it with purpose to bring in Popery', but also 'these wretches
[of Sunderland] ... to say ... each of them in particular to be
as glorious as the Blessed Virgin herself'. The claim to equality
is still a religious claim, being referred only to 'their abundant
faith'.[1] Yet the affective disposition which it expressed was not
easily reconcilable with the dominant traditional system of
values in the region, whose keynote whether in religion, politics,
or social order had always been hierarchy.

RECUSANCY: THE CATHOLIC MINORITY

When Father William Palmes (or Palmer), S.J., wrote his
Life of Mrs. Dorothy Lawson of St. Anthony's near Newcastle,[2] the
formidable matriarch of north-eastern Recusancy during the
generation before her death in 1632, he spoke of her father's
family, the Constables of Burton Constable as follows: 'The
condition of this family might compete for divers ages with any
lord in the realme for greatness of state and prerogative ... In
prerogative it came near the highest, having privilege to make
vassals or slaves, and receive homage as their native prince,
with chair and cloth of state in equipage of sovereignty.'[3] The
Constables were a substantial and influential family of Yorkshire squires, but they are seen here through a haze of nostalgia
for a romanticized past, and endowed with a fictional grandeur and prerogatives far beyond what they actually possessed,
'incomparable', so it was thought, 'till these sad times'. The
mood is very much like that of John, Lord Lumley, or Robert
Hegg, who turned from the 'decay' of the present to contemplate the glories of antiquity. From one point of view the attitude reflects the viewpoint of a group standing for everything
that was most traditionalist in the gentry way of life. This was
particularly true of the hard core of the Durham Recusants
(those who persisted in their Recusancy during the worst

[1] Ibid.   [2] See Lawson.   [3] Ibid., p. 6

persecuting years of the 1580s and 1590s), which was made up of the families, many of them respectably ancient and long-established, who had risen with the Nevilles in 1569, and who in one way or another had suffered the consequent penalties. These had imposed burdens on their estates to which the fines and disabilities involved in Recusancy were subsequently added. Amongst them the Trollopes of Thornley were prominent. There were the Claxtons of Old Park and their relatives, as well as the Salvins, the Blakistons of Blakiston, and the surviving connections of the exiled Tempests and Swinburns.[1] Most of them would, in the course of the next century, disappear from the Durham scene, shipwrecked by the burden of fine and proscription their estates had to carry.[2]

But the Recusants cannot be simply put in the category of 'old' or 'mere' gentry afflicted with political and social decline. For an interesting feature of Durham Recusancy is the powerful reinforcement it received from the urban and mercantile background of Newcastle, and particularly from the great coal-owning families. Already in the 1560s Richard Hodgson, mayor of Newcastle in 1555, 1566, and 1580, and founder of the coal-owning family which eventually settled at Hebburn, had been notable for his friendship with the Nevilles, and his brother participated in the Rising. Subsequently he and his relatives remained Recusants, and in the 1590s, in association with the earl of Westmorland's daughters, received and maintained seminary priests in various centres around Lanchester.[3] The Hodgsons were related to another prominent Newcastle merchant stock, the Lawsons, with whom they intermarried. By the end of the century, with estates at Byker near Newcastle, and in Durham and Yorkshire, the Lawsons, like their Hodgson relatives, had risen into the upper gentry. By then both families were intermarrying with old-established, but Recusant, gentry houses, thus forming alliances which confirmed and strength-

---

[1] Recusant families none of whose members were ever identified as rebels (although some, like the Hodgsons, were in fact involved) were the Hedworths and Lambtons (who abandoned their Recusancy in the seventeenth century), the Forcers, and the Hodgsons. The Recusant group also included families which had served the earls of Westmorland, like the Welburies, the Lees, and the Radcliffes. Bishop Matthew's list of Recusants of January 1592/3 (P.R.O., S.P.12/244/8) gives a conspectus of the group as it was in the later years of the reign of Queen Elizabeth.   [2] See above, p. 67 ff.   [3] Foley, iii.130 ff.

ened their Catholic orientation. Edmund Lawson, some time before 1613, made a match with the above-mentioned Dorothy Constable, of the famous, but Catholic, Burton Constable family. Sir Robert Hodgson, at about the same time, married Frances Ingleby, of the Recusant Inglebies of Ripley, near Ripon, who was proudly singled out in the Hodgson family pedigree as a great-granddaughter of the last earl of Westmorland. Probably the contacts made in the time of Richard Hodgson between the bourgeois Hodgsons and the noble Nevilles were still remembered two generations later.[1] In the 1620s the Hodgson house at Hebburn and Dorothy Lawson's at Saint Anthony's in Heaton near Newcastle became important link-points for the passage of priests between the north and south banks of the Tyne, 'and for harboringe of persons of all sorts ill-affected to the state'. At about this time a further marriage alliance linked the two families.

Marriages of newly risen Newcastle (or in some cases Durham) families into established landed houses of Catholic background seem to have been the principal means whereby Rucusancy infiltrated into the ownership of the new fortunes created out of commerce, coal, or office. The Riddells of Gateshead and Fenham, one of the leading Tyne coal-owning families, owed their Catholicism to Sir Thomas Riddell senior's wife, Elizabeth, daughter of Sir John Conyers of Sockburn, who by 1625 had converted her eldest son Sir William,[2] and whose younger son Sir Thomas had also turned to Catholicism by the time of his death in 1654.[3] John Jenison, of Walworth, heir to a Durham estate bought by his father out of the fortune he had made as auditor of Ireland, and connected also with Newcastle wealth, was carried into Recusancy by his marriage into the ancient Lancashire Gerard family in 1614.[4] The Maires of Hardwick, a Durham family founded on a legal fortune, turned Catholic after marrying into the Trollopes.[5]

These newly risen gentry tended to be strongly status-conscious, and the prestigious marriages which had brought them into the Catholic fold were remembered by their descendants.

---

[1] Sur. *Hist. Durh.*, ii.77; *Lawson*, p. xvii; *N.C.H.*, vol. xiii (1930), pp. 392 ff.

[2] *Lawson*, ibid. Sir Thomas Riddell was disarmed in 1625, his wife and eldest son being identified as Recusants (*Barnes*, p. 310).

[3] Foley, v.659. [4] Sur. *Hist. Durh.*, iii.320; *N.C.H.*, xii.247.

[5] Sur. *Hist. Durh.*, i.52–3.

Thomas Jenison, a priest, stated on his entry into the English College at Rome, 'My father ... John Jenison ... spent his life at his own house called Walworth, from whence he married a lady of the ancient family of Gerard, of Lancashire ... I have an elder brother possessing a large property...'[1] Michael Jenison, of the Jenisons of Neasham, stated 'I am of a family of the higher class. My father is an esquire, my mother's name was Bowes ... They were always Catholics.'[2] Sir Thomas Riddell's grandson described him as of 'a noble and ancient family'.[3] Part of what it meant to be a Recusant was the sense of belonging to an exclusive élite. But it was the wives who appear to have contributed most to the religious formation of these families, the exemplar in this respect being Dorothy Lawson. Over-riding her easy-going husband 'who comply'd with the times' she first ensured that her household was staffed exclusively with Catholic servants, 'while her children, through her sedulous industry, were all bred Catholicks, solidly instructed in Christian doctrine, and had the company of a priest freely ...'[4] It is not surprising then that the government should have become alarmed at the inroads made as a result of Catholic marriages into the Protestant establishment, so that legislation of 1606 sought to penalize such unions by denying public office to Protestants who took Catholic wives, and by excluding them from any claim on the latters' property. The widowed Catholic wife of a mixed marriage forfeited two-thirds of her dowry, as well as the right to be the executrix of her husband's will.[5]

Catholic organization, and such vestiges of a Catholic church structure as could be kept going, came to depend during these years on the houses and estates of the gentry who formed part of the Recusant community. When in the 1570s and 1580s Catholic missionary priests trained in the seminaries newly founded abroad for Englishmen at Douai, Rome, and elsewhere began to enter Durham by way of Newcastle, Hartlepool, or from the south, the earliest centres for their activities were the Trollope house at Thornley, and the Claxton house at Water-

---

[1] Trans. from the Latin in Foley, v.634.
[2] Ibid., iii.117. The Boweses of Ellerbeck are the family referred to here.
[3] Foley, v.647. The importance and wealth of the Riddells dated from their settlement in Newcastle in the sixteenth century; but they soon boasted a pedigree which traced them back to a medieval sheriff of Northumberland.
[4] *Lawson*, pp. 19–20.   [5] 3 Jac. I, c. 5 (1606), Statutes, iv(2), 1077.

house.[1] In the 1590s we hear of the shelter given to priests at the Manor House in Lanchester, the home of the Hodgsons; and at Greencroft in the same parish by Lady Catherine Neville, the earl of Westmorland's daughter.[2] In the seventeenth century new centres grew up in association with the seats of the Recusant gentry. There was a Catholic chapel at the Hodgson house at Hebburn, and another at Stella, also the estate of a New-castle coal-owning dynasty, the Tempests, descended from the rebel family of 1569. There was a chapel attached to the Rid-dell house at Gateshead, another at the Forcer house at Harber-house, the Maires had one at Hardwick, and presumably the Jenisons too at Walworth.[3]

This reliance of Catholicism on a leadership of gentry back-ground made it inevitable that the Recusant community should consist in the main of gentry households with their dependent bodies of servants and tenants.[4] For the prestige and influence of the landlord, and his ownership of the land, worked to pro-duce a solidly Catholic community dependent on the great house. There were instances of a yeoman or middle-class Recus-ancy, and perhaps the Jackson family of Bishop Auckland may have been an example of this.[5] Others may be the two isolated Catholics in Bishop Wearmouth parish, and the four in Monk-wearmouth, or more certainly the Emerson clan in Weardale, who refused to sign the anti-Catholic Protestation circulated by Parliament in the tense days of 1642.[6] But given the prohibition by law of Catholic preaching and missionary activity, the estate Catholicism of the great house was much the most important. Thus the most considerable of the little knots of Recusants bold enough to refuse the Protestation are found in association with a Catholic landlord—like the twenty-one who withheld their signatures with Sir William Selby in Ryton parish, the twenty with John Claxton in Brancepeth, and the thirty-five headed by the Hodgsons at Jarrow and Tanfield.[7] Dorothy Lawson's bio-grapher tells us that although there was only one Catholic family in the parish of Heaton when she went to live there, by the time of her death in 1632 the district had been converted to

---

[1] *C.S.P. Dom. Eliz., 1591–4*, pp. 305, 377.   [2] Above, p. 138.
[3] Foley, iii.126 ff.   [4] cf. Bossy, 'Character'.
[5] *C.S.P. Dom. Jas. I, 1603–10*, p. 278; ibid., *Eliz., 1591–4*, p. 262.
[6] *Durh. Prot.*, pp. 34, 103, 110, 111.   [7] Ibid., pp. 24, 39, 45, 78.

Recusancy, and not a single Protestant family still survived.[1]
The leadership of the gentry was inevitably reflected too in the
ranks of the clergy. The Jenisons for example sent some half
dozen of their sons into the priesthood in the course of the
seventeenth century, and one of these died in Newgate during
the Titus Oates persecution. Another, Robert Jenison, became
a Jesuit in 1617, rising to be head of his Order's Mission in
England; others became chaplains in Recusant households.[2]
The Tempests, Forcers, and the Maires provided recruits for the
priesthood.

    Throughout these years the Recusant minority remained, in
the nature of things, a small one. The reports of the authorities,
ecclesiastical and secular, usually speak of between 125 and 200
Recusants as belonging to the gentry and their immediate dependants, the number rising to the upper level after the accession of the Stuarts.[3] Estimates of the total number of Catholics
were bound to be vaguer, but the assize judges put this at 400
in 1609, a fall from 700 earlier in James I's reign, before the renewed persecution which followed the Gunpowder Plot.[4] In
1625/6 a round figure of 1,000 was put forward for 'convicted
recusants'; but only half this number refused the Protestation
in 1642.[5] Considerable determination and strength of religious
commitment, as well as a powerful sense of group adhesion,
must have been necessary for the Recusant gentry to persist in
their Catholicism, in view of the political, economic, and social
disabilities which it involved.[6] But the group was sustained by

---

[1] *Lawson*, p. 26.   [2] Foley, v.632 ff.
[3] e.g. *C.S.P. Dom. Eliz., 1595–7*, pp. 348, 431; ibid., *Jas. I, 1603–10*, p. 36.
[4] Ibid., p. 543.   [5] Ibid., *Ch. I, 1625–6*, p. 420; *Durh. Prots., passim.*
[6] The main disabilities involved were exclusion from office and the professions,
restrictions on travel, and in the case of women those (mentioned above) which
followed on marriage to a Protestant; the estates of Catholics were burdened with
a fine of £20 a month for non-attendance at the services of the Church of England.
There were further penalties for attending Mass and harbouring priests. The latter
were much more severely treated than Catholic laymen, their mere presence in
England exposing them to the penalties of treason. If rigorously applied the laws
against Catholics might well have rendered the survival of a Recusant community impossible. But in practice enforcement was erratic, and severity varied
from year to year and place to place according to the views of local J.P.s and
government policy. The fines were the most irksome burden from which Recusants, particularly the gentry leadership, suffered. After 1625 it became usual to
'compound' for Recusancy fines, i.e. pay an annual sum supposed to represent
two-thirds of the rental of the property (one-third after 1635). But once again
Recusants tended in practice to be leniently treated and the full amount of the

hopes of dynastic change, and of shifts in political power which might transform a persecuted minority overnight into a favoured dominant group. In the bad years of the 1580s and 1590s the Recusants looked hopefully forward to the death of Queen Elizabeth, with the change of régime which it was hoped would follow, particularly if James VI of Scotland, son of the Catholic Queen Mary, were to succeed. The hopes placed on James did not survive the Gunpowder Plot and the renewed persecution which followed. But in the 1630s tolerance of Recusancy increased (so that Bishop Morton was reproved by the Privy Council for attempting to impose harsh penalties for Durham Catholic christenings and marriages)[1] and Catholic influence at Court grew. Of the structure of religious practice and emphasis of belief which sustained the solidarity and persistence of the Recusant leadership something can be gathered from the case of Dorothy Lawson, her influence being an important one on Durham as well as Northumberland Recusancy.

After the death of her husband in 1613/14 Dorothy Lawson moved from Byker to the neighbouring parish of Heaton, where she built the establishment called Saint Anthony's. There she aimed to realize in ideal form the kind of organization which the circumstances and setting of an excluded and persecuted, but gentry and upper class group forced on the Recusant society. That organization, as has been seen, came to be based on the gentry household, with its associated community of servants and tenants; but a household whose inner cohesion was strengthened by its sense of isolation, and whose characteristics reflected the sense of separation from the dominant establishment which Recusancy implied. In Dorothy Lawson's household these characteristics were articulated into a religious way of life, that of the gentry Catholicism of the Recusants. This was displayed, however, on a scale and with an elaboration

---

composition was rarely exacted. Resusancy fines rarely ruined a Recusant family unless there were other factors in the situation which made the burden intolerable. However, in spite of these mitigations, which made survival possible, the price of Recusancy was isolation, insecurity, and exclusion from the main stream of social and political life. For a summary of the legislative disabilities placed on Recusants during this period, see M. J. Havran, *The Catholics in Caroline England* (Stanford, 1962), ch. i; for the process of compounding, see ibid., pp. 92–9.

[1] *Cowper MSS.*, ii.80. Baptisms and marriages outside the established church were penalized by 3 Jac. I, c. 4 (1606), Statutes, iv(2), 1071.

which suggests the degree of non-interference and freedom enjoyed in practice by Recusants who, like the Lawsons, belonged to the local governing class, in this case the Newcastle mercantile and coal-owning aristocracy.[1] Saint Anthony's was used as a headquarters and training centre by the Jesuits in the northeast, retreats and devotional exercises being regularly held there by members of the Order. There was an elaborate chapel 'according to the fashion in Catholic countries', and a daily and seasonal routine of ceremonies and liturgical services.

As in Puritan families, the household became the vehicle of a close religious discipline, in which servants participated as well as parents and children. The servants at Saint Anthony's attended daily services, heard a sermon on Sundays, were catechized and instructed in Scripture and the lives of the saints. But the religious routines and disciplines were supplemented by and intertwined with the traditional code of 'magnanimity' and (the older term) 'good lordship' which ideally ought to inform relations between the nobility and gentry and their dependants. Thus Dorothy Lawson was 'a bountifull mistress' who gave her servants 'more than was their due in temporalls'. She visited the poor and the sick, bringing 'relics for the soul' and 'cordialls for the body'.[2] At Christmastide the solidarity of mistress and dependants received expression in the feasting of neighbours and tenants with music and dancing, as well as in elaborate liturgical services.[3] Dorothy Lawson's biographer identified her virtues with those traditionally ascribed to the patriarchal family head. She was praised for 'her authority,

---

[1] A good example of the kind of protection she enjoyed is provided by the case of Anthony Vandenhaupt, a servant of Sir Robert Hodgson, who was intercepted in November 1629 while attempting to smuggle in a consignment of 82 theological and devotional works intended for the library at Saint Anthony's. Bishop Neile complained to the mayor of Newcastle (Thomas Liddell) about Mrs. Lawson, and the contact afforded by Saint Anthony's via the Hodgson house at Hebburn between the Recusants north and south of the Tyne. But Liddell took no action, and merely reported that the contacts with Hodgson were but 'idle reports, other than their keeping boats to cross the river'. One of her priests, Henry Morse, was arrested shortly afterwards, but Mrs. Lawson was allowed to visit him in gaol, and was not herself molested. Throughout her life she enjoyed this kind of immunity. Sir Robert Hodgson, being within Bishop Neile's jurisdiction, was more roughly treated, in that his house was searched by the sheriff; but he avoided further unpleasant consequences by absenting himself until the storm had blown over. See *Barnes*, pp. 309–12; *C.S.P. Dom. Ch. I, 1625–6*, pp. 310–11, 325, 358; Caraman, chs. 4–5.

[2] *Lawson*, p. 45.   [3] Ibid., pp. 44–5.

prudence, sweetness and gravity', and because 'every one loved her with fear, and fear'd her with love'.[1] But it is interesting that the family at Saint Anthony's should in fact have been a matriarchy, thus reminding us once again of the important part played by wives, particularly those like Dorothy Lawson from older and more prestigious families than their husbands, in strengthening and enlarging the bonds and bounds of Recusancy. The matriarchal household had its appropriate symbol and exemplar at hand moreover in the cult of the Mother of God, Dorothy Lawson being 'singularly devoted to the service of the Blessed Virgin' and also 'zealous to advance her glory, by herself, her children, her servants, and her neighbours'.[2]

At a deeper level this whole way of life was founded on an intense moralism. We are told that Dorothy Lawson made a general examination of conscience twice a day, but supplemented this by offering her thoughts, words, and deeds to God at waking, and renewing her 'intention' in this respect at regular intervals throughout the day. In addition, in 'particular actions' or situations in which the strengthening of the will by divine grace might be thought particularly necessary, again there was a renewal of 'intention', 'like a considerate archer who takes his aim deliberately before he shoots'.[3] Where this kind of Catholic moralism differed from its Puritan counterpart, in spite of the superficial resemblances, was in its emphasis on the will, choice, and on the human initiative (the 'intention') whose weaknesses and inadequacies were then supplemented by the assistance of divine grace, mediated through the ministry of the Church. The Puritan on the other hand threw overboard the Aristotelian and Stoic psychology of will and intention which lay behind Dorothy Lawson's self-questionings, relying solely on the lore and images of Scripture, and the application of these to individual decisions and situations; an attitude which rejected more of the inheritance of the past, and particularly that of classical antiquity and medieval scholasticism. Characteristically, the kind of Catholicism practised at Saint Anthony's seems to have shied away from the more affective and mystical elements in the tradition, Dorothy Lawson's constitution being such that it would 'permit her to spend but half an

---

[1] Ibid., p. 48.   [2] Ibid., p. 38.   [3] Ibid., pp. 39, 40.

hour every day in meditation';[1] this side of her religious practice being plainly less important than the active life of virtue
and good works. The essence of Recusant Catholicism as it re-
veals itself in this setting might well be seen as this training of
the will to graft the life of virtue on to those inherited merits
which came with blood and descent to the heirs of ancient
stocks, a training which it was the duty of parents to provide and
for which the family provided the primary context. As William
Palmes put it: 'The glory of children is in their parents . . . not
only because the same blood runs in their veins which framed
their posterity, but chiefly for that by a peculiar influency or
reflection their glory shines in their posterity, and makes their
merits by a natural participation . . . theirs'; but he adds,
'. . . as St. Ambrose says, there is no prerogative in succession of
kindred . . . this good is to be ascribed to nobility and stemm
of progenitors, that children from them may learn to live well,
by whom they first began to live . . .'[2] This 'learning to live
well' seems to have been the heart of the Recusant discipline at
its best; it accounts for the degree of resistance which the Recusant society could put up to the environment of social and cultural change which increasingly challenged the foundations on
which it rested.[3]

[1] Ibid., p. 38.   [2] Ibid., pp. 5, 7.
[3] A resistance strengthened however by the increasingly in-turned and isolated
quality of Recusant society. After the first half of the seventeenth century there
were no further recruits from the Newcastle milieu, and families like the Hodgsons,
Tempests, Riddells, and Lawsons withdrew increasingly from industrial activities,
contrasting in this respect with for example the Protestant Liddells.

6

POLITICS: FROM SINGLE-FACTION
RULE TO BREAKDOWN

THE NEW POLITICAL PATTERN

THE main result of the Rising in the North, as far as
Durham was concerned, was to destroy the ancient
counterpoise of ecclesiastical and secular power in the
region.[1] For the exile of the earl of Westmorland, and the with-
drawal of Lord Lumley from the Durham scene left the Bishop
(particularly if reinforced by his Dean and Chapter) in a position of unchallenged leadership as the sole surviving Durham
magnate, and one whose landed resources in the area were now
approached in extent only by those of the Crown. The conditions were therefore created for single-faction rule, although
some time elapsed before the changed pattern, and all it implied,
emerged. For Protestantism tended to deprecate the political
and secular functions of the episcopate, emphasizing instead the
pastoral role of the Bishop, the 'father in God' of his clergy and
people, to whom notions of 'lordship' and 'prelacy' ought to be
alien. Bishops therefore like Pilkington (1561–76) and Barnes
(1577–87) who were essentially Protestant intellectuals, were
allergic to an energetic political role. Both had the support of
Cecil (and Pilkington of the earl of Leicester), but neither were
courtiers, neither enjoyed the favour of the Queen, and each
remained essentially within the university and clerical world.[2]
Both also showed a certain incompetence where matters of control and leadership were concerned: Pilkington by his passive
role during the Rising, when he fled leaving the rebels in
possession;[3] Barnes by the insouciance with which (so it seems)

[1] Above, p. 51.
[2] For Pilkington and Barnes, see *D.N.B.*, and references there given; Sur. *Hist.
Durh.*, i.lxxii–lxxxii; Hutch., i.445–66; *Durh. Eccles. Proc.*, intro. For Pilkington's
firm assertion of the priority of the spiritual over the temporal duties of bishops
(but a loophole is left for the latter, as commissioned by royal authority), see
Pilkington, *Works*, pp. 491–2.
[3] A few weeks before the Rising, Pilkington was approached by Dean Whitting-

he entrusted the administration of his affairs to his oppressive
and profiteering brother John Barnes, as well as by his readi-
ness to become involved in quarrels between his servants and
his tenants.[1] Both bishops complained of their isolation and
powerlessness in their Palatinate. It was the 'Papists' who ruled
all, and Durham was an 'Augean stable' whose cleansing presented a herculean task. Barnes, particularly, was mainly concerned with attempting the reform of his clergy, and though
'affable and good' took less interest in the secular aspects of his
responsibilities.[2]

Inevitably then after Elizabeth's accession there was more lay
support, oversight, and control. Tunstall was not followed as
lord lieutenant by his Protestant successors. Under Pilkington
this office was conferred on the earl of Bedford, warden of the
East March; under Barnes on the earl of Huntingdon, lord
president of the Council in the North.[3] The Queen's financial
needs led also to a pruning of the Durham episcopal estates,
with Pilkington on his appointment handing over lands to a
value of nearly £700 a year, to be 'detained' in the Queen's
hands. These were eventually returned, but at the price of a
rent-charge in perpetuity to the Crown of £1,020 a year.[4]
Pilkington, after the Rising, also had to surrender to the Queen,
by Act of Parliament, the forfeitures of rebel lands to which he
was entitled as Palatine.[5] Barnes had to make long leases to the

---

ham who suggested (according to the latter's biographer) 'that he would send
for his tenants to come to his castell at Durham, with their warlike furniture; which
if he would doe, he [i.e. Whittingham] would cause all the tenants of the church
[i.e. the Cathedral] to join likewise with them, which would be a means to awe
the collecting rebels, and be a stay and refuge for many . . .' But Pilkington refused,
answering that 'he had a great deal of the Queen's money in his hand, and durst
not hazard it'. Nothing was done to mobilize the Church tenantry. See *Whittingham*, pp. 23–4.

[1] See Carleton, pp. 151–4, and above, p. 82.

[2] *Cal. S.P. Dom.*, *1547–80*, p. 187; *Durh. Eccles. Proc.*, pp. ix–xi. Hence Barnes's
indifference, affirmed by persistent tradition, to John Barnes's misdoings, and
Bernard Gilpin's reproofs 'God hath exalted you to be bishop of this diocese, and
requireth an account of your government thereof. A reformation of all those things
which are amiss in this church is required of your hands. And now lest, perhaps,
while it is apparent, that so many enormities are committed every where, your
lordship should make answer, that you had no notice of them given you, and that
these things escaped your attention . . . behold I bring these things to your knowledge this day.' Carleton, pp. 153–4.

[3] Thomson, pp. 53–5.   [4] Strype, *Annals*, ii(1).438–42.

[5] Sur. *Hist. Durh.*, i.lxxvi.

Crown of further bishopric lands and possessions, including Whickham and Gateshead, which thus passed out of the episcopal control, with all their rich coal resources, for a term of ninety-nine years—to the profit, as has been seen, of Newcastle, whose Corporation secured the lease from the Queen's grantee, Thomas Sutton.[1]

The most remarkable feature of the situation, however, was the continued survival of the bishopric within a now established and permanent Protestant context. A survival moreover which involved the persistence of its landed possessions (pruned, but none permanently alienated), of its jurisdiction and Palatine privileges, and of the way of life which the sheer weight of its lands and institutions imposed on the region. Paradoxically this outcome must be ascribed to the rule of Bishop Pilkington. For not even this ardent Protestant, with his Calvinist sympathies, could escape the traditional role (or the abuses) which the institution over which he presided imposed on him. In the administrative documents of his see Pilkington appeared as bishop 'by the grace of God', or *miseratione divina*, and was described as *reverendissimus*, phrases inherited from his medieval predecessors, but not without incongruity in relation to his own principles.[2] Like his medieval predecessors too, he sued for and obtained from the Queen a confirmation of the liberties and charters of the bishopric in 1564.[3] It was the same pressure on the present of a position inherited from the past which also required him, in the same year, to sue for the return of the Palatine estates still 'detained' in the Queen's hands. For while they were withheld from the possession of their rightful lord, lands could not be sold or alienated, or estates in law conveyed, a state of affairs which, Pilkington affirmed, 'I am sorry should chance in this time, or by occasion of any that professes Christ's gospel. And surely the people say, this is the fruit of our religion, to procure such mischiefs.' The argument linked Protestantism and common sense, and so was likely to appeal to the Queen, who gave in. A heavy price had to be paid for the restored possessions, but it was important that the Bishop's title to the whole of the landed endowment of his see had been preserved.[4]

Pilkington also has to his credit the maintenance of the feudal

---

[1] Strype, *Annals*, ii(2).531. Trevor-Roper, p. 55.   [2] Hutch., i.456.
[3] Ibid., i.447.   [4] Strype, *Annals*, ii(2).440–2.

prerogatives of the Bishop as Palatine. These were curtailed by
the Act of 1571,[1] which gave the Queen the forfeitures of rebel
lands after the Rising, but only after the Bishop had put up a
fight in defence of his rights involving a law-suit with the Queen
herself. As a result they were not abolished, but merely suspended *pro hac vice*.[2] Cosin at the Restoration owed it to
Pilkington that he was able to bargain them away to Charles II
in return for the rent charge exacted by Queen Elizabeth in
1566.[3] Thus Pilkington, in spite of his timidity and unworldly
doctrinal preoccupations (which put him on the radical, anti-
government side in the 'Vestiarian controversy' of the 1560s),
proved himself as obstinate and tenacious as any of his predecessors in the defence of the possessions and privileges of his see. He
prepared the way too for the defeat of the renewed attempt of
the Corporation of Newcastle, just before the Parliament of
1576, to annex the town of Gateshead and reduce the liberties
of the Palatinate.[4] Of course, in the background there was the
determination of the government to maintain the hierarchical
structure of the Church, with most of its property and privileges.
Pilkington therefore could rely on the support of Cecil. He also
owed much to the clever lawyer, William Fleetwood, Puritan
and recorder of London, whom he appointed as his temporal
chancellor[5]—to the disgust of such local families as the Meynells,
Tempests, and Chaytors, from whom it had been previously
usual to appoint this official.

The survival of the bishopric, with its Palatine jurisdiction
intact, and with its endowment of landed possessions still placing at its disposal all the offices and perquisites of a great estate,
meant the reassertion, sooner or later, of its role as the centre of
a gentry affiliation aspiring to a leading role in the region's
politics. This increasingly dominant 'Church interest', which
had its roots in the wealth and influence of the Cathedral as well
as of the bishopric, can be seen emerging during the rule of
Bishop Hutton (1589–95) and Bishop Matthew (1595–1606).
Landmarks from this point of view were the marriage of
Hutton's heir to a daughter of Sir George Bowes of Streatlam,

---

[1] 13 Eliz., c. 16; *Statutes* iv (1), 549.
[2] Sur. *Hist. Durh.*, i.lxxvi; Coke, Pt. iv, p. 219.
[3] Strype, loc. cit., p. 442.   [4] Trevor-Roper, p. 52; Longstaffe, pp. 219–25.
[5] Ibid., p. 224, and *D.N.B.* under Fleetwood; *C.S.P. Dom.*, *1547–80*, p. 187.

the first episcopal alliance into the dominant upper gentry; and the purchase in 1591 of the manor of Neasham by prebendary Bunny, the first of the upper clergy to found one of those landed families of clerical connection subsequently prominent in the ranks of the Church interest.[1] These same years also saw the rise of other Church families, but of lay background, their fortunes founded or sustained by office under the bishopric, or by Church leaseholds. Amongst them were the Calverleys, the Wrens of Binchester, the Frevilles, Tailboys, and Bellasises. The Church interest thus constituted, well represented on the commission of the peace, providing stewards, receivers, and legal advisers to the Bishop and Cathedral, also formed a centre around which gravitated such respectable 'ancient' families as the Hiltons, Conyers, and Bowes (from whose ranks the Bishop frequently appointed his sheriff). It stood for a formidable concentration of office, wealth, and influence.[2] The more because the identification of the Crown, since Elizabeth's accession, with Protestantism meant that the opposition Catholic families of the Neville and allied connection were gradually pushed outside the political pale. As a result dissidence was forced to assume a Protestant colour. It could emerge only from within the Protestant establishment itself, and was not long in doing so.

These developments were of more long-term and permanent importance than the attempt put in hand, at the end of Bishop James's episcopate (1603–17), to revive the power of the Neville connection in the bishopric on behalf of the King's Scottish favourite, Robert Carr. This episode, however, drives home once again the persisting impact of the pattern of landownership, and particularly of the structure and traditions of the great estate, on politics and the distribution of influence. For the mere memory of the role vacated by the fallen earl of

[1] Sur., *Hist. Durh.*, i.lxxxv ff.; iv.40–1. See also above, p. 72 ff.

[2] Thomas Calverley was temporal chancellor and steward to bishops Barnes, Hutton, and Matthew, and had begun his career as steward to Bishop Pilkington in 1564; Richard Tailboys was attorney-general to Barnes and Hutton, and Robert Tailboys escheator to Hutton; the Wrens were constables of Durham castle under bishops James, Neile, Mountain, Howson, and Morton, and farmed prebendal lands at Binchester; the Frevilles farmed the episcopal demesnes at Bishop Middleham, and the Bellasises the episcopal grange at Morton. The Bowes, Hilton, and Conyers families monopolized the shrievalty from Pilkington's accession to 1608, when the Newcastle coal-owner Sir George Selby was appointed, to be succeeded by Sir William Bellasis in 1625.

Westmorland, sustained by the continued existence of the Neville inheritance, now in the hands of the Crown, proffered to the great men in the King's immediate circle a recurring temptation to fill the place formerly occupied by the head of this family as leader of the anti-Church interest in the bishopric. Robert Carr's aspirations in this respect emerged with the conferment on him in 1613 of the Durham title of baron of Brancepeth, at the same time as he was made earl of Somerset. In this year he advanced money for the purchase from the Crown of the former Neville lordships of Brancepeth and Raby.[1] Somerset's connection, through his mistress and subsequent wife Frances, countess of Essex, with the Howard interest underlines how the political pattern of the Rising in the North was still liable to return to life in the ambitions of a later generation. For Lady Essex (divorced from her first husband and married to Somerset at the end of 1613) was the daughter of Thomas Howard, earl of Suffolk, second son of that same duke of Norfolk who, before his execution in 1572, had headed the northern connection of lords and gentry, mainly Catholic, with which the last earl of Westmorland had been involved. The countess's great-uncle was Henry, earl of Northampton, James I's lord privy seal, younger brother of the late duke, political head of the Howard family, and leader of the pro-Catholic and pro-Spanish faction at James's Court.[2] The Howard family had approved of the plan for Frances's remarriage to Somerset, the object in view being to strengthen the Howard influence with the King by means of the favourite; and also to renew and extend the Howard connection in the North by reviving the Neville influence in favour of Somerset, like the last earl of Westmorland a Howard son-in-law.

Thus early in 1615 Somerset was made lord lieutenant of Durham, much to the distress of Bishop James, who begged that 'the country may be informed that it was for no neglect on his own [James's] parts, having discharged the service for six years, with great pains'.[3] There can be little doubt that the new office was intended as a snub to the Bishop, and it is clear that

---

[1] G.E.C., xii(1).67; *C.S.P. Dom. Jas. I, 1611–18*, p. 211.

[2] Until Northampton's death in 1614, when Somerset succeeded him as lord privy seal; Suffolk now presided over the Howard interest, and was made lord treasurer. See *D.N.B.*, under Robert Carr, Thomas Howard, and Henry Howard.

[3] *C.S.P. Dom. Jas. I, 1611–18*, p. 270.

Somerset hoped to play an active role in Durham. For at the Saint George's day feast of the same year he was attended by leading Recusant gentry from the Palatinate, including Sir William Blakiston and Sir John Claxton, although these (as Bishop James pointed out), being Recusants, 'should not leave their bounds or come within ten miles of the court'.[1] It seemed then as though the politics of the 1560s were about to re-emerge. But already in 1615 Somerset's influence with James I was declining before the rising star of the new favourite George Villiers. In November the scandal broke of the murder of Sir Thomas Overbury in the Tower, and the supposed involvement of Somerset and his wife in this. The result was their arrest and trial, and the end of Somerset's political career. His role in Durham did not survive his fall. But it was revived in the 1630s, this time in favour of the courtier Vanes—Sir Henry, treasurer of the King's household, later secretary of state, and his Puritan heir of the same name—who during these years were establishing themselves as lords of Raby castle and Barnard Castle, purchased from the Crown.[2] It did not take long for this new great family to become the centre of the anti-Church interest, now Puritan in its religious orientation.[3] By the end of the century the Vanes would head the Whig interest in the Palatinate, renewing the traditional pattern which the fall of the Nevilles had disrupted, but in terms of a very different world of Parliamentary and party politics.

THE BISHOPS AND THE CROWN

The difficulties of Bishop James, confronted by the re-emergence of a powerful Recusant interest, led by Somerset, in his Palatinate, and passed over for the lord lieutenancy, illustrate the extent to which the bishops depended on the favour of the

[1] Ibid., p. 291.
[2] The first step in Sir Henry Vane's acquisition of Barnard Castle and Raby seems to have been taken in 1626, when both lordships were vested in trustees from the City of London on his behalf by the Crown. He entertained Charles I at Raby in 1633, but the final transfer of the privileges etc. annexed to both lordships did not take place until 1640. See Sur. *Hist. Durh.*, iv.68, 166; Brydges, iv.511, 505; *C.S.P. Dom. Ch. I, 1633–4*, p. 174. The price was £18,000. See also *D.N.B.*
[3] See, for example, the approaches made to Vane by John Richardson, the Durham lawyer who was clerk of the peace, but an opponent of Bishop Neile, who had probably dismissed him from his solicitor-generalship. See *C.S.P. Dom. Ch. I, 1637–8*, p. 475, and ibid., *1639–40*, p. 412.

Crown. James's troubles can largely be attributed to his failure to secure the confidence of his namesake King James I, with whom his relations were uneasy. Partly the reason lay in the Bishop's own background and disposition, for James was in the tradition of Pilkington and Barnes, having little contact with the Court (long ago he had been briefly chaplain to the now forgotten Elizabethan magnate, the earl of Leicester); like them his career had been exclusively in the field of university and Church administration.[1] He had not been happy in the one assignment which might have brought him closer to the King— his brief custodianship of Arbella Stuart. There was also the complication of the curiously 'medieval' wrangle over Palatine regalities and prerogatives, inherited from Bishop Matthew, relating particularly to the incorporation of boroughs.[2] The case which had caused the trouble was that of the city of Durham, which had sought and received a royal charter of incorporation in 1601. But the legality of this had been successfully contested in the court of Exchequer by Matthew, and an episcopal charter substituted for it. The latter caused trouble all through Bishop James's episcopate, the townsmen seeking the intervention of the Privy Council 'concerning the vindication of the City liberties from the encroachment of the late lord Bishop'. The matter was raised again in 1617 when the King visited Durham, causing a confrontation between him and the Bishop which (according to tradition) hastened the latter's death a few months later.[3] The role planned for Somerset in the bishopric (and the harassment which Bishop James also suffered from the vocal Durham Puritan faction) owed much to this disharmony between him and his royal master.

Other bishops managed better in this all-important matter. Already in the late sixteenth century, under Bishop Hutton (1589–95) and Bishop Matthew (1595–1606), a break is apparent with the style of the scholar-intellectual Bishops Pilkington and Barnes, their two successors prefiguring the

[1] See *D.N.B.* under William James; Sur. *Hist. Durh.*, i.216; ii.41, 43, 159n; Hutch., i.479.

[2] The trouble had begun under Hutton, when the Queen had encroached on the Durham regalities by granting a royal charter to Hartlepool, at the suit of Lord Lumley, in 1593. See Sharp, *Hartlepool*, p. 63.

[3] *C.S.P. Dom. Jas. I, 1603–10*, p. 573; ibid., *1611–18*, p. 487; Sur. *Hist. Durh.*, i.lxxxvii; iv(2).14–16; *V.C.H. Durh.*, iii.34 ff.

great courtier-prelates of the seventeenth century. Both Hutton and Matthew (in spite of the latter's determination to defend his regalities)[1] were liked by Queen Elizabeth, and Matthew was a royal chaplain and favourite Court preacher. Hutton contrasted with Barnes in the strength of his character, and the self-confidence with which he dealt with the magnates of the Court towards whom Barnes behaved subserviently.[2] Court favour made it easier for both these bishops to revive the note of the 'prelatical' statesman-bishop avoided by their predecessors; and it was characteristic that Hutton should leave Durham not only to become archbishop of York, but also lord president of the Council in the North, the second bishop of the Protestant establishment to hold this post.[3] Matthew was an energetic and able administrator, who established his reputation as such during his tenure of the Durham deanery, from 1583–95; he was very much involved in Border affairs and Scottish diplomacy, and the determined foe of the Recusants in his diocese.[4] During his rule the earl of Huntingdon died, but no new lord lieutenant of Durham was appointed in his place, Matthew instead assuming the burdens and duties of the office, although never given the title, as would be the case with Bishop James after him.[5] By the latter's accession in 1606 the Bishop had already emerged as the effective temporal ruler of the Palatinate. Only the title of lord lieutenant was still withheld, and once Bishop James was out of the way and the Somerset episode over, this was granted (with much else) to the King's episcopal favourite and model bishop, Richard Neile.

Bishop Neile (1617–28)[6] was remarkable for the harmonious relationship which persisted during his rule between bishop and

---

[1] He was a good deal more determined than Hutton in this respect, who not only did not resist the grant of a royal charter to Hartlepool, but also surrendered the nomination to the Twelfth Stall in the cathedral to the Crown. Hutch., i.474.

[2] For Hutton, see *D.N.B.*, and *Hutton*. Thus Barnes, when in trouble because of his disputes with his tenants over customary tenures, which were referred to the Council, could humbly seek 'the testimony' of the earl of Huntingdon, lord president of the North, 'who knows my doings and the estate of the same' (P.R.O. S.P.12/159). Hutton on the other hand confidently asserted, while still only dean of York, that 'he needed neither the favour of the Archbishop [of York] nor yet of the lord president, and therefore he would join with neither of them' (Sur. *Hist. Durh.*, i.lxxxiii, n).

[3] But he was not well regarded as President. See *Hatf. MSS.*, ix.317.

[4] For Matthew's activities in the Border Administration, see e.g. *Hatf. MSS.*, vol. vi, *passim*.   [5] *Hatf. MSS.*, vi.72; *C.S.P. Dom. Jas I, 1611–18*, p. 270.

[6] See *D.N.B.*; Sur. *Hist. Durh.*, i.lxxxviii–lxc; Hutch., i.482–7.

Crown. He was essentially the courtier-prelate, more noted for his Court sermons and friendship with James I than for his learning or university contacts. Endowed with a strong sense of the deference due to his superiors and patrons, he had been lucky in the latter. For he owed his start in the world to the Cecils, still all-important in the first decade of James's reign, having been chaplain to Lord Treasurer Salisbury, before becoming chaplain to the King himself.[1] Neile, while modest about his own intellectual pretensions, nevertheless held strong views on the political and social role of the Church, derived from the teaching of those 'Arminian' divines already discussed above.[2] Throughout his career, he saw the Church and its organization as unconditionally committed to the maintenance of the authority of the Crown. This he conceived to be the foundation of that whole traditional structure of Church and State now increasingly exposed to the assaults of unruly Parliamentarians and Puritans. Neile's policy was to give the King absolute support in pulpit and Parliament. He thus aroused the fury of the Commons in the Parliament of 1614, and emerged in due course as a principal clerical bugbear of the parliamentary opposition. As a result he was highly regarded by King James well before his arrival in Durham, to which he was promoted from the see of Lincoln. Subsequent events were to prove that throughout his episcopate he could rely on the backing of the Crown in Palatine affairs. An early and significant indication of the favour in which he was held was his appointment, on 14 November 1617, as lord lieutenant 'of the bishopric and county of Durham'.[3] Neile was the first of the bishops to occupy this post since Tunstall, but subsequently it would remain in episcopal hands as long as there were Stuart kings on the throne. No layman was appointed until after the flight of James II in 1688. In Durham therefore King James, in the person of Neile, confirmed the union of ecclesiastical and secular (including

---

[1] In an early version of his will, made while still dean of Westminster, he refers to 'My old master, the Lord Treasurer Burleigh, and my most honourable master, the Earl of Salisbury, by the goodness of which my two most honourable masters, I am what I now am; and without the goodness of which my most honourable foundress and patroness [i.e. Mildred, Lady Burleigh] I think I should never have been sent to the University; but that the best of my fortunes should have been to have become some bookseller's apprentice in St. Paul's Churchyard . . .' (Sur. *Hist. Durh.*, i.lxxxviii).

[2] pp. 112 ff.   [3] *C.S.P. Dom. Jas. I, 1611–18*, p. 497.

military) power in the hands of the Church. He thus abandoned the policy of a balance of a Church and aristocratic interest in the Palatinate which he had recently been willing to revive in favour of Somerset. Here then the 'Arminian' and 'Laudian' doctrine of the interdependence of Church and State was given comprehensive expression.

No monarch was more aware than James I, with his 'No bishop, no King', of the political importance of the episcopate, even if his appointments to bishoprics were not always of the wisest. The English monarchy had no professional body of officials controlled from the centre to represent it in the regions, like its counterpart in France or Castile. The justices of the peace, unless carefully watched, were liable to be more responsive to local interests and needs than to the tasks imposed from London. The bishops, on the other hand, were appointed by the Crown, and depended on it for advancement. They were outside the local web of kinship and common interest which involved both the gentry families from which J.P.s were recruited, and the great landlords of peerage status who became lords lieutenant. No bishop was better suited to act as the agent of government in his region than the bishop of Durham, who was not only a great landowner, justice, and after 1617 lord lieutenant (as well as a member of the Council in the North and the northern High Commission), but also in a special relationship of dependence on and obedience to the Crown.

His importance as the agent for the effective implementation of government policies had been apparent already in Elizabeth's reign, in the struggle with Recusancy. For this had drawn the State into the novel task of imposing an ideological conformity which met with frequently effective forms of evasion and passive resistance on the part of powerful kinship groups in the local societies. In the relatively tolerant 1560s and 1570s Pilkington had been prone to confess his helplessness in face of the strength and cohesion of the Recusant interest in his diocese. For in Durham even after the failure of the Rising the Catholics still survived as an active and self-confident faction,[1] though now without the leadership of the Nevilles, or the support of the Norfolk interest at Court. But in the 1580s the issue of Recusancy became urgent and immediate following the influx of seminary

[1] See e.g. P.R.O., S.P.12/81.

priests. As tension with Spain mounted and the threat of a Spanish invasion materialized, so the priests were treated as the agents of a foreign power. Bishop Hutton and Bishop Matthew after him were therefore forced into a much more sustained and determined struggle with the Recusants, and the draconian penal Acts of 1581 and 1585 provided the means.

This resolved itself into a conflict between the cohesive power of kinship, social class, and local interest, working in favour of Recusancy, but opposed by new forms of police power supplemented by spy and intelligence networks. These were usually operated by private entrepreneurs, themselves often fanatical Protestants. In the Palatinate they were set to work by the Bishop, as the representative both of the Crown and of the dominant Protestant order, but acting in close association with the Council in the North and northern High Commission.[1] The Catholics were not easy to lay by the heels. As Bishop Matthew pointed out in the 1590s, the magistrates would take no action against Recusant families harbouring priests or attending Mass, if these (often their relatives) belonged to the gentry or to the Newcastle ruling families.[2] The Newcastle men in particular (as has already been seen in connection with Dorothy Lawson) re-fused to allow their solidarity of social and political interest to be disrupted by religious differences. The leading Durham Recusant and coal-owner, Nicholas Tempest of Stella, was safe as long as he remained in Newcastle, for 'nothing in Newcastle can prevail against him, being both in affinity and consan-guinity with both factions there . . .' He was too seldom at Stella, so it was claimed, for the sheriff of Durham to apprehend the priest he harboured; and Matthew had to confess that 'as diocesan I cannot reach to the height to enquire effectively into persons of that quality'. He therefore required the direct inter-vention of the Council.[3] But there were other Recusants in the Palatinate who could defy the authorities equally effectively, as the case of Sir William Blakiston showed, 'the most dangerous Recusant in all these parts, whom no man these seven years durst lay hands upon'.[4]

Nevertheless it was during these years of the later 1580s and 1590s that the pressure of authority on the Recusants began to

---

[1] See Cross.   [2] *Hatf. MSS.*, vi.62–3.   [3] Ibid.
[4] Ibid., x.204.

tell. Its main weight did not, however, fall on the estate and household communities of Catholic tenants and dependants with their gentry heads, even if they too now began to find evasion more difficult that in the past. The victims were rather the activists of Recusancy, the missionary priests and their organization, against whom the heaviest penalties of the law were directed. It was from the latter alone that the death penalty was exacted, the first priests executed being Edward Waterson and Joseph Lampton at Newcastle in 1593.[1] But in the following year three more were put to death at Gateshead, Durham, and Darlington respectively, one of them being the famous John Bost, who had landed in Durham at Hartlepool.[2] The decade closed with further executions, that of the priest Thomas Palliser at Durham, and of two of the only three laymen who suffered in this way, both characteristically not gentlemen.[3] Behind this offensive against the seminary priests, and the increased harassment to which even the Catholic gentry was now subjected was the energy of Matthew. Even during Hutton's rule, when still dean of Durham, he was the most determined enemy of the Recusants.[4]

Matthew's indispensable tool, however, was the Newcastle 'searcher' and customs official Henry Sanderson. He was employed to organize a police force and spy network to hunt down the priests and harass the Recusants; and in return for government and episcopal support and rewards he was willing to defy the power of the Catholic kinship groups.[5] It was Sanderson who in 1589 broke the organization at South Shields for landing Jesuits and seminary priests, and checked the smuggling of Catholic books and literature through Newcastle. In 1592 he apprehended the redoubtable William Blakiston, who was imprisoned under his charge at Brancepeth castle, with Lady Margaret Neville, daughter of the earl of Westmorland. In this same year thirty Recusants, mostly gentry, were rounded up

[1] See Pollen, i.228, 231, 293; Sykes, i.81.

[2] Pollen, i.215–23, 242–3, 293, 286; Sykes, loc. cit.

[3] Sykes, p. 82; *Hatf. MSS.*, x.202, 204–5.

[4] Hutton was suspected of leniency towards Recusants. See e.g. his intervention on behalf of the prominent Recusant Nicholas Tempest of Stella in 1597, *C.S.P. Dom. Eliz., 1595–7*, p. 370.

[5] The 'searcher' Anthony Atkinson was also active in Durham, but only it seems in 1593, when he played a prominent part in the capture of John Bost. Pollen, i.218–19.

and imprisoned in Durham castle and other Palatine prisons, fifty more being forced into hiding. Sanderson also dared to levy the full fines on Recusant lands, 'for which he was hated and persecuted, to the wreck of his estate'. He organized the arrest of Palliser in 1600.[1]

Sanderson was well rewarded, being made constable of Brancepeth castle, and given leases of episcopal coalmines and Recusant lands. He founded a gentry family which played a prominent part in the Puritan and parliamentary interest in the region.[2] There can be little doubt that it was the work of his organization which so weakened the Durham Recusants as to force them into an awareness of their role, no longer as the powerful alternative faction in the bishopric to the Protestant establishment, but as an oppressed and barely tolerated minority. But the encouragement and support which he received from Matthew also underlined the importance of the whole Church interest in the region. This was the agency whereby the Crown could bring its policies to bear and make its will felt against that local 'affinity and interest' which was such a powerful defence for the Recusants.

In the seventeenth century the importance of the bishops as the agents and representatives of the government in the region grew, particularly after Bishop Neile became lord lieutenant; and so also their influence and power. And the trust accorded the office by the Crown was further emphasized by the special status given Durham under the so-called Book of Order of 1631, instituting a system of closer supervision over local authorities. This provided for monthly reports by the J.P.s in each county to the sheriff, reports by the latter to the judges at each assizes, and terminal reports by the judges to a commission of councillors. But in Durham the implementation of the whole scheme was put in the Bishop's hands, to whose temporal chancellor the assize judges made their reports.[3] The Bishop too was not only consulted about those put on the commission of the peace, but also presided over the bench of justices, and represented them in contacts with the Council in London. As lord lieutenant a con-

[1] *Hatf. MSS.*, x.202–5.

[2] Foster, p. 277. The family leased episcopal mines were at Hedleyhope, and Henry Sanderson's heir Samuel married into the Liddells of Ravensworth. During the Civil War he was a member of Parliamentary County Committee of Durham.

[3] *A.P.C.*, *1630–1*, nos. 604, 606.

siderable patronage was at his disposal. He appointed the deputy lieutenants, the captains of the musters and trained bands in each ward, and such officials as the muster-master. In addition the offices of the Palatine courts, from that of temporal chancellor downwards, were at his disposition, with that of sheriff. The Bishop was also consulted about the appointment of officers to the Crown lands, at least in central and north Durham; so that it would be surprising if he had no say too in the disposition of the more lucrative royal leaseholds. It was also the Bishop, since the grant of this patronage by Queen Mary to Tunstall, who appointed to all but one of the prebendships of the Cathedral foundation.[1]

Thus in Durham, already before the Civil War, the Bishop exercised powers, and controlled a great interest, similar to those entrusted to the magnates appointed as lords lieutenant after the Restoration—the linchpins of local administration under the later Stuarts and subsequently. In return he had to work hard, active now in matters of religion, now of the Poor Law; now seeing to the state of fortifications on the coast, now to that of the trained bands; taking the musters, or sending in lists of suitable contributors to a forced loan. A bishop like Morton (1632–59), who was not subservient to the Court, on occasion also represented and pressed Durham interests in London, as well as those of the government in the region. Indeed, as a result of the power and influence of the Church, Durham (paradoxically, in view of its Palatine 'liberties') was one of the counties which, under the Stuarts, probably received most 'government'. The Church even provided in-built controls ensuring that the bishops would not stray over-much from the orders of their London masters, these being provided by the persistent groups of dissident cathedral clergy, prone to use their contacts with highly-placed patrons at Court to make trouble for bishops whose ways and policies they disliked.

CHURCH DOMINANCE AND LAY OPPOSITION

Under Bishop Neile the rule of the Church and its associated interest, assured now of the support of the Crown, asserted itself with a consistency and comprehensiveness previously lacking. One feature of the situation that consequently emerged was that

[1] Hutch., i.436.

the clergy now counted for more in the political affairs of the Palatinate, and in its secular government. Throughout his career Neile had been adept at mobilizing élites, bringing their intellectual abilities and capacity for affairs to bear at the strategic points where these would have most effect. No sooner had he risen to episcopal status than he hastened to provide patronage and advancement for those able university clergy who were attracted to the teachings of Hooker, Overall, and Andrewes, and were committed to the defence of the established Church against the Puritan threat. Many of the 'Arminian' Church meritocracy, including Laud himself, had begun their ascent as chaplains in one or other of Neile's episcopal establishments, or as prebends in one of his cathedral churches. He had a strong sense of the capacity of a gifted minority to transform the Church and support the State in the face of what he saw as the disintegrative tendencies of the time, much as the Jesuits (to whom Neile's 'Arminians' were unflatteringly compared) had done in Romanism. These were convictions which would in fact be subsequently implemented by Archbishop Laud, the ablest of Neile's protégés, with his policy of 'Thorough'; Neile willingly accepting the leadership of this former disciple. Once he became bishop of Durham, Durham House in the Strand became the London headquarters of his Arminian followers, with quarters permanently available there for Laud, Lindsell, Buckeridge, and other members of the group.[1] Inevitably, as has been seen, a nucleus, all former Neile chaplains—Cosin, Clark, Lindsell, and the rest—were fitted into Durham prebendships.[2] They formed in the Chapter a self-confident group conscious of its direct links with the great world of the Court, and sure of support there, even after Neile had left Durham.

The sense of the rise of a clerical élite which was self-assured, already aware of itself as one of the great interests in the State, and increasingly impatient of the Erastian attitudes of an earlier and more submissive clergy, emerges in Cosin's strongly expressed views on the Royal Supremacy; these were made the basis of the attempt to convict him of treason in the Parliament of 1628–9. Cosin's emphasis was on the merely coactive power of the Supremacy, the King, he pointed out, being 'Supreme Governor', not 'Supreme Head' of the Church, Queen

[1] Heylin, pp. 74–5.   [2] See above, p. 112.

Elizabeth having repudiated the latter title. By contrast, 'the power of the spirituall itself was from Christ, who had given it unto his disciples, and they to their successors in ordination', i.e. to the clergy.[1] There was nothing unorthodox or innovative in this position, nor did it necessarily contradict views of the Supremacy held by Puritans and their like. Yet to raise it at that time, and with Cosin's emphasis on the 'ordained' ministry, touched the raw nerve of anti-clerical Erastianism, as well as of the Puritanism, in the ranks of the governing class. Fears were roused of a revived clerical caste whose power the Reformation was supposed to have drastically and effectively pruned.

Confirmation of this had been seen in the increasing role played by Neile's men, at the expense of the gentry, in the rule of the Palatinate. In the Parliament of 1621 it was claimed that the clergy now outnumbered the gentry, to the number of thirteen against twelve, on the Durham commission of the peace.[2] This was an exaggeration, for there were nineteen gentry J.P.s on the commission of 1620, to only nine clerical justices, with six clergy to thirteen gentry on the quorum.[3] Nevertheless, under Neile there was a sharp upswing in the number of clerical J.P.s, which until his advent had usually consisted only of the Bishop himself, the Dean, and the 'spiritual chancellor', or diocesan ecclesiastical judge.[4] But now the two archdeacons (of Durham and Northumberland) and a selection of prebendaries were included in the commission, the ubiquitous Marmaduke Blakiston being one, with Burgoyne, Birkhead, Moorcroft, Lindsell, and others.[5] In the later years of Neile's rule the clerical J.P.s were indeed dominant, since although (in 1625) there were only nine clergy to seventeen gentry on the commission, the former had a majority (nine to six) on the inner

[1] Cosin, *Corres.*, pp. 147–52; *Durh. High Comm.*, pp. 199–201, 231–2; Cosin, *Works*, iv.371.

[2] *C.D., 1621*, ii.334, 425; iii.113; v.125.

[3] Commission of the peace, Durham, 8 July 1620; P.R.O., C/181/3, fo. 9d. I owe to the kindness of Miss Shirley King this reference and others which follow to Durham commissions of the peace.

[4] See e.g. the commissions for 1558 (B.M., Lansdowne MS. 1218); 1575 (B.M., Egerton MS. 2345); 1584 (B.M., Lansdowne MS. 737, fo. 178d–179); and 1596 (P.R.O., C/66/1468d).

[5] Commission of the peace, Durham, 1 Feb. 1618 (P.R.O., C/66/2147d), and 8 July 1620 (P.R.O., C/181/3, fo. 9d).

circle of justices appointed to the quorum.[1] The régime of the clerical office-holders was also seconded by a more extensive employment of families of the Church interest. Thus Neile appointed Sir William Bellasis, a Church leaseholder, and descendant of Wolsey's confidential agent, to the office of sheriff,[2] and in 1621 of deputy lieutenant. In the latter office Bellasis had two coal-owners as his colleagues, the oppositionist Sir Henry Anderson and the courtier Sir George Selby; but also representatives of two other Church families, a Calverley and a Fetherstonhaugh.[3] The Church influence also increasingly predominated in the offices of the lieutenancy. By 1625 the four captains appointed to command the trained bands in each of the four Durham wards were all of Church families—a Bowes, a Calverley, a Wren, and one of Marmaduke Blakiston's sons; so was the provost-marshal appointed in the following year, Sir Timothy Whittingham.[4] By contrast, under Neile the Newcastle men were thinly represented in office, only Anderson and Selby being appointed to the commission of the peace, and when the latter dropped out, Sir Thomas Riddell.[5] It was the clergy, the Church families, and the 'ancient gentry' who formed the dominant faction; while the Wear coal-owners and Sunderland men were completely unrepresented.

Single-faction rule was not easy to maintain in the conditions of the early seventeenth century, when economic and social changes were bringing powerful new interests, greedy for power, into the Durham political scene. As early as the episcopate of Bishop James opposition was forthcoming, and not so much from the survivors of the Neville connection, increasingly crippled, in spite of the Somerset episode, by their Recusancy; but from the Newcastle coal-owners recruited into the gentry. Accustomed as they were to the politics of the town council chamber, of debate, of property and economic interest, these men found the ramifications of the Church interest, its traditionalism, legalistic ethos, and clerical bent difficult to come to terms with. A standing grievance on their part was the lack of a Durham parliamentary representation, apart from the Bishop's

[1] Commission of the peace, Durham, 1625 (P.R.O., C/66/2367).
[2] Hutch., i.490.
[3] Allan MS. The Calverleys were descended from an episcopal chancellor; the Fetherstonhaughs were employed under the bishopric as bailiffs of Stanhope.
[4] Mickleton MS., 30(5).   [5] Riddell appears in the commission of 1625.

seat in the House of Lords. The point of view of the Newcastle families required the wider opportunities for participation in parliamentary politics which seats in the Commons provided, and closer connections with London and the Court. For these became increasingly important as the coastal coal trade tied the north-east ever more closely to the capital. The new-style opposition was therefore anti-clerical and 'Puritan', but in a wide non-dogmatic sense, for some of the Newcastle men involved were in fact of Recusant affiliation; and in Newcastle there was reluctance, as has been seen, to put religion before common interest. The main point in its programme was seats in the House of Commons for the Durham gentry, a demand which also interested some of the older families, particularly the Bowes of Streatlam.

Both the anti-clericalism and the demand for parliamentary representation first found expression in the Parliament of 1614, a Bill being moved on 21 May to the effect that 'knights and burgesses to have place in Parliament for the County Palatine and the City of Durham, and the town of Barnard Castle'. It was introduced by one of the Newcastle M.P.s, William Jenison, of Recusant as well as Puritan affiliation; but its principal proponent was the other, Sir Henry Anderson, of Haswell Grange in the Palatinate, head of one of the first Newcastle families to settle on a Durham estate.[1] Anderson, according to Cosin, 'hated Bishop James', and had probably been involved in the latter's troubles with the Crown over the contested charter of the City of Durham.[2] He made the demand for representation the occasion for an attack on the Bishop, whom he proposed should be proceeded against by Petition of Grievance.[3] But his Bill came to nothing with the rapid dissolution of the 'Addled' Parliament of 1614. In the Palatinate, however, an anti-clerical and Puritanically inclined opposition persisted, with the former 'searcher' and favourite of Bishop Matthew, Henry Sanderson, emerging as a leading opponent of Bishop James (the appointment of Sir Charles Wren, of the Church interest, as steward of

---

[1] *C.J.*, i.492.

[2] The Andersons, who bought Haswell before 1571 were connected with the Wrights of Durham, who provided the first mayor of the city; see *C.S.P. Dom. Ch. I, 1628–9*, p. 349; Cosin, *Corres.*, p. 212. Sometime in the 1630's the family sold its Durham estates, and moved to Long Cowton in Yorkshire.

[3] *C.J.*, i.502.

Brancepeth lordship over his head probably had something to do with this.[1] From him and his associates came attacks on James's 'covetousness', and that of his officers, and on his slackness in dealing with Recusants. There were suggestions that 'the royalties be taken from the Bishop, who is King in his country', and that another lay lord lieutenant (but one more acceptable to the Puritans) be appointed in Somerset's place.[2]

Probably the strains and tensions arising during the rule of Bishop James, and the baiting which he received from the opposition, were the result of this bishop's poor standing with the King, commented on above. There was a drastic change in the fortunes and tone of the oppositionists, once it became clear under Neile that the latter could be sure of the 'countenance' and support of the Crown. This became obvious when the movement to secure a Durham representation in the House of Commons was revived in the Parliament of 1621–2. The objectives were more ambitious than in 1614, no less than fourteen M.P.s being proposed for the county and various towns within it, including the City, Barnard Castle, and Hartlepool; but only six were approved (two each for county, City, and Barnard Castle) by the committee to which the Bill was referred.[3] Once again the coal-owners were in the forefront of the Bill's sponsors, these including Sir Henry Anderson, Sir Thomas Riddell, and Francis Brandling, both the latter also Durham men. But there was support too from the Bowes family, for Sir Talbot Bowes expected to control the representation of Barnard Castle.[4] At the same time a broad-fronted attack was developed on the Durham Church interest, with complaints about the over-representation of the clergy on the commission of the peace, and about the 'corruptions' of Dr. Cradock, Neile's spiritual chancellor.[5] But this time all was saved not only by a dissolution but probably too by the use of the royal veto to preserve the Bishop's monopoly of Durham's parliamentary representation. This was certainly brought into play when a third Durham representation Bill passed the Commons in May 1624; James I rejected it

---

[1] *C.S.P. Dom. Jas. I, 1603–10*, p. 461.
[2] *C.S.P. Dom. Jas. I, 1611–18*, pp. 329, 395.   [3] *C.J.*, i.539, 553.
[4] Sir Henry Anderson made this clear in the debate on the Durham Representation Bill of 1624, when he stated that 'Sir T. Bowes hath power there, by reason of his inheritance, to procure the election against all letters . . .' (*C.J.*, i.697).
[5] *C.D., 1621*, v.167.

on the grounds that the House was in any event already too large.[1] The Bishop, thanks to the support of the Crown, had his way, and Durham would not get its M.P.s, except for a brief period during the Protectorate, until well after the Restoration. Yet in many respects it was a pyrrhic victory, the lack of Parliamentary representation becoming a standing Durham grievance, raised for example in 1627 in connection with the forced loan,[2] and again in 1640 in connection with Ship Money.[3] As such it was felt by a broad spectrum of not particularly radical gentry opinion, and so helped to isolate the Church interest in the Palatinate.

FROM EIRENICISM TO BREAKDOWN: BISHOP MORTON (1632–1640)

This isolation was only one of the respects in which Neile's rule, in spite of the authority he enjoyed in the Durham scene, revealed its drawbacks; and the inadequacies of the methods and outlook on which it relied were not long in making themselves increasingly felt. In the first place there was the failure to take seriously local prejudices, needs, and interests, and to present these, in so far as they became grievances, to the government. Neile and his men were above all the determined representatives of metropolitan authority and of metropolitan trends, particularly in matters of religion. The roots they were able to put down into the life of the region itself were neither deep nor widespread. Neile was a conscientious justice and lord lieutenant, diligently responding to the tasks laid on him by the government whether these related to the musters, trained bands, and fortifications, or to matters fiscal, religious, and the multitude of other assignments which claimed his attention as bishop and J.P. Yet this same meticulous response to government pressures and requirements often made him neglect to temper and adapt these to local conditions. Hence the quarrel with his tenants resulting from his prompt response to the King's command 'to abide strictly by the King's proclamation against tenant right . . . to countenance no claim founded thereon, and to acquaint the tenants of His Majesty's pleasure therein, giving

---

[1] *C.J.*, i.747, 749, 766, 782, 786; *C.S.P. Dom. Jas. I, 1623–5*, p. 265.

[2] *C.S.P. Dom. Ch. I, 1627–8*, p. 121.

[3] *C.S.P. Dom. Ch. I, 1639–40*, pp. 592–3.

them no hopes to the contrary',[1] so fastening on the Church the image of an oppressive landlord. Similarly, and with much more spectacular results, local customs and practices were allowed to count for nothing against the imposition of the new Church model proposed by the Arminian divines, underwritten not only by Neile, but also by the increasingly formidable authority of Laud. Cosin, Lindsell, and their supporters were self-confident and even violent in their determination to impose the new religious styles, yet the result was to divide that very Church interest on which Neile's rule had been based. As a result the opportunity for the Parliamentary attack of 1629 on the Durham 'Arminians' was provided from within the Cathedral establishment itself, Peter Smart's sermon unleashing the storm which broke soon after Neile's departure. This in turn became the catalyst which precipitated an increasingly hard dividing line between 'Puritan' and 'Arminian' in the region.[2]

It is not surprising then that Bishop Howson (1628–32) should have attempted (although an Arminian himself) to change some of the courses set by his predecessor. He tried to tone down the religious innovations in the cathedral, and to conciliate Peter Smart. But he soon found that his authority as Bishop counted for little against the contacts of Cosin and Lindsell in London, both with Neile, now bishop of Winchester, and with Laud, who had direct access to the King. Howson, as has been seen, was ordered by Charles I to leave Cosin and Lindsell alone, and not to meddle with the cathedral. He was effectively humiliated ('I conceave I have suffered more than was ever offered so any Bishop of Durham' he told Laud).[3] But again such tactics were profoundly divisive, setting the influence of a party against the established structure of authority in the Church. In the case of Bishop Morton (1632–59),[4] however, the last of the bishops before the Civil War, there was a more prolonged and determined attempt at conciliation, with a view to healing the breaches which had opened, and widening the basis of consent on which the established order rested. Morton, the friend of Casaubon and Dury, was in spite of his determined opposition to Catholicism, a relatively eirenic figure, belonging

---

[1] *C.S.P. Dom. Jas. I, 1619–23*, p. 430. See above, p. 83.
[2] See above, pp. 119 ff.   [3] Cosin, *Corres.*, p. 207.
[4] See *D.N.B.* and Baddely & Naylor.

more to the Broad than the High or Puritan trends in the Church. But like Howson he had to meet the opposition of an entrenched and powerful Arminian party. This did its best to oppose his policies even before the pressure of Laud's statesmanship of 'Thorough', particularly as applied to Scotland, eventually brought about their collapse. But Morton was not without his successes, and his rule points forward to the kind of balance of forces which would eventually establish itself, but only after 1688.

We can see that one of the first of Morton's preoccupations should be to preserve the solidarity of the Church interest over which he presided. Thus, for example, in spite of the distrust in which he was held by the dominant Arminian faction in the Cathedral, there were no public quarrels with the Chapter; nor did Morton resume the Howson policy of curtailing the Cosin innovations in the Cathedral services. As prebendships became vacant, he ensured that moderates of his own sort, like Ralph Brownrigg or his chaplain and biographer John Barwick, were gradually infiltrated into the Chapter. But his appointments also included Isaac Basire, a man more in the Cosin than the Morton tradition.[1] Secondly, and as far as the wider affiliations of the Church interest with the gentry families occupying Church offices and leaseholds were concerned, Morton's object was to damp down potential resentments and conflicts by conforming his estate policies to what gentry opinion would be likely to regard as just and fair. He therefore turned over the sensitive issue of the renewal of those under-rented leases of Church lands on which many Church fortunes depended to a commission of four gentlemen, probably presided over by the

---

[1] Morton's effective appointments, taking place before the collapse of his authority in 1640, were few. They included the two Scots ministers, Anthony Maxton and John Weemes, recommended to him by Charles I, and his chaplain Joseph Naylor, collated to a stall in 1636. Isaac Basire was brought into the diocese as rector of Egglescliffe in 1640, but had been Morton's chaplain for several years before this; he was not made a prebend until 1643. Ralph Brownrigg, a 'Low' churchman who had been archdeacon of Coventry under Morton when the latter had been bishop of Lichfield, was also not made a prebend of Durham till 1641, in the same year as Barwick. Morton's only other prebendal appointment was that of John Neile, Archbishop Neile's nephew, in 1635. Throughout Morton's rule during the 1630s there was a majority of Neile appointees on the Chapter. See Hutch., ii.141–225, *passim*; *Alumn. Cantab.* and *Alumn. Oxon.*; *Walker Rev.*; for Brownrigg, Basire, and Barwick see also *D.N.B.*

sheriff, Sir William Bellasis. Similar commissions were also appointed to keep an eye on Morton's officers during his absences in London, and to mediate in differences arising between him and his tenants.[1] Morton was concerned therefore to expunge the image established by some of his predecessors of the Bishop as a grasping landlord.[1] This was easier for him to do since being unmarried he had no children to be provided for; nor did he surround himself with a circle of greedy relatives. As a result he could afford to be relatively moderate with regard to such windfall gains as fines and feudal payments, which often formed an important component in the build-up of Durham clerical fortunes.[2] All this made for prestige and moral authority in relation to the gentry class, those most affected particularly by the irritations of feudal incidents, which sometimes fell with crushing weight on an estate. Whether Morton was as popular with the rank and file of his humbler tenants seems more doubtful. We could feel more sure about this if we knew more of what exactly was behind the enclosure riots which broke out on the episcopal estates in 1641, after his flight from the bishopric.[3]

Such measures helped to strengthen the solidarity of the Church families, clerical and lay. But Morton also saw that the whole basis of the Church interest needed to be broadened, and its rule made acceptable to a wider spectrum of the expansive, changing society over which it presided. Under him there was a wider distribution of power, Sir Henry Vane the new Durham magnate appearing on the commission of the peace, with a larger representation of the Newcastle men.[4] Morton's most remarkable initiative, however, was the grant in 1634 of an episcopal charter which incorporated the community of coal-owners and shippers at Sunderland into a borough, thus giving their leaders, including George Lilburne, a place on the bench of magistrates.[5] This move probably owed a good deal to Sir William Bellasis, the first mayor of Sunderland before he was succeeded in this office by Lilburne. With the latter Bellasis had 'much dealing and commerce, shipping and colliery'. But the

---

[1] Barwick, pp. 93–5.   [2] Ibid., Baddely & Naylor, pp. 93, 109.
[3] Above, p. 78.
[4] P.R.O., C66/2654.
[5] For the text of the charter, see Summers, ch. vii.

Sunderland charter was much disapproved of by Morton's opponents, the Arminian upper clergy.[1]

Inevitably such a policy of political comprehension also had its religious implications. Here Morton's object was to provide assurances that Puritan beliefs and attitudes, provided they were not extravagantly pressed, could find a place within the established Church. Hence his protection of the Puritan lecturers Lapthorne and Vincent,[2] the consideration he showed Peter Smart,[3] and the blind eye turned to the Puritan preachings at Sunderland, carried on at Monk Wearmouth church, where Lilburne's father-in-law John Hicks was vicar.[4] At the same time, Morton's use of his fortune to augment the income of benefices in his gift, so making them more attractive to an educated clergy, emphasized his sympathy with the ideal of a 'preaching' ministry,[5] so congenial to the Puritans. The latter were also likely to be reassured by the anti-Catholic polemics in which Morton specialized, and his pursuit of Recusants, policies which placed him firmly (unlike his Arminian opponents) within the Protestant fold.[6] In these various ways Morton provided something for a wide range of political and religious opinion. Consequently, for the Puritan, although a bishop, he was one who differed 'in nothing considerable from the rest of the reformed churches except in church government'[7] while for the wide central range of establishment opinion outside the Arminian high churchmen, he was one of the 'less formal and more popular prelates',[8] differing in this respect from 'the great bishop' Neile.[9]

But Morton's conciliatory initiatives had to operate under the mounting pressures, fiscal, administrative and political, brought to bear on the Palatinate by the prerogative rule of Charles I, and the policy of 'Thorough' operated by Archbishop Laud, the King's chief minister. And although his sym-

---

[1] *C.S.P. Dom. Ch. I, 1639–40*, p. 426; see ibid., p. 516 for Triplet's denunciation of the policy of suffering 'little towns to grow big, and anti-monarchy to boot', ascribed in the case of Sunderland to the King; but it is unlikely that this fanatical Laudian was unaware that Sunderland's charter had been granted by Morton, not Charles I.
[2] See above, p. 130–1.   [3] *C.S.P. Dom. Ch. I, 1638–9*, p. 457.
[4] Ibid., *1639–40*, p. 519.   [5] Hutch., i.499.
[6] See *D.N.B.*, and above, p. 143.
[7] Richard Baxter, quoted *D.N.B.*, xiii.1061.   [8] Clarendon, i.409.
[9] So described ironically by John Richardson, *C.S.P. Dom. Ch. I, 1625–6*, p. 420.

pathies probably lay with Laud's rival, the Broad churchman Bishop Williams of Lincoln, his position required him to act as the former's executive agent. Ship Money was the principal fiscal burden on the Palatinate, but this was combined with heavy charges on the county for the conveyance of large quantities of timber for the navy, felled in Durham. The latter imposition caused particular resentment because of the obstinacy with which neighbouring counties resisted contributing to it.[1] This was probably the reason for the growing feeling that Durham was disproportionately taxed by comparison with the rest of the kingdom, a state of mind which stimulated tax evasion. So did the unequal distribution of the fiscal burdens amongst the taxpayers, because the county rate-book had not been revised since the reign of Queen Elizabeth, being therefore neither 'equal' nor 'indifferent'. While these grievances affected the gentry first and foremost, their effects were also felt in the ranks of the tenantry and the poor, for those in authority were liable to shuffle off the tax burden on to their inferiors. Thus in the city of Durham the mayor (so Morton informed the Privy Council) instead of cessing the inhabitants for Ship Money 'with an equality, that the service be not disgraced, or the poor oppressed', made the levy 'disproportionately in the most, and unworthily upon the poor ones', which 'has caused the greatest clamour that I have hitherto heard of . . .'[2] Nothing was done about Sir William Bellasis's insistence that the rate-book should be revised and the incidence of taxation more evenly distributed;[3] and his plea that Durham should not be overcharged (probably in any case made too late) was ignored. 'If they could bear that other countries paid they would do the like,' he told Secretary Windebank in 1640, 'but that this county should be the first in all charges and most of them higher than in other part of the kingdom, seems much to trouble them. . . .'[4]

Dissidence and discontent began first in the ranks of the gentry, manifesting itself in resistance to Ship Money. The payments due on the first two writs, those of 1634 and 1635, collected by Bellasis, with the help of the old oppositionist Sir

---

[1] *C.S.P. Dom. Ch. I, 1635*, pp. 113, 134, 156, 308.

[2] Ibid., *1637–8*, p. 294; the tobacco monopoly, and the attempts of the patentees to enforce it, also caused trouble in Durham city. See ibid., *1639–40*, p. 139.

[3] Ibid., *1636–7*, p. 382.   [4] Ibid., *1639–40*, p. 593.

Henry Anderson, were made in full.[1] But subsequently the re-
fusals multiplied, with Lilburne in the lead at Sunderland, and
the Tyne coalowners withholding payment on their stocks of
coal, mostly stored in Newcastle, and so out of the jurisdiction
of the sheriff of Durham.[2] Yet when the Scottish crisis broke in
1639, with a Scottish invasion to be faced in 1640, it was to this
already alienated class that the government had to turn for support and military service. In the broad ranks of the gentry there
was still a fund of loyalty which might have been exploited, expressed for example by Bellasis in April 1640. He told the
Secretary of State 'I hope His Majesty shall be well satisfied,
that as I have never been wanting in my power to do him faith-
ful service, I shall not now be slack, being very sensible of the
state of these times, which require the duty of every good subject . . .'[3] Yet courtier officers were pushed into commands in
the Durham trained band companies, to the exclusion of the
local gentry, in spite of the latters' protests;[4] while the renewed
demands for representation in Parliament were ignored.[5] These
mounting discontents would soon contribute to the tenantry
agitation against the Dean and Chapter,[6] the mutiny of the
Durham trained bands in April 1640, and the Derwentdale
Puritan agitation.[7] Finally, there came the inevitable climax;
the military collapse before the Scottish invasion in August of
the same year.

Morton's eirenic policies were amongst the first casualties as
the government moved towards the crisis with Scotland. As it
did so, the note of uncompromising intransigence in its demands hardened; and in Durham it was not the Bishop, but the
Laudians and Arminians amongst the clergy who were listened
to. The latter were eager to exploit the climate of mounting in-
tolerance in order to sharpen the ideological content of the local
controversies, and to harden the line between 'Churchmen' and
'Puritans', the Sunderland men being the main target for their
attacks. In particular the ambitious and fanatical rector of
Whitburn, Thomas Triplet, offered himself at the beginning of

---

[1] Ibid., *1635–6*, p. 528.

[2] Ibid., *1639–40*, p. 516; *1636–7*, pp. 229, 382; *1638–9*, pp. 4, 80; *1639–40*,
p. 593; *1640*, p. 133.

[3] Ibid., *1639–40*, p. 593.   [4] Ibid., *1638–9*, pp. 450, 490, 527.

[5] Ibid., *1639–40*, p. 593.   [6] See above, pp. 85–6.

[7] *C.S.P. Dom. Ch. I., 1640*, pp. 73, 75.

1640 to Laud, 'if I may have protection and encouragement,
and any reasonable power authorizing me', as an informer
against the local Puritans, undertaking to 'have such an eye
about my quarter, and so unkennel the seditious cubs, that not
a man of them shall be earthed about me'.[1] Implacable conflicts defined themselves in Triplet's violent assertions: 'I am . . .
right for the King and Church . . . and it would better appear in
me if the times were as I hope they never shall be, when Puritanism shall rise . . .';[2] and also in the sympathetic response of
Duncan, Neile's old chaplain, and still one of the Cathedral
clergy, 'What you [Triplet] do against Puritans, God reward
you for; I think the generation of them most dangerous to this
Church and state'.[3] It was Duncan who claimed the credit for
silencing the Puritan lecturers Lapthorne and Vincent, whom
Morton had tolerated, charges being brought against Lapthorne
for which he was called up to answer before the Council.[4] On
the Puritan side, George Lilburne took the lead as the situation
became increasingly embittered. Not only did he 'murmer
against the Ship Money', and suffer a distraint before he would
pay it, but he was also summoned before the High Commission
'for saying that all such as used to give thanks in particular for
the Blessed Virgin, did it with a purpose to bring in Popery'.[5]
As the Scottish crisis deepened, so the religious and political
offensive against the Sunderland men merged into one, Triplet
bringing a charge against a servant of Lilburne's for treasonable
words spoken in defence of the Scottish Covenanters. As a result both Lilburne and the then mayor of Sunderland, Richard
Cottrill, were summoned up to London to account for themselves before the Council, Triplet denouncing the latter for his
'perfect and intestine malice against our church discipline,
which will be sufficiently proved against him'.[6] Once again
Morton was ignored and bypassed. He was increasingly in disfavour with the government, the King himself ordering the
alteration of certain passages in one of his sermons 'relating to
Church government',[7] and his policy in Durham was in ruins.
The Sunderland Puritans were now increasingly forced outside

---

[1] Ibid., *1639–40*, p. 519.   [2] Ibid., p. 518.   [3] Ibid., p. 542.
[4] Ibid., *1638–9*, p. 434; *1639*, p. 469; *1639–40*, p. 542.
[5] Ibid., *1639–40*, p. 516.   [6] Ibid., pp. 539–40.
[7] Ibid., p. 212.

the religious pale as 'most dangerous to this church and state', the irreconcilable enemies of 'our church discipline'. Thus the latter were forced, as a result of their firm rejection by the dominant Church and political order, to make the progression from a religious to a political radicalism as soon as circumstances provided the opportunity.

The end came in August 1640, when the badly led and demoralized army of Conway and Astley, which included the Durham trained bands, tried to hold the Tyne crossing at Newburn against Leslie's well-trained and professionally led troops. The English defence soon crumpled, and the English army retreated into Yorkshire. Morton and the Cathedral clergy had already fled, the former never to return, and Durham and Northumberland were abandoned to a Scottish military occupation. As the Scottish troops entered the Palatinate, Durham was plunged into the climate of crisis, military occupation, and exploitation by armed force which would persist on and off for the next five years, creating an unprecedented state of affairs hardly conceivable before the crisis broke. Rushworth has left a graphic description of the confusion in the early days of the invasion, with the coal mines of the Tyne valley 'that had wont to employ 10,000 people all the year long . . . now not a man to be seen, being possessed with fear that the Scots would give no quarter'. In Newcastle the shops were shut, no ship would dare enter the port, and 'many families gone leaving their goods to the Scots'. As far as Durham city was concerned, 'it became a most depopulated place; not one shop open for four days . . . not one house in ten had man, woman or child in it . . . in sad condition for want of food.' Cattle and sheep had been driven into Yorkshire, and many families went with them. Instructions had been left to the high constable to break the upper millstones in each parish.[1]

Thus Durham had to pay the price for its possession of those coal resources whose exploitation in the previous generation had brought about such changes in its own pattern of life, but which also made the Palatinate the strategic objective of the Scottish army. For by cutting off coal shipments pressure could be brought to bear on London, now dependent on the northeast for its fuel supplies. The extent of the price due emerged

[1] Ibid., *1640*, pp. 645, 647; Rushworth, iii.1236–8, 1239.

when in September Bellasis and Sir William Lambton were summoned to Leslie's camp near Newcastle to give security on behalf of the county to supply the Scottish forces with forage and provisions.[1] The rents of the bishopric and Chapter and those of Recusants were immediately sequestered to the Scots' use, and in October under the terms of the Treaty of Ripon it was agreed that the cost of the occupation should fall on Northumberland, Newcastle, and Durham at a rate of £850 a day, the Durham proportion being £350.[2] These two unfortunate counties, it was said, were 'totally lost for the present, and the inhabitants totally undone'.[3] Exactions now began which made Ship Money ludicrously insignificant. Over £12,000 were paid over to the Scots between September and October alone, and the total cost of the year-long occupation, as represented by the unpaid balance due by the government to Durham in August 1641, was over £25,000.[4] On this supervened the Civil War, and early in 1644 another Scottish invasion. 'Our country is in a miserable plunge', wrote Sir George Vane in that year 'and at a stand what to do . . . in most lamentable distress . . .'[5] Out of this background of dislocation and confusion the extraordinary would emerge: a king be executed, a Republic rule, with the bishopric dissolved; and Durham be subjected to the military government of a local squire, in the garb of a major-general.

---

[1] *C.S.P. Dom. Ch. I, 1640–1*, p. 27; Rushworth, iii.1254.
[2] Ibid., p. 75; Rushworth, iii.1308–9.
[3] *C.S.P. Dom. Ch. I, 1640–1*, pp. 147–8.
[4] Sur. *Hist. Durh.*, i.xcvi, xcvii; Rushworth, iii.1274.
[5] *C.S.P. Dom. Ch. I, 1644*, p. 289.

life, in which entrepreneurial, professional and administrative preoccupations, with a strongly Protestant religious commitment, increasingly blurred the traditional chivalric image.

Not only the gentry, but society as a whole, was involved in this pattern of change; and particularly after 1570, when the speed at which the kaleidoscope revolved markedly increased. The years between the Northern Rising and the Civil War were characterized by economic and demographic growth, and by exceptionally rapid social transformation. To this the fall of the Nevilles, the rise of the coal industry, the changes in agriculture all made their contribution. At the same time, it was during these years that the new outlook and mentality implicit in the rise of a Protestant culture began to work their way into the texture of society, instead of remaining, as in the early days of the Durham Reformation, the mark of a small, mainly clerical, élite. The society of 1500 was not without its competitive tensions and social strains; but the process of change altered the character of these, while generating stresses specific to a rapid social and cultural transformation. Economic growth brought increased prosperity, but this did not extend much below the upper and middle reaches of society. Population growth and inflation helped to keep the poor poor, and the real value of miners' wages, for example, did not rise during the period, in spite of the spectacular expansion of the coal industry. At the lower levels of society the recurring crises of plague, so often accompanied by dearth, generated intense anxieties and promoted instability, often precipitating the small husbandman or shopkeeper into the ranks of the poor. Increased mobility of labour, promoted by new economic opportunities, may have helped, in the lower ranges of society to weaken the family, and so remove the support which this provided for those unable to stand on their own feet in times of stress. The Reformation did away with the protective powers, the saints, rites, relics, and miracles which had given the Catholicism of the simple and illiterate its appeal and potency; for these the established Church of the new Protestant order failed to provide adequate substitutes. And as literacy and access to the Scriptures spread further down the social scale, so larger numbers of those who had been accustomed to articulate their world in terms of what tradition or their betters imparted, were compelled to decide for themselves in religious matters. Thus the tension of choice and conflict entered the inner world of attitudes and basic convictions.[1]

For the upper classes the strains and stresses were different, arising partly from the decline or disappearance of established elements in their ranks. Many newcomers had to be assimilated, their rise throwing into disarray the accepted hierarchy of esteem and leadership, and the place which individual families held in this. The process of rising in the social scale bred its own anxieties. Parvenu fortunes were often as soon lost as made, particularly in the coal industry, the most prolific source of new recruitment into the gentry. While the pitmen gambled with their lives, and remained poised on the verge of poverty and unemployment, their masters gambled with their capital, and constantly confronted the risk of ruin from flooded pits and collapsed workings. Monopolies and privileges, like those which protected the Newcastle Hostmen, were the best guarantee of security, as distinct from survival. But these generated a further cycle of tension, for they aroused the resentment of those excluded from their advantages. Moreover, securely founded though the fortune of a newcomer to the upper class might be, whether his wealth came from coal, the law, trade, agriculture, or the Church, he nevertheless still confronted the stresses involved in securing acceptance in the ranks of the gentry. He had to adopt the life-style of a landed society which was often different from that of his own background, and promote his own standing in this new setting. The process was only completed when, usually within a generation or two, intermarriage signalized an unqualified recognition of the incoming families, at an appropriate level in the hierarchy of esteem, by the established stocks. Many newcomers, like the Wear coal-owners, the yeomen-gentry, or some of those who owed their rise to the Church, remained on the fringe of the county establishment, and never achieved total acceptance. They were uncertain of their status, and distrustful of authority.[2]

Social change, with the revolution in outlook, religion, and culture which went with it, also confronted the 'ancient' gentry with problems of adjustment and adaptation. The whole traditional concept of 'gentility' was brought in question by

---

[1] See above, pp. 52 ff; 125 ff.   [2] Above, pp. 89 ff.

the large-scale recruitment of those who often owed nothing to the hereditary nobility conferred by gentle 'blood'; while the fall of the Nevilles, and the disappearance of the great households and aristocratic affinities undermined the traditional values of faithfulness, service, lordship, and loyalty to the lineage. These were further weakened by the rise of Recusancy, which made religion the touchstone of attachment and solidarity. At the same time the critique of many of the traditional values associated with gentility, as incompatible both with the 'Christian nobility' of the Gospels and with the 'nobility of virtue' of the humanists, was given a new immediacy by the procedures of grammar school education. Increasing numbers of the gentry were subjected to these, and also to the disciplines of the universities or perhaps of the Inns of Court. Thus the way of life of the class gradually conformed itself to a new pattern. The emphasis on privacy in the new-style housing displaced the traditional gregarious household routines. The environment of the school was substituted for that of the great household, while religion and humanism took the place of a style of training in which the arts of ceremony, war, and the chase had been given first place.[1]

Finally, the immemorial pattern of society as a hierarchy in which an upper class ruled while others unquestioningly obeyed lost much of the total acceptability which it had once possessed. No doubt it was as true in 1640 as it had been a century before that 'in countries some must rule and some obey'. Yet by the eve of the Civil War the old 'simplicity of obedience' had in important respects decayed. It was not so much that riots and disorders were liable to occur—such as no doubt had always threatened particularly in times of stress and dearth. But rather that those previously assumed to be 'rude and ignorant, having of themselves small light of judgement, but ever in simplicity ... so follow they their masters', now showed a tendency to articulate coherent claims, to assert rights which the law was liable to uphold, and to have opinions in matters of religion. In the process they were liable to follow leaders other than those on whom they were 'naturally' dependent as landlords or religious mentors. Such were the implications of the tenant movements, the subversive disobedience of Sunderland under Lilburne,

[1] Above, pp. 100 ff.

Puritan intransigency, and the connection liable to be built up between the latter and the parliamentary oppositionists. Once again, and particularly as far as landlord–tenant relations were concerned, the traditional personalized dependence of inferiors on their 'governors' tended to give way to an impersonal texture of legal relationships in terms of which rule was determined and subordination defined, and to ties and loyalties founded on religious allegiance. This did not mean that the traditional governing class ceased to rule; but simply that those in authority had to come to terms with new styles of leadership which now emerged.[1]

Of these various aspects of the changing scene in Durham, some are relatively easy to categorize; and those in particular which involve social and economic changes constitute familiar features of the total landscape of English social history.[2] Similarly the political scene, as it shapes itself by 1640, with the gentry alienated by unacceptable fiscal burdens and rebuffed in their military self-respect, with dislike of the Arminian clergy widespread, conforms to a familiar pattern. The failure of Bishop Morton's moderate policies, the polarization of significant sectors of opinion between the two extremes of Puritan and Arminian, and the support given the hot-heads amongst the latter from London, with tension mounting as the Scottish crisis gathered momentum; all this conforms to the accepted picture of the almost suicidal folly of the government of Charles I.[3] Other aspects of the total development over the whole period, on the other hand, are much more specific to Durham. Particularly there is the sense of sharply defined contrasts, summed up for example in the continued survival of a traditionalist style of society, vital enough, as late as 1569–70, to mount the formidable demonstration of the Northern Rising. But at the other extreme, there is the environment of the coal industry, a world whose way of life was remote from that of the great households and lineages; and one in which the distinctive marks of an industrial and technological future can be discerned. The Durham development drives home sharply the sense of a tension of old and new; of basic shifts in beliefs and mentality, in religion and culture, in the domestic setting of the

[1] Above, pp. 79 ff., 83 ff., 173 ff. [2] Cf. Lawrence Stone, 'Social Mobility'.
[3] Cf. Lawrence Stone, *Causes*, pp. 128 ff.

individual, and in the relationship between these and the general social and political setting. By 1640 the pattern of change has blended into the still persisting continuities; a new style of society, its stability still precarious, has constituted itself.

It remains to interpret the pattern of development, and to generalize from it. As attempted below, this involves the use of a few improvised terms. It will be suggested that between 1500 and 1640 Durham made the transition from a 'lineage society' to a 'civil society'.[1] Under the lineage society, the mental world was articulated in terms of 'bounded horizons' and 'particularized modes of thought', which also reflected themselves in the social and political arrangements; the civil society, on the other hand, involved the rise of systems of 'generalized discourse, claiming universal validity'. These terms—the sense given them will emerge in the further course of this chapter— are not intended as contributions to social science, nor does their use imply any all-embracing sociological interpretation of the period. Rather they are put forward as useful periodizing phrases in terms of which the development from one kind of social pattern towards another, which took place in Durham during these years, may be understood. Other expressions are of course available for this purpose, like the well-worn 'from medieval to early modern', or from 'a custom and status society' to 'a possessive individualist society'.[2] It is hoped that those chosen have a special suitability for discussing and relating some of the themes developed in the course of this book, which it is contended have a special transformative significance

---

[1] The term 'lineage', used here for the kind of great landed family which stood at the centre of a 'connection' or 'affinity' of relatives, servants, and followers was suggested, *mutatis mutandis*, by G. Duby's description of the role of the extended family in the setting of a French regional society of the earlier medieval period, in *La Société au XIe et XIIe siècles dans la région Maconnaise* (Paris, 1953), and by *L'Enfant et la Vie familiale sous l'Ancien Régime* (Paris, 1960), by P. Ariès; the latter using the term to distinguish the extended family from the nuclear family which evolved out of it. The use made of 'civil society' is close to that of Hobbes, according to which it designates the state upon which men enter when they agree to abandon rights possessed in the state of nature (the essence of which being the right of self-preservation), these being conferred on a single sovereign lawgiving power. In civil society an association of political equals is constituted by contract, consisting of patriarchal family heads who include women, children, and servants, the latter in themselves possessing no political rights. On Hobbes's adhesion to the patriarchal family in spite of his rejection of a patriarchal origin for political power, see Thomas, 'Hobbes', p. 189.

[2] See Macpherson.

in the Durham scene. In particular they enable emphasis to be given not only to changes in economy and social structure, but also to the ways in which the intimate environment and mental world of the individual was being altered by a changed domestic and family organization, by the effects of a new-style educational system, and by the dissemination of literacy; also by the displacement of a religion of rite and visual symbol by one of preaching and the Word. At the same time these same terms leave a place open for the development whereby traditional dependencies and allegiances, conceived in personal and family terms, gave way to a more complicated pattern of greater and lesser 'interests', related to each other within the pattern of law, now the dominant bond between them.

THE LINEAGE SOCIETY: BOUNDED HORIZONS AND PARTICULARIZED MODES OF THOUGHT

Still essentially medieval, this society and its associated culture centred on the great household,[1] gregarious and hospitable, with its swarms of servants and dependants. The setting was the castles and larger manor houses of the great families; it was in the context of Raby, Lumley, Witton, Hylton, and their like that the characteristic attitudes formed themselves, with their related forms of political assertion and competitiveness, and indeed the whole way of life. The tone of the latter, the outlook cultivated, and the objectives pursued were appropriate to the same great families whose houses and resources sustained it, the house of Neville being the most striking and obvious example; families that is whose dominance over the region was already traditional, and which collectively made up the lineage society. The emphasis in this society was on the cult of 'lordship', the exercise of which in the course of time had come to be thought the natural and inherent prerogative of the leading lineages. The tough persistency of the lineages over the generations received recognition in the reverence accorded 'ancient blood'. Inherent in lordship were claims to service, fidelity, and obedience, not only from the servants and the tenants who occupied the family lands, but also from the dependent gentry who constituted its 'affinity'. In return patronage and protection were made available.

[1] See above, pp. 31 ff.

Involved too in lordship was the need to assert and maintain family 'honour', this requiring in the first place that the lineage should enjoy a wealth, dignity, and authority commensurate to its inherited status and right. Disputes about the extent and limits of the latter imparted to the society its competitive edge, giving rise to feuds and lawsuits, contributing to revolts and rebellions. On the one hand therefore, this was a society geared to tension and conflict. But on the other these same 'connections' and affinities into which the lineage society was divided, since they also generated an inner solidarity based on obedience, fidelity, and service to the dominant lineage, could contribute to political and social stability. It was the Crown which, already by the early sixteenth century, constituted the most important extraneous factor with a role to play in Durham lineage politics; this was to mediate between, damp down, or exploit in its own interest the tissue of local grievance and aspiration in which the lineages were involved. In spite of his Palatine status, the effectiveness of the Bishop in this respect depended on the degree of support available from London.[1]

One aspect of the bounded horizons and particularized modes of thought characteristic of the lineage society emerges in the rarity with which it was possible for lineage politics to be articulated in terms of generalized political principles or constitutional positions. For there were few with access to the kind of legal or university formation which might have opened up a perspective wider than the grievances and aspirations of the lineage itself, these forming the framework within which the values of lordship, fidelity, and service were contained. What lay beyond the latter was firstly a sense of the kingship as constituted within a context of law, and as possessing a divinely legitimated status which made the person and authority of the King in the last resort inviolable.[2] Secondly there was an awareness of the restraints imposed on all exercising lordship and rule, including kings, by the Christianized cult of Fortuna, which predicted the inevitable downfall of those who lapsed into injustice and tyranny, so stirring up their own subjects to overthrow

---

[1] Above, pp. 35, 41 ff.

[2] Circumstances could arise, however, as during the Pilgrimage of Grace, when the possibility of resistance to the supposed unjust exercise of authority by the Crown could commend itself at least to some of the Durham lineages. See above, pp. 46 ff.

them.[1] These convictions did not provide much of a basis for ideological crusades and causes, but tended rather to fasten on rights, grievances, and personalities of a specific and particularized kind. Thus the Durham contribution to the common political stock of the Pilgrimage of Grace was a particularly vehement distrust of the government, and an assertion of the 'liberties of Saint Cuthbert'.[2] The attempt to work up a 'religious' revolt in 1569, by which time the lineage society had already lost much of its confidence in its own values, was, as such, a failure.

The concern with bounded horizons and particularized situations, rather than with any total world outlook is also encountered in the religious aspects of the culture of the regional lineage society. Pre-Reformation Durham was permeated by the organization, wealth, and authority of the Church; but to a much lesser extent by the system of values and belief which the Church claimed to represent. This did not penetrate very deeply beyond the élite of university-trained clergy, most of them connected with the abbey and episcopal entourage at Durham itself. Lower down the social scale, and even amongst the gentry, there is not much evidence of lineage solidarities, or those of neighbourhood which reinforced family ties amongst the husbandmen and commonalty, receiving more than spasmodic Christianized expression, as for example, in funeral rites. Indeed it seems to have been parish feuds and rivalries, rather than parish solidarities, which emerged when the parish community assembled at church; the latter and its churchyard being the commonest setting for frays, brawls, and assaults between rival *coqs de paroisse*, subsequently cited before the ecclesiastical courts.[3]

But although there was not much sense of a specifically Christian total world view, or of much more than a mechanical and legalistic Christian code, a wide recognition nevertheless

---

[1] The most popular and widely disseminated vehicle of the cult of Fortuna in early Tudor England was probably Lydgate's *Fall of Princes*, of which MSS. have survived from the circle of both the Nevilles and Lumleys; see above, p. 4 and n. For the socio-political implications of the cult, see James, 'Obedience', pp. 69–78.

[2] See above, p. 47.

[3] Cf. *Durh. Eccles. Proc.*, pp. 93–4, 257. Brawls in churchyards and churches were specifically prohibited by Act of Parliament in the reign of Edward VI.

persisted that the Church disposed of reserves of spiritual power profoundly relevant to those situations of crisis and peril, for example birth and death, in which the sacraments were needed, or which required the intervention and protection of the angels and saints. As a result after the Reformation doubts about the credentials of the new Protestant minister, and whether these were adequate for the due performance of the traditional rites, particularly baptism, rather than any hankering after points of traditional Catholic doctrine, about which most had little knowledge, were a common cause of dissent from the Protestant establishment in the parishes.[1] This then was not a religious culture of generalized dogma and belief articulating an all-embracing world outlook, in terms of which the individual, or a whole society, might be expected to make sense of its total existence; but rather one of specific situations and times, each ruled by its relevant spiritual powers, which, given the right conditions, could be invoked to good effect. This religion of 'the dark places of the land'[2] had much in common with the folk beliefs relating to witchcraft and wizardry which flourished side by side with it, and reflected the failure of the Church to carry christianization deeper than a shallow upper social crust. In religion, therefore, the culture of the region reflected again bounded horizons and a concern with particularity divorced from any deep involvement with the total structure of Catholicism.

The decline of the framework which sustained this kind of social and religious culture and its accompanying political style is aptly dramatized by the defeat of the Northern Rising of 1569. This, by doing away with the power of the Nevilles and finalizing the fall of Catholicism, opened the way for new tendencies at work in the region to establish themselves as the dominant pattern. One of these, reflecting in the most basic way what was involved in the decline of the lineage society, was the rise, over the course of a century before 1640, of the new-style gentry and upper-class housing, which implied a new pattern of domestic living.[3] It has been contended that the centre of the way of life

---

[1] See e.g. *Durh. Depos.*, pp. 228–51 for an incident at Wolsingham, when an Elizabethan incumbent was compelled to hand over his surplice to 'the old priest' in order that the latter might baptize a child.

[2] See Hill, *T.R.H.S.*; Hill, *Society*, pp. 55 ff. [3] See above, pp. 13 ff.

characteristic of the lineage society had been the community of the great household, its solidarity receiving expression in a public and open-handed style of living focused on the hall-space with its open hearth, which formed the centre of the traditional layout of the great houses. Here close contact was maintained between the family and its dependent service community, and here hospitality was dispensed to allies and friends. The new house-plan, however, developed into a more compartmentalized kind of domestic setting, with greater privacy for the family, servants relegated to specialized quarters, and hospitality increasingly restricted to relatives and close friends.[1] The Nevilles themselves may have set the example for the new patterns of domestic living, the earls of Westmorland having by the early sixteenth century divided up the public great chamber at Raby castle into smaller private rooms; and at their modest manor house at Kirkby Moorside in north Yorkshire,[2] to which it was their pleasure to 'come hunt and take pastime', they could escape from the gregarious and oppressively ceremonious routines of Raby and Brancepeth.

The growing emphasis on domesticity and privacy, however, tended to disintegrate the social setting basic to the values of lordship, fidelity and service, and so the way of life which those values projected, which had been the mark of the great households. Once the latter had largely disappeared in the wake of the collapse of the Northern Rising, and the affinities related to them dissolved, what remained? Essentially a gentry society made up of an association of nuclear families, a 'civil society' of patriarchal family heads, in Hobbes's sense, whose members, although wide variations in wealth and standing might exist amongst them, were equal in status before the law; and in which it had become difficult for any single house to command the kind of unquestioned deference and leadership ascribed to the Nevilles. At the same time, the entrance of an increasing number of new recruits into the ranks of the gentry, as a result of economic and social changes, further blurred the traditional social and political pattern, and the values and beliefs associated with it.[3]

[1] Cf. Stone, *Crisis*, pp. 583–4; Hoskins, 'Rebuilding', p. 54.
[2] P.R.O., E164/37, Survey of Kirkby Moorside.
[3] See above, pp. 67 ff. Cf. Stone, 'Social Mobility', pp. 28–9.

CIVIL SOCIETY AND POSSESSIVE MARKET SOCIETY

As the lineage society dwindled in the wake of the collapse of the Rising, so the disciplines involved in the production and sale of commodities (one of which was increasingly the land itself, and another the labour of those who worked it) asserted themselves with greater prominence and strength. The economy of the region now responded increasingly to the rhythm of the coal trade, whose fluctuations began to supplement the traditional cycle of good and bad years of the agricultural economy, the latter itself becoming more and more keyed to the needs of the growing market of Newcastle and the coal districts. In the wake of these economic developments, a powerful tendency emerged for the society of the region to reshape itself in terms of something like a 'possessive market society', of a 'society of possessive individualism', in place of the older 'customary or status society'.[1] This emerges most strikingly in the pit communities, where relations between master and man have been divested of the domestic setting and patriarchal overtones which formed the background for the labour of the apprentice, journeyman, or farm labourer. The pitmen sold their labour to a remote employer, who played little part in the day-to-day disciplines and solidarities which held these communities together. Even more irrelevant to the pit background was the traditional style of relationship between lord and tenant.[2]

As commercial and industrial activity expanded, so 'possessive individualism' invaded the Durham countryside. Perhaps it is most obvious in the rapidly changing and competitive world of the lower Wear valley, where a society of coal-owners, merchants, quarrymen, and salt producers had to clear a space for itself out of an environment of peasants, fishermen, and yeomen, dominated by the rich clergy and such great families as the Lambtons, Bellasises, and Lumleys. Above all perhaps in this sector of the Durham scene we come closest to the competitive and contractual pattern of relationships given prominence in C. B. Macpherson's interpretation[3] of Harrington, Locke, and Thomas Hobbes. The Wear men, at loggerheads with the Crown, with the Newcastle monopolists, and with local landowners, would surely have been amongst those least in-

---

[1] See Macpherson, op. cit.   [2] See above, pp. 91 ff.   [3] Op. cit.

clined to contest the Hobbesian dictum that the commonwealth existed to uphold 'the Liberty to buy, and sell, and otherwise contract with one another; to choose their own abode, their own diet, their own trade of life'. Similarly Hobbes's view that the '*Value*, or worth of a man, is of all other things, his Price',[1] was illustrated by the transformation of the character of the gentry by newly made mercantile, yeoman, or official fortunes. Such fortunes could establish as leading squires and landowners men who were often of obscure background, but who nevertheless displaced old-established houses, or settled on lands which had belonged to the Nevilles.

In connection with the new modes of enterprise, whether industrial or agricultural, and the wider market possibilities, a weakening of old-established solidarities can be detected. The prosperous yeoman in lowland Durham depended less on his family, and more on hired servants. The extension of customary tenure made the tenant less inclined to rely on 'good lordship', and the favour of his landlord, so that he and his like came to 'accounte themselves for ther rent payinge to be lordes of ther tenementes'. Amongst the gentry the traditional lineage loyalties had to come to terms with the increasingly individualized style of living of the nuclear family under its patriarchal head, and with an emphasis on profit and property to which they were often irrelevant.[2] It is difficult not to assume that in Durham, as elsewhere, a growing sense of the defensive isolation of the individual, entrenched with his family in the fortress of his property, was forming itself. Soon, in the pamphlet warfare of the next generation, the sentiment would become articulate: '. . . every man is an island; and hath somewhat which he may call his own, and which he not only lawfully may, but also out of duty to God ought to defend . . . against all other men . . .'[3]

The interest of each man in his 'propriety' was founded on the law, and this constituted a system whose machinery was 'national' and centred on London, as did the market into which the rise of the coal trade had incorporated Durham. The law required a single enforcing authority, and consequently in

---

[1] Hobbes, *Works*, pp. 76, 199.   [2] See above, pp. 13, 23, 102–3, 79–80.
[3] L.S., *Nature's Dowrie; Or, the People's Native Liberty Asserted* (1652), quoted Gunn, p. 11.

some quarters the traditional prerogatives of the bishop of Durham began to be seen as an anomaly,[1] in spite of the fact that regionalism remained a powerfully felt sentiment in the Palatinate, just as in other comparable county societies.[2] A strong sense of local community emerged in the opposition to Ship Money, in jealousy of the supposed disproportionate burdens placed on Durham by comparison with other and neighbouring shires, and in dislike of the metropolitan religious trends imported from the universities and the Court by the Arminian upper clergy. But what is significant is the ineffectiveness of this regional sentiment, in so far as it drew solely on its own resources, as a political force. It was unable to prevent the increasing permeation of Durham society by policies, influences, and tensions having their roots in London; and it was there alone, through Parliament, that regional grievances could find effective expressions and redress. Thus politics too came to be seen as oriented towards London, and as requiring participation in the sessions of the House of Commons. Hence the increasingly vocal demand, under the Stuarts, for Durham M.P.s, the gentry no longer being content with a vicarious representation in the House of Lords through their bishop and the local peers.[3] The extent to which Durham had become soldered to the general body of the kingdom emerged when the region was opened to military occupation and the irruption of civil war as a result, not of any local conflict, but of one over national issues giving strategic importance to the Durham coal resources. For although the regional society was divided, particularly over matters of religion, its inner tensions would have been unlikely to explode into violence but for the pressure of the inflamed national situation.

The pressure of market forces made for a national economy,

---

[1] See above, pp. 165–6. The point of view of the civil society on regional autonomies and immunities was put in its developed form by a Durham deputy sheriff, John Spearman, early in the eighteenth century: 'The subjects of this kingdom of England having the same interest, and an equal right to his Majesty's protection, and to the benefit of the laws of the realm, ought in all reason and justice to be put on the same level, and governed by the same laws, as well in one part of that dominion as in the other; and why this part of the country should be under singular rules, and embarrassed by the interposing power of a fellow subject . . . a Count Palatine of Durham, it seems not consistent with their interest, nor the common benefit of the realm . . .' (Spearman, p. 36).

[2] Cf. Everitt.   [3] See above, pp. 164 ff.

10. *Cosin's Gothic Revival:* the chancel of Brancepeth Church

legal system, and political pattern, and carried Durham a long way towards the emergence of a 'society of possessive individualism' out of a 'customary or status society'. Yet to see the situation in these terms does not do full justice to the range of tensions and pressures at work, or to the strong resistance which market values, in important respects, still encountered. Not even Hobbes could commit himself consistently and whole-heartedly to the values of possessive individualism. For in his thinking the compulsions of the market-place were qualified by the disinterested ethic of the 'generous nature', stoical and aristocratic, who could rise above them.[1] And Harrington similarly held that the commonwealth required 'the genius of a gentleman' who was free from the pressures which buying and selling imposed.[2] Again, Leveller thinking, in spite of its strong possessive and individualist bent, also manifested a strong sense of social solidarity, since 'no man is born for himself only,' all being obliged 'to employ our endeavours for the advancement of a communitive happinesse'.[3] It is this kind of tension which marks the pattern of 'civil society' as it constitutes itself in the Durham scene, and which differentiates it from a consistently 'market' or 'possessive' society.

For the Durham 'possessive individualist' was hemmed in by attitudes, aspirations, and disciplines, which if not directly hostile to the market society, were at any rate irrelevant to it. Some of these were in part inherited from the older status or lineage society, like the cult of gentility; others rooted in such associations for mutual aid and support as the neighbourhood groupings in which yeoman and husbandman families were involved in the lowland, and the powerful kinship loyalties of the upland. Above all there was the influence of the religion and humanism disseminated by the grammar schools, which more than any other factor was responsible for the framework of assumptions, fundamentally conservative, yet making room for change, in which the civil society acquired its fundamental characteristics. It was in terms of humanism and religion, for example, that gentility acquired different connotations from those thought to go with gentry status in the lineage society. As far as the latter was concerned, the characteristics of gentility,

[1] Thomas, 'Hobbes', pp. 202 ff.   [2] Macpherson, p. 166.
[3] Gunn, p. 25; Macpherson, p. 157.

---

11. *Arminian liturgical splendour:* Cosin's Communion Plate at Auckland Castle chapel

as summarized by Laurence Humphrey, had been those of 'hawkynge, huntynge, pastimes, mightye power, vayne vauntes, traynes of horse, and servauntes, ryot, myschyfes, bravery, roysteringe porte, or greate lyne'.[1] But the crude competitive edge of the lineage society whose last fling had been the Northern Rising gave way, as literacy and education spread among the upper classes, to an insistence on magnanimity and a cultivated taste as the marks of true gentility. As a result, the essence of nobility came to be seen as the marriage of ancient lineage and decorous deportment; or, as Humphrey put it, 'that, whyche with the renoune and fame of ancestry, hath coupled excellent, Chrystian and farre spread vertue'.[2]

Gentility therefore came to reflect the humanist ideal of the cultivated and Christian gentleman, while at the same time, thanks to the activities of the heralds and antiquarians, retaining its roots in tradition and the past. As a result, in 1640 as in 1500, a social structure dominated by a hereditary élite remained the rule, in spite of the rise of a wide range of functional and occupational hierarchies promoting social mobility in industry, the professions, and even in agriculture. Hobbes would have encountered in the mobile setting of the functional hierarchies confirmation for his view that differences in rank and degree rose solely from agreement and convenience.[3] But in the civil society it was the concept of a hereditary gentility, based on supposed innate capacities transmitted by 'blood' and descent which kept the upper hand, and constituted the social ideal. The persisting and obsessive attraction of gentility and 'ancient blood' even for those whose natural ambience was that of the market society emerges for example in the consequences of the intermarriage of Newcastle coal-owning and mercantile families like the Riddells and the Lawsons with Recusant stocks endowed with long pedigrees; matches which eventually carried the former out of their urban and monied origins into the back-woods isolation liable to become the lot of the Recusant squires.[4]

The civil society, with its emphasis on order and decorum, and as far as its conservative aspects and sense of continuity with the past are concerned, can be seen as the mould into which

---

[1] *Of Nobilytie* (1563).   [2] Ibid.

[3] Thomas, 'Hobbes', p. 188, and above, pp. 91, 92.   [4] Above, pp. 138 ff, 146 n.

Durham society sought to stabilize itself as a period of exceptionally rapid economic growth drew to its close and as the
opportunities which the market made available contracted.
Land remained the most attractive investment, providing
security, as well as making status available. It is not surprising
therefore that in the world of the Wear men, enterprising and
free-trade, but also without the security which the mono-
polistic privileges enjoyed by their Tyne counterparts made
available, should have been assiduous in their pursuit of land
and gentility. Families like the Greys, Jacksons, Sheperdsons,
and the Sunderland Lilburnes all established themselves on
landed estates, and gradually assimilated themselves, in the next
generation or two, to the world of gentility and status values,
abandoning their original entrepreneurial roles.[1] The underlying trend, which the upheaval of the Civil War could inter-
rupt but not reverse, is perhaps most aptly expressed by the
descent order which increasingly prevailed in the parish
churches, with the gentry in the places of honour, their servants
and tenants grouped around them, with the people in the humbler seating according to their status and degrees. This was the
model of the civil society which had emerged by the 1630s, its
decorum contrasting with the brawls and feudings liable to
assail the congregations of an earlier age. Similarly the implications of the new-style gentility, with its sober demeanour,
strong sense of duty, and *noblesse oblige* are encountered in the
character of Sir William Bellasis, Bishop Morton's sheriff of
the 1630s, conscientiously discharging the tasks laid on him by
the Crown, in spite of his distaste for many of them, because he
was 'sensible of the state of these times, which require the duty
of every good subject'.[2]

The conservative and traditionalist, yet flexible attitudes,
responsive to change, which gathered around the implications
of gentility, were a significant aspect of the emerging civil
society. They illustrate the character of the latter as a framework within which the forces of social mobility and change
could be received, but also contained and assimilated to the
conventions and values of an earlier age. One of the problems of
the time was to construct a structure of religious beliefs and
organization, and of cultural values which might play a similar

[1] Above, pp. 89–90.   [2] Above, pp. 122 ff., 173.

assimilative and conservative role. 'Arminianism' was an attempt at such a structure which failed through over-rigidity, Bishop Morton's Broad Church eirenicism being nearer the kind of flexible, yet authoritative Church structure which the situation demanded. It was a problem which Protestantism and humanism could not resolve, with the result that it was in the religious, cultural, and mental world that civil society showed its greatest instability. For here authority had come to be qualified by the possibility of freedom and choice.

GENERALIZED DISCOURSE AND THE UNIVERSALLY VALID VIEWPOINT

As far as beliefs, mental attitudes, and values are concerned, it has been suggested above that the transition from a lineage to civil society involved a break with the bounded horizons and particularized modes of thought characteristic of the former, and that this was one of the most significant new experiences which the transition brought in its wake. It was made available partly in the context of the grammar school, partly in that of the new religious climate resulting from the Reformation, in which the choice between alternative forms and emphases of religious belief became available.[1] In both these settings there was the opportunity to develop a relationship with a universalized cultural system (that of humanist rhetoric) and with a total religious point of view claiming general validity. In the process something was learnt of the power of generalized discourse, and of what was involved in choice and individual self-determination. At a simple, but nevertheless significant level this was the experience in which a grammar school education immersed increasing numbers of the Durham upper class. First, there was the break with family background and setting in favour of the specialized environment and meritocratic hierarchy of the school, accompanied by the inculcation of the values and modes of expression of the system of humanist rhetoric. But at the same time the discipline contemplated was not one of mere conformity to the system, but aimed rather to encourage initiative in the choice of words, phrases, and expressive forms from the texts studied, and the adaptation of these by

[1] Cf. Stone, 'Educational Revolution', pp. 69 ff.

the pupil to his own communicative needs and purposes.[1] The rhetorical medium was something plastic which could be manipulated to meet the needs of rational or imaginative discourse.

The experience of the kind of Calvinist Puritanism, disseminated amongst the Muggleswick parishioners through the preaching of Lapthorne, and finding expression too in the Biblicism and anti-Arminianism of the Sunderland men, had a similar quality, involving a break with the particularized situations and specialized spiritual powers and forces of folk belief in order to come to terms with a total and all-embracing world view, that of Calvinist dogma, presented in the preaching.[2] But the latter had to be freely appropriated and internalized as God's Word speaking within the hearer himself, with its relevance to his own specific needs and situation, otherwise (as the Newcastle Puritan Robert Jenison put it) 'no profit will redound . . . from it, as not to young Samuel till he left running to old Eli, and acknowledged God speaking to him . . .'[3] The Puritan who responded to an effective preaching had no need to run to the minister for explanation and reassurance. He had merely to listen to and freely appropriate the Word which had sounded in his own heart just as much as in the preacher's mouth. As far as the Sunderland community was concerned, the element of liberty and choice which Puritanism involved suggests a parallel with the social experience of these men, involved as they were in novel forms of economic enterprise and community-building, and who had many reasons to be ill at ease with the dominant 'Arminianism' disseminated by the Cathedral establishment. But at the same time the total and all-embracing character of Calvinism, and its harsh dogmatism, provided an element of discipline, stability, and reassurance in a fluid situation in which so many traditional landmarks had been removed or discredited.

But on the other hand it is also clear that the appeal of the imagery and lore of Puritanism was not limited to the emergent capitalist society of Sunderland, but could reverberate over a range of contrasting situations, extending to a peasant and traditionalist society such as that of Derwentdale.[4] Here the remote tenant community of Muggleswick, which had always

---

[1] Above, p. 98; Watson, p. 6.   [2] Above, pp. 130 ff., 135 ff.   [3] Jenison.
[4] Above, p. 131.

taken for granted its humble social status and its subordination to extraneous authority, by making choice of Lapthorne's 'preaching' Puritanism and rejecting the 'dumb dogs' imposed by its clerical landlords, was enabled to become aware of itself, in religious terms, as a distinctive group with its own specific needs and requirements. At the same time the harsh Calvinist moralism of Lapthorne's preaching surely both defined and internalized the social disciplines, family and economic, characteristic of such poor upland societies. It also provided a clearer understanding and more compelling justification of these in terms of divine decrees and purposes than had previously been available, raising the hope of their spontaneous and effective implementation on the part of those who had become 'regenerate' and counted amongst the Calvinist 'Elect'. But it is probably an index to the differential social context of the Sunderland and Derwentdale Puritanism that under the Commonwealth the latter evolved towards the spontaneous and decentralized kind of church organization favoured by the Baptists. Sunderland on the other hand remained 'Presbyterian', and so in favour of a centralized state Church retaining some of the property basis of the old establishment, like tithes. But no doubt the differences which grew up between the Sunderland Lilburnes and their Cromwellian relative Colonel Robert Lilburne, patron and protector of the Baptists, were also a factor in this development.[1]

What is clear at any rate is that by 1640 a range of different religious points of view (Catholic Recusancy should of course be included amongst these as well as the various kinds of Protestantism) existed which it was increasingly difficult to unify into a single religious culture presided over by an established Church. The various religious alternatives thus emerging tended to be identified with specific social environments, and with a background outside the ambience of the university trained clergy and educated gentry who assimilated and absorbed the dominant culture. They constituted in fact the novel phenomenon of a cultural initiative arising from outside the clerical and social establishment, and as such were thought to present a threat to this. The threat might, perhaps, have been met if a conservative Puritanism of the Peter Smart variety had

[1] See Douglas, ch. i; Robson, 'Lilburne', pp. 117, 118.

continued to predominate in the Church, and if effective measures had been taken to provide preaching in the parishes. But the increasingly dominant Arminian party distrusted such a solution on the grounds that a religion of preaching and spontaneous prayer would unleash disorder in the Church, and threaten its authority. Instead a strongly episcopal establishment was to rely increasingly on a religious practice of rite and visual effect, and on a set liturgy; sermons being supplemented by set 'homilies' of approved content which could be read from the pulpit by an uneducated clergy.[1] It was the monotony and mechanical uniformity of this recipe which was one of its weaknesses. By such means the Church could not possibly even approach the needs of the upland peasantry for whom Lapthorne's preaching provided an illuminating centre around which the pattern of their lives could appear more clarified and more coherent. Nor could the sophisticated Anglicanism of men like Cosin and Bishop Morton enter the world of folk belief, dominated by demonic possession, witchcraft, and spiritual powers good and evil.[2] Puritanism could confront these powers with that of charismatic prayer, Catholicism with the invocation of angels and saints; but the tendency of Anglicanism was to minimize their importance or deny their existence.[3]

Less obvious perhaps in Durham, from the point of view of the Church establishment, were the fissiparous tendencies within the dominant culture itself, and the emergence out of the humanist educational system of a lay intelligentsia qualified, through such spokesmen as Hobbes and Harrington, to challenge the claim of the clergy to monopolize the terms in which the political, social, and metaphysical world could be ordered. Nevertheless the case of John Lilburne should not be forgotten, for the great Leveller was a Durham man who thought it worthwhile to boast that 'besyde other education, the best which the country afforded, I was brought up well night ten years together, in the best schooles in the North, namely at Auckland and Newcastle . . .' Nor, in the next generation, that of the atomist Henry Power, who not only set his 'free' mechanical

---

[1] Above, pp. 129 ff.

[2] See above, pp. 125 ff. Morton, while still bishop of Lichfield, had been notable for his scepticism about witchcraft, and had rescued a woman falsely accused of this from the gallows. See Webster, pp. 275 ff.

[3] Above, pp. 126, 132, n. Cf. Thomas, *Religion*, pp. 75–7 and 484–6.

APPENDICES

A: *Bishops, Priors, and Deans of Durham, 1500–1640*

BISHOPS OF DURHAM

Richard Fox	1494–1501
William Senhouse	1502–5
Christopher Bainbridge	1507–8
Thomas Ruthall	1509–23
Thomas Wolsey	1523–9
Cuthbert Tunstall	1530–59
James Pilkington	1561–76
Richard Barnes	1577–87
Matthew Hutton	1589–95
Tobias Matthew	1595–1606
William James	1606–17
Richard Neile	1617–28
George Mountain	1628
John Howson	1628–32
Thomas Morton	1632–59

PRIORS OF DURHAM

Thomas Castell	1494–1519
Hugh Whitehead	1524–40

DEANS

Hugh Whitehead	1541–?8
Robert Horn	1551–3
Thomas Watson	1553–8
Thomas Robertson	1558–9
Robert Horn	1559–60
Ralph Skinner	1561–3
William Whittingham	1563–79
Thomas Wilson	1580–1
Tobias Matthew	1583–95
William James	1596–1606
Adam Newton	1606–20
Richard Hunt	1620–38
Walter Balcanqual	1639–45

B. *The Nevilles*

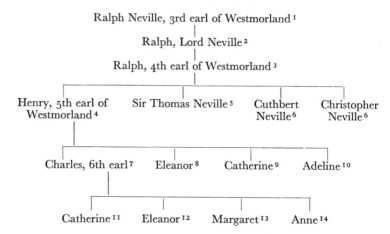

Ralph Neville, 3rd earl of Westmorland [1]

Ralph, Lord Neville [2]

Ralph, 4th earl of Westmorland [3]

Henry, 5th earl of Westmorland [4] Sir Thomas Neville [5] Cuthbert Neville [6] Christopher Neville [6]

Charles, 6th earl [7] Eleanor [8] Catherine [9] Adeline [10]

Catherine [11] Eleanor [12] Margaret [13] Anne [14]

1. Ralph Neville, 3rd earl of Westmorland. Succeeded 1484; died 1499. He married a niece of Archbishop Booth of York.

2. Ralph, Lord Neville. He died in 1498, during the lifetime of his father, the 3rd earl. His second wife was Edith Sandys, who after his death married Thomas, Lord Darcy, subsequently a leader of the Pilgrimage of Grace.

3. Ralph, 4th earl of Westmorland; son of Ralph, Lord Neville, by Edith Sandys, and step-son of Lord Darcy, he was born in 1498 and died in 1549. As a child he was a ward of the attainted Edward, duke of Buckingham, whose daughter he married. He was officially 'loyal' during the Pilgrimage of Grace, but his heir took an active part in it.

4. Henry, 5th earl of Westmorland, born 1525, died 1564. The most successful and powerful of the Neville earls, he held many offices and commands on the Border, and was lord lieutenant of Durham. He received large grants of Crown lands in Yorkshire and elsewhere from Queen Mary, who also made him her lieutenant-general in the North. His first wife was a daughter of the earl of Rutland; his second and third Cholmleys of Roxby. One of his sisters married Henry, earl of Rutland, another Thomas, Lord Dacre, a third the earl of Oxford. His youngest sister became the wife of Sir Fulke Greville; her son was the poet, dramatist, and courtier of the same name.

5. Sir Thomas Neville. Died without children.

6. Cuthbert and Christopher Neville. Both attainted for their part in the Rising of 1569, and died in exile.

7. Charles, 6th earl, and last of the Neville earls of Westmorland. Aged 21 in 1564, he was attainted in 1571, and died in exile thirty years later. He married Jane Howard, daughter of Henry, earl of Surrey, executed for treason in 1547, and sister of Thomas, duke of Norfolk, executed in 1572. His mother was the 5th earl's first wife, Anne Manners.

8. Eleanor. Married Sir William Pelham of Newstead.

9. Catherine. Married to Sir John Constable of Kirby Knowle, Yorks.

10. Adeline. Died at Willington, Durham, *c.* 1613.

11. Catherine, living 1604. She married Sir Thomas Grey of Chillingham.

12. Eleanor. Died unmarried.

13. Margaret. Her husband was Nicholas Pudsey of Barforth, Yorks.

14. Anne. She married David Ingleby, son of Sir William Ingelby of Ripley, head of a notable Recusant family which subsequently intermarried with the coal-owning Hodgsons of Hebburn.

C. *The Lumleys*

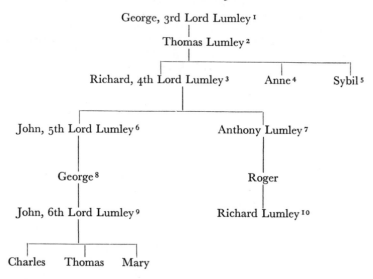

George, 3rd Lord Lumley[1]

Thomas Lumley[2]

Richard, 4th Lord Lumley[3]   Anne[4]   Sybil[5]

John, 5th Lord Lumley[6]   Anthony Lumley[7]

George[8]   Roger

John, 6th Lord Lumley[9]   Richard Lumley[10]

Charles   Thomas   Mary

1. George, 3rd Lord Lumley, born 1445, succeeded 1485, and died 1507. He was sheriff of Northumberland, and served on the Border under Richard III while the latter was still duke of Gloucester. Richard made him a knight banneret. In Durham he was keeper or forester of Weardale. He married Elizabeth Thornton, daughter of a wealthy Newcastle merchant.

2. Thomas Lumley, the third lord's only son, died during the lifetime of his father. He is probably the Lumley who married a natural daughter of Edward IV, known as Elizabeth Plantagenet, the King's daughter by Elizabeth Lucy.

3. Richard 4th Lord Lumley, 1507–10. He held the family office of forester of Weardale, and was surveyor of the Bishop's parks, mines, and forges. He married a sister of William, Lord Conyers.

4. Anne. Married George, Lord Ogle.

5. Sybil. Married William Hilton of Hylton.

6. John, 5th Lord Lumley, born *c.* 1492; died 1545. Fought at Flodden, and present at Field of the Cloth of Gold. Joined Pilgrimage of Grace 1536. The peerage forfeited by the attainder of his heir.

7. Anthony Lumley, who married a daughter of Richard Grey.

8. George, the only son of the 5th lord, was attainted and executed 1537 for his part in Bigod's rising.

9. John, 6th Lord Lumley, born *c.* 1533, restored in blood 1547, and by Act of Parliament I Edw. VI created Lord Lumley. Died 1609. A prominent magnate of the reign of Mary, after Elizabeth's succession he became in-

volved in dissident politics and in the scheme for a marriage between the duke of Norfolk and Mary Queen of Scots. Imprisoned in Tower, 1569–73. Subsequently a commissioner in several important state trials, including that of Queen Mary and Secretary Davison. Famous for his library and scholarly interests. By his marriage to Jane daughter and co-heiress of Henry, earl of Arundel, he inherited the greater part of the Arundel fortune. His children died during his lifetime, leaving no heirs, and he bequeathed the family properties to his distant relative Richard Lumley.

10. Richard Lumley, born *c.* 1589, died *c.* 1661–2. He inherited in 1609 the family properties in Durham and Yorkshire from John, Lord Lumley, and was created in 1628 Viscount Lumley in the Irish peerage. A prominent royalist during the Civil War, and garrisoned Lumley castle.

D. *The Boweses*

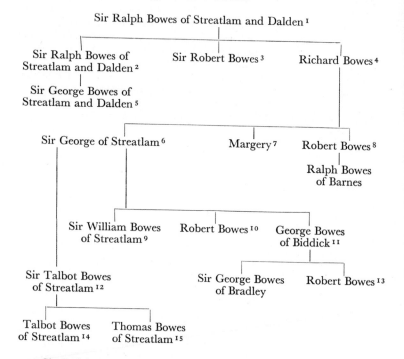

Sir Ralph Bowes of Streatlam and Dalden [1]

Sir Ralph Bowes of Streatlam and Dalden [2] — Sir Robert Bowes [3] — Richard Bowes [4]

Sir George Bowes of Streatlam and Dalden [5]

Sir George of Streatlam [6] — Margery [7] — Robert Bowes [8]

Ralph Bowes of Barnes

Sir William Bowes of Streatlam [9] — Robert Bowes [10] — George Bowes of Biddick [11]

Sir Talbot Bowes of Streatlam [12]

Sir George Bowes of Bradley — Robert Bowes [13]

Talbot Bowes of Streatlam [14] — Thomas Bowes of Streatlam [15]

1. Sir Ralph Bowes of Streatlam and Dalden married a daughter of Richard Conyers of South Cowton, Yorks; his will dated 1482.

2. Sir Ralph Bowes of Streatlam and Dalden. Sheriff of Durham, he fought at Flodden, and died in 1516. He married a daughter of Henry, Lord Clifford.

3. Sir Robert Bowes, died 1555. He was a privy councillor, and member of the Council in the North, as well as Master of the Rolls, and in Durham, steward of the lordship of Barnard Castle. His wife was a daughter of Sir James Metcalfe of Nappa, Yorks. He was a prominent participant in the Pilgrimage of Grace. His four sons all died young.

4. Richard Bowes. Married the heiress of Roger Aske of Aske, Richmond-shire.

5. Sir George Bowes of Streatlam and Dalden, 1517–46. His wife was a daughter of William, Lord Eure. He left no male heir, and after his death Dalden passed to the heirs of Sir Cuthbert Collingwood of Eslington, Northumberland, who married his youngest daughter, Jane. Collingwood was an officer of the earls of Northumberland, of Recusant sympathies, and, at Dalden, a big farmer and stock raiser.

6. Sir George Bowes of Streatlam, died 1580. Member of the Council in the North and steward of Barnard Castle. A prominent opponent of the 1569 Rising, and made knight marshal to punish those involved. Marshal of Berwick.

7. Margery. Married the Scottish reformer, John Knox.

8. Robert Bowes, born *c.* 1535, died 1597. Ambassador to Scotland, and treasurer of Berwick, sheriff of Durham, 1562–75. A member of the Council in the North.

9. Sir William Bowes of Streatlam, eldest son of Sir George by his first wife. Ambassador to Scotland, treasurer of Berwick, and steward of Barnard Castle, he died in 1611, leaving no heirs.

10. Robert Bowes, killed in an accident in the Keswick mines.

11. George Bowes of Biddick, coal and mining entrepreneur.

12. Sir Talbot Bowes of Streatlam, eldest son of Sir George Bowes by his second marriage, and by the latter's entail succeeded Sir William in the family inheritance. M.P. for Richmond, he died 1637.

13. Robert Bowes. Married a daughter of Robert Hutton rector of Houghton-le-Spring.

14. Talbot Bowes of Streatlam, 1603–54.

15. Thomas Bowes of Streatlam, succeeded his brother. Died 1664. He married a daughter of Anthony Maxton, rector of Wolsingham and prebend of Durham.

E. *The Tempests*

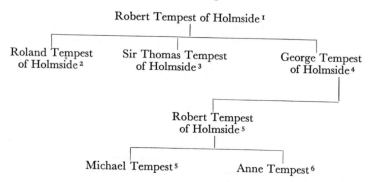

Robert Tempest of Holmside [1]

Roland Tempest of Holmside [2]   Sir Thomas Tempest of Holmside [3]   George Tempest of Holmside [4]

Robert Tempest of Holmside [5]

Michael Tempest [5]   Anne Tempest [6]

1. Robert Tempest of Holmside, living 1497, married a daughter of Thomas Lambton of Lambton. In the seventeenth century the coal-owing Tempests of Stella, whose head Sir Nicholas Tempest was created a baronet in 1622, claimed to be descended from one of his sons.

2. Roland Tempest of Holmside. He died leaving no children.

3. Sir Thomas Tempest of Holmside. He was steward to Bishop Ruthall, Cardinal Wolsey, and Bishop Tunstall. Took part in the Pilgrimage of Grace, and subsequently became a member of the Council in the North. A serjeant-at-law and recorder of Newcastle, he died 1545, leaving no children. His widow married George Smith of Nunstainton, father to William Smith, a prominent rebel of 1569.

4. George Tempest of Holmside, died before 1540.

5. Robert Tempest of Holmside. Sheriff of Durham 1558–62. A leader of the 1569 Rising, attainted, and died in exile, with his heir, Michael.

6. Anne Tempest. Married Anthony Hebburn of Hardwick, another attainted rebel.

F. *The Bellasises*

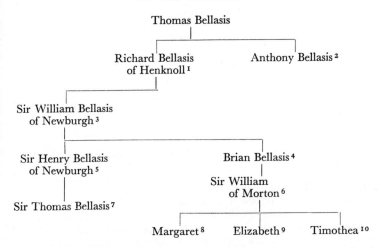

Thomas Bellasis

Richard Bellasis
of Henknoll[1]

Anthony Bellasis[2]

Sir William Bellasis
of Newburgh[3]

Sir Henry Bellasis
of Newburgh[5]

Sir Thomas Bellasis[7]

Brian Bellasis[4]

Sir William
of Morton[6]

Margaret[8]   Elizabeth[9]   Timothea[10]

1. Richard Bellasis of Henknoll, co. pal., died 1542. He was appointed constable of Durham castle by Wolsey in 1527, and granted a lease of the episcopal estate of Morton and Morton Grange. A member of the Council in the North.

2. Anthony Bellasis, died 1552. A doctor of laws and master in chancery, archdeacon of Colchester, and prebendary of Lincoln and Westminster. One of Thomas Cromwell's secretaries, he was granted Newburgh priory, Yorks, which he gave to his nephew Sir William Bellasis. A member of the Council in the North.

3. Sir William Bellasis of Newburgh, Yorks, died 1604, aged 81. He married a daughter of Sir Nicholas Fairfax of Gilling.

4. Brian Bellasis, born 1559, of Morton House, co. pal. He married a daughter of William Lee of Brandon, a former officer of the earl of Westmorland.

5. Sir Henry Bellasis of Newburgh; created a baronet 1611.

6. Sir William Bellasis of Morton, sheriff of Durham 1625–40. Died 1641. His wife was a daughter of Sir George Selby of Whitehouse, a rich coalowner.

7. Sir Thomas Bellasis. Created Lord Fauconberg of Yarm 1627, and Viscount Fauconberg 1642.

8. Margaret. Married Sir Thomas Davison of Blakiston.

9. Elizabeth. Married Francis James of Hetton.

10. Timothea. Married Ralph Davison.

G. *The Hodgsons*

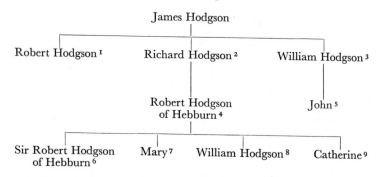

James Hodgson

Robert Hodgson [1]   Richard Hodgson [2]   William Hodgson [3]

Robert Hodgson
of Hebburn [4]   John [5]

Sir Robert Hodgson   Mary [7]   William Hodgson [8]   Catherine [9]
of Hebburn [6]

1. Robert Hodgson, doctor of physic, died 1576.
2. Richard Hodgson. Sheriff of Newcastle, 1549; mayor 1555, 1566, and 1580. Died 1585. Purchased Hebburn, 1562. One of the Newcastle syndicate of coal-owners which, in 1569, purchased the manor of Winlaton from the last earl of Westmorland for £2,000. His wife was a Lawson.
3. William Hodgson. Married a daughter of Sir Christopher Hildyard, of the Manor House, Lanchester. A follower of the earl of Westmorland, and involved in the 1569 Rising.
4. Robert Hodgson of Hebburn, died 1624. Married a daughter of Christopher Place of Halnaby, Yorks. His children all made Recusant matches.
5. John, living 1637. Married Jane, daughter of Henry Lawson of Nesham.
6. Sir Robert Hodgson of Hebburn. Married Anne Ingleby, a grand daughter of Charles, earl of Westmorland. He left no male heir.
7. Mary. Married Gerard Salvin of Croxdale.
8. William Hodgson, who succeeded his brother at Hebburn, and died 1662. He married a Haggerston.
9. Catherine. Married to Peter Forcer of Harberhouse.

H. *The Lilburnes of Thickley Puncharden and Sunderland*

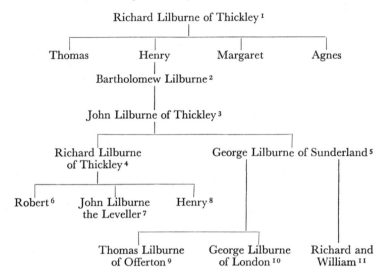

1. Richard Lilburne of Thickley came of a family which had settled at Thickley early in the fifteenth century; his father had served the earl of Northumberland as constable of Alnwick castle. He died at the turn of the fifteenth and sixteenth centuries, but the exact date, like the name of his wife, is unknown.

2. Bartholomew Lilburne, died 1562. Although he, like his father and son, seems to have married outside the gentry, he was reputed to have been 'at Bullen [Boulogne] with Henry VIII', and was acquainted with the earl of Westmorland. In his will he left goods worth £60, including a few pieces of plate and armour.

3. John Lilburne of Thickley, died 1604. He took part in disorders connected with the Northern Rising, 1569.

4. Richard Lilburne of Thickley. He married in 1599 Margaret, daughter of Thomas Hixon, keeper of the standing wardrobe at Greenwich to Queen Elizabeth. He returned from Greenwich to Thickley in 1619.

5. George Lilburne of Sunderland, merchant, born *c.* 1586. He acquired one-third of the manor of Offerton from Henry Wycliffe in 1630. His first wife was a daughter of Thomas Chamber of Cleadon; his second of John Hicks, vicar of Monk Wearmouth, then rector of Whitburn. His will is dated 1676.

6. Robert, born 1614, died 1667. Colonel of a parliamentary regiment of foot, and signed Charles I's death warrant. M.P. for East Yorks. 1656.

7. John Lilburne, the Leveller, born 1614, died 1657.

8. Henry; lieutenant-col. in his brother Robert's regiment. Declared for the King 1648, and died in the siege of Tynemouth castle.

9. Thomas Lilburne of Offerton, George Lilburne's eldest son by his first marriage. Born 1622, died 1665. He was an officer in Monk's army, and Cromwellian M.P. for county Durham. He supported the Restoration.

10. George Lilburne of London, druggist. He eventually inherited Offerton.

11. George Lilburne's two surviving sons by his second marriage, Richard and William, were barristers of Gray's Inn. A daughter of this marriage married a Newcastle merchant, Benjamin Ellison.

I: *The Blakistons of Newton Hall*

Marmaduke Blakiston, M.A. [1]

Toby Blakiston [2] · John Blakiston [4] · Thomas Blakiston, M.A. [6] · Frances [8]

Ralph Blakiston, M.A. [3] · Margaret [5] · Robert Blakiston, M.A. [7]

1. Marmaduke Blakiston M.A., was fifth son of John Blakiston of Blakiston; he matriculated at Trinity College, Oxford in 1579, aged 16, and married Margaret James, probably a relative of Bishop James, in 1593. He was vicar of Woodhorn and rector of Redmarshall (1589); rector of Sedgefield (1599). He was also archdeacon of the East Riding, and a prebendary of York. Prebendary of the 7th stall in Durham cathedral. He died in 1639. In the 1600s he acquired the estate of Newton Hall.

2. Toby Blakiston, eldest son and heir, succeeded to Newton Hall. He died *c.* 1646.

3. Ralph Blakiston, M.A., Christ's College, Cambridge; rector of Ryton. Died 1677.

4. John Blakiston, born 1603. M.P. for Newcastle 1641, and a regicide. He married Susan Chamber, probably one of the Chambers of Cleadon, and died 1649.

5. Margaret. Married in 1631 Thomas Shadforth of Eppleton. He held on lease the episcopal manor of Tunstall.

6. Thomas Blakiston, M.A., Queen's College, Oxford, vicar of Northallerton 1628. Succeeded his father in his prebendship of York Minster.

7. Robert Blakiston, M.A., Christ's College, Cambridge, succeeded his father as rector of Sedgefield and prebendary of the 7th stall at Durham cathedral. He married a daughter of Bishop Howson, and died in 1635.

8. Francis. Married John Cosin, prebendary and later Bishop of Durham, to whom his father-in-law resigned his archdeaconry of the East Riding, 1625.

SELECT BIBLIOGRAPHY

WITH ABBREVIATIONS USED IN TEXT

MANUSCRIPTS AND PRINTED SOURCE MATERIAL

Allan: Durham Cathedral Library, Allan MSS.

A.P.C.: Acts of the Privy Council. Edited by J. R. Dasent. 32 vols., Lond. 1890–1907.

Barnes: Memoirs of the life of Ambrose Barnes, Merchant and sometime Alderman of Newcastle upon Tyne. Surtees Society, vol. 50.

Carr: Select Charters of Trading Companies. Edited by C. T. Carr. Selden Society, vol. 28.

C.B.P.: Calendar of Letters and Papers relating to the . . . Borders of England and Scotland. Edited by J. Bain. 2 vols., Edinburgh, 1884–6.

C.D., 1621: Commons' Debates, 1621. Edited by W. Notestein, F. H. Relf, and H. Simpson. 7 vols., New Haven, 1935.

Chronicon: Cuthbert Sharp, *Chronicon Mirabile.* Lond. 1841.

Church Comm., Durh.: University of Durham, Department of Palaeography and Diplomatic, Church Commission MSS.

Cons. Ct. Bks.: University of Durham, Department of Palaeography and Diplomatic, Durham Consistory Court Deposition Books.

Cosin, Corres.: The Correspondence of John Cosin, Bishop of Durham, vol. i. Edited by G. Ornsby. Surtees Society, vol. 52.

Cott: British Museum, Cotton MSS.

Cowper MSS.: Calendar of the Manuscripts of Earl Cowper. Historical Manuscripts Commission, 3 vols., Lond. 1888–9.

C.P.R. Edw. VI: Calendar of Patent Rolls, Edward VI. 6 vols., Lond. 1924–9.

C.P.R. Eliz.: Calendar of Patent Rolls, Elizabeth. 5 vols., Lond. 1939–66.

C.P.R. Ph. & M.: Calendar of Patent Rolls, Philip and Mary. 3 vols., Lond., 1937–8.

C.S.P. Dom. Ch. I: Calendar of State Papers, Domestic, of the reign of Charles I. Edited by J. Bruce, W. D. Hamilton, and S. C. Lomas. 22 vols., Lond. 1858–93.

C.S.P. Dom. Edw. VI:⎫ *Calendar of State Papers, Domestic, of the reigns of*
C.S.P. Dom. Eliz.: ⎪ *Edward VI, Mary, Elizabeth, and James I.* Edited by
C.S.P. Dom. Jas. I: ⎬ R. Lemon and M. A. E. Green. 12 vols., Lond.
C.S.P. Dom. Mary: ⎭ 1856–72.

Dep. Kpr., 36th Rep., App. I.: Deputy Keeper of the Public Records, 36th Report, Appendix I.

Diaries, I: North Country Diaries, vol. i. Edited by J. C. Hodgson. Surtees Society, vol. 118.

Diaries II: North Country Diaries, vol. ii. Edited by J. C. Hodgson, Surtees Society, vol. 124.

Dugdale: The Heraldic Visitation of Yorkshire by Sir William Dugdale in 1665. Edited by R. Davies. Surtees Society, vol. 36.

Durh. Ch. Accnts.: Durham Churchwardens Accompts. Edited by J. Barmby. Surtees Society, vol. 84.

Durh. D. & Ch.: Durham Dean and Chapter MSS., Prior's Kitchen, Durham.

Durh. Eccles. Proc.: The Injunctions and other Ecclesiastical Proceedings of Richard Barnes, Bishop of Durham (1577–87). Edited by J. Raine. Surtees Society, vol. 22.

Durh. Depos.: Depositions . . . and other Ecclesiastical Proceedings from the Court of Durham. Edited by J. Raine. Surtees Society, vol. 21.

Durh. Halm. Rolls: A Selection from the Halmote Court Rolls of the Prior and Convent of Durham. Edited by W. H. D. Longstaffe and J. Booth. Surtees Society, vol. 82.

Durh. High Comm.: The Proceedings of the High Court of Commission for Durham and Northumberland. Edited by W. H. D. Longstaffe. Surtees Society, vol. 34.

Durh. Prots.: Durham Protestations in 1641–2. Edited by H. M. Wood. Surtees Society, vol. 135.

Durh. Rites: The Rites of Durham. Edited by J. T. Fowler. Surtees Society, vol. 107.

Durh. Stats.: The Statutes of the Cathedral Church of Durham. Edited by A. Hamilton Thompson. Surtees Society, vol. 143.

Egerton: British Museum, Egerton MSS.

Es. Accnts.: Estate Accounts of the Earls of Northumberland, 1562–1637. Edited by M. E. James. Surtees Society, vol. 163.

Foley: H. Foley, *Records of the English Province of the Society of Jesus.* 6 vols., Lond. 1875–80.

Foster: Joseph Foster, *Durham Visitation Pedigrees.* Lond. 1887.

Fox: The Register of Richard Fox, Bishop of Durham, 1494–1501. Edited by Marjorie P. Howden. Surtees Society, vol. 147.

Gairdner: J. Gairdner, *Materials Illustrative of the Reigns of Richard III and Henry VII.* 2 vols., Rolls Series, Lond. 1861–3.

Hatf. MSS.: Calendar of the Manuscripts of the Marquess of Salisbury at Hatfield House. Historical Manuscripts Commission, 18 vols., Lond. 1883–1940.

Hunter: Durham Cathedral Library, Hunter MSS.

Hutton: The Correspondence of Dr. Matthew Hutton, Archibishop of York . . . Edited by J. Raine. Surtees Society, vol. 17.

Lansd.: British Museum, Lansdowne MSS.

Lawson: William Palmes, *Life of Mrs. Dorothy Lawson of St. Anthony's near Newcastle.* Edited by G. B. Richardson. Lond. 1885.

L. P. Hen.: VIII Letters and Papers, Foreign and Domestic, of the reign of Henry VIII, 1509–47. Edited by J. S. Brewer, J. Gairdner, and R. H. Brodie. 21 vols., Lond. 1862–1910, and *Addenda,* 2 vols., Lond. 1929–32.

Lum. Libr.: The Lumley Library: The Catalogue of 1609. Edited by S. Jayne and F. R. Johnson.

Memorials: Cuthbert Sharp, *Memorials of the Rebellion of 1569.* Lond. 1840.

Mickleton: Durham University Library, Mickleton and Spearman MSS.

Parl. Survey: University of Durham, Department of Palaeography and Diplomatic MSS. of the Parliamentary Surveys of the Bishopric of Durham.

Pollen: J. H. Pollen, *Unpublished Documents relating to the English Martyrs.* 2 vols., Catholic Record Society, vols. v, xxi, 1908–14.

Prob.: University of Durham, Department of Palaeography and Diplomatic, Probate MSS.

P.R.O., C.: Public Record Office, Records of the Chancery.

P.R.O., Durh.: Public Record Office, Records of the Palatinate of Durham.

P.RO., E.: Public Record Office, Records of the Exchequer.

P.R.O., S.P.: Public Record Office, Records of the State Paper Office.

Roy. Comp. Pps.: *Royalist Composition Papers in the Counties of Durham and Northumberland.* Edited by R. Welford. Surtees Society, vol. 111.

Statutes: *Statutes of the Realm.* 11 vols., Lond. 1801–28.

Sy. H. (Aln): Syon House MSS (at Alnwick castle).

Tonge: *The Heraldic Visitation of the North of England made in 1530 by Thomas Tonge.* Edited by W. H. D. Longstaffe. Surtees Society, vol. 41.

Weardale: University of Durham, Department of Palaeography and Diplomatic, Weardale Chest MSS.

Whittingham: *The Life and Death of Mr. William Whittingham, deane of Durham, who departed this life Anno Domini 1579, June 10.* Edited by M. A. E. Green. Camden Society Miscellany, vol. vi, 1870.

Wills & Inv. i: *Wills and Inventories . . . (Chiefly from the Registry at Durham), vol. i.* Edited by J. Raine. Surtees Society, vol. 2.

Wills & Inv. ii: *A Volume of Wills from the Registry at Durham.* Edited by W. Greenwell. Surtees Society, vol. 38.

Wills & Inv. iii: *Wills and Inventories from the Registry at Durham, vol. iii.* Edited by J. Crawford Hodgson. Surtees Society, vol. 112.

Wills & Inv. iv: *Wills and Inventories from the Registry at Durham, vol. iv.* Edited by H. M. Wood. Surtees Society, vol. 142.

OTHER WORKS

Ag. Hist.: *The Agrarian History of England and Wales, vol. iv (1500–1640).* Edited by Joan Thirsk. Cambridge, 1967.

Alumn. Cantab.: J. and J. A. Venn, *Alumni Cantabrigienses. Part I, to 1751.* Cambridge, 1922.

Alumn. Oxon.: *Alumni Oxonienses, Being the matriculation register of the University, 1500–1714.* Edited by J. Foster, 4 vols., Oxford, 1891–2.

A most: *A most lamentable Information of Part of the Grievances of Muggleswick.* Lond., 1641.

Ariès: P. Ariès, *L'Enfant et la Vie familiale sous l'Ancien Régime.* Paris, 1960.

A true: *A true narrative concerning Sir Arthur Haslerigs possessing of Lieutenant-Colonel John Lilburnes estate in the County of Durham.*

Aubrey: John Aubrey, *Remaines of Gentilisme and Judaisme.* Lond., 1886. Edited by James Britten, Lond. 1881.

Aveling: H. Aveling, *Northern Catholics*, Lond. 1966.

Baddely & Naylor: Richard Baddely and Joseph Naylor, *Life of Dr. Thomas Morton, late Bishop of Duresme.* York, 1669.

Bailey: John Bailey, *The Agriculture of the County of Durham.* Lond. 1810.

Barley: M. W. Barley, *The English Farmhouse and Cottage.* Lond. 1961.

Barwick: 'Ιερονίκης, *or the fight victory and triumph of St. Paul, accommodated to Thomas, late L. Bishop of Duresme in a sermon preached at his funeral, . . . together with the life of the said bishop.* Lond. 1660.

Basire, *Sermon:* Isaac Basire, *Sermon preached at the funeral of Jo. Cosin, Bishop of Durham . . . with a brief life.* Lond. 1673.

Birch: Thomas Birch, *The History of the Royal Society of London.* 4 vols., Lond. 1756–7.

Blakeborough: R. Blakeborough, *Yorkshire Wit, Character, Folklore and Customs.* Lond. 1898.

Bossy, 'Character': John Bossy, 'The Character of Elizabethan Catholicism'. *Past and Present,* No. 21, April 1962, pp. 39 ff.

Brand: John Brand, *History and Antiquities of Newcastle upon Tyne.* 2 vols., Lond. 1789.

Britannia: William Camden, *Britannia.* Translated by P. Holland. Lond. 1637.

Brydges: Arthur Collins, *The Peerage of England.* Edited by S. E. Brydges. 9 vols., Lond. 1812.

Caraman: P. Caraman, *Henry Morse.* Lond. 1957.

Carleton: George Carleton, *Life of Gilpin* (1629), in Christopher Wordsworth, *Ecclesiastical Biography,* vol. iv.

Carlisle: N. Carlisle, *A Concise Description of the Endowed Grammar Schools of England and Wales.* 2 vols., Lond. 1818.

Child: *The English and Scottish Popular Ballads.* Edited by F. J. Child. 5 vols., Boston (Mass.), 1882–5.

C.J.: Journals of the House of Commons, 1547–1714. 17 vols., s.l.s.a.

Clarendon: Edward Hyde, earl of Clarendon, *History of the Rebellion.* 6 vols., Oxford, 1826.

Coke: Sir Edward Coke, *Institutes of the Laws of England.* 4 parts, Lond. 1797.

Collingwood: C. S. Collingwood, *Memoirs of Bernard Gilpin.* Lond. 1884.

Compl. Coll.: C.J., *The Compleat Collier.* Edited by M. A. Richardson. *Newcastle Tracts,* vol. vii, Lond. 1848.

Cooper, *Muker:* Edmund Cooper, *The Story of a Yorkshire Parish.* Clapham, 1948.

Cosin, *Works:* John Cosin, *Works.* Edited by J. Sansom. 5 vols., Oxford, 1843–55.

Cross: M. Claire Cross, 'The third Earl of Huntingdon and the trials of Catholics in the North'. *Recusant History,* vol. viii, 1965–6, pp. 136 ff.

Curtis: M. H. Curtis, *Oxford and Cambridge in Transition, 1558–1642.* Oxford, 1959.

D.N.B.: Leslie Stephen and Sidney Lee, *Dictionary of National Biography.* 22 vols., Lond. 1908–9.

Dodds: M. H. and R. Dodds, *The Pilgrimage of Grace . . .* 2 vols., Lond. 1915.

Douglas: D. Douglas, *A Brief History of the Baptist Churches in the North of England.* Lond. 1846.

Duby: G. Duby, *La Société au XIe and XIIe siècles dans la région Maconnaise,* Paris, 1953.

Ellis: H. R. Ellis, *The Road to Hel: A Study of the Conception of the Dead in Old Norse Literature.* Cambridge, 1940.

Erasmus, *De Civ.*: Erasmus, *De Civilitate, A Lytel Booke of good maners for Chyldren.* Edited Latin and English by R. Whittington, Lond. 1532.

Everitt: Alan Everitt, *Change in the Provinces in the Seventeenth Century.* Leicester, 1969.

Examples: *Examples of Printed Folklore concerning Northumberland.* Collected by M. C. Balfour and edited by Northcote C. Thomas. Lond. The Folklore Society, 1904.

F. & D.: C. H. Firth and Godfrey Davies, *The Regimental History of Cromwell's Army.* 2 vols., Oxford, 1940.

Fearefull: *Most Fearefull and Strange Newes from the Bishoppricke of Durham.* Lond. 1641.

Fiennes: Celia Fiennes, *Diary.* Edited by the Hon. Mrs. Griffiths. Lond. 1888.

Filmer: Sir Robert Filmer, *Patriarcha and other Political Works.* Edited by Peter Laslett. Oxford, 1949.

Galloway: R. Galloway, *Annals of Coal Mining and the Coal Trade.* Lond. 1898.

Gard. *Hist. Eng.*: S. R. Gardiner, *History of England . . . 1603–42.* 10 vols., 1883–4.

Gardner: Ralph Gardner, *England's Grievance Discovered in Relation to the Coal Trade* (1655). Reprinted 1849.

G.E.C.: G. E. Cockayne, *The Complete Peerage.* Edited by V. Gibbs, H. A. Doubleday, Lord Howard de Walden, G. H. White, and R. S. Lea. 13 vols., Lond. 1910–53.

Gibb: M. A. Gibb, *John Lilburne The Leveller.* Lond. 1947.

Girouard: M. Girouard, *Robert Smythson and the Architecture of the Elizabethan Era.* Lond. 1966.

Gray: H. L. Gray, *English Field Systems.* Cambridge (Mass.), 1915.

Gray: William Gray, *Coreographia, or A Survey of Newcastle upon Tyne.* Newcastle, 1649.

Greenslade: S. L. Greenslade, 'The Last Monks of Durham Cathedral Priory'. *Durham University Journal*, vol. xli, June 1949, pp. 107 ff.

Gregg: P. Gregg, *Freeborn John.* Lond. 1961.

Gunn: J. A. W. Gunn, *Politics and the Public Interest in the Seventeenth Century.* Lond. 1969.

Haller: W. Haller, *Tracts on Liberty in the Puritan Revolution,* 2 vols, New York, 1954.

Harrison: William Harrison, *Description of England.* Edited by George Edelen. New York, 1968.

Havran: M. J. Havran, *The Catholics in Caroline England.* Stanford, 1962.

Hegg: Robert Hegg, *The Legend of Saint Cuthbert, or the Historie of his Churches at Lindisfarne, Cunecascestre and Dunholm.* Lond. 1663. Reprinted at Darlington 1777.

Henderson: W. Henderson, *Notes on the Folklore of the Northern Counties.* Lond. 1879.

Heylin: P. Heylin, *Cyprianus Anglicus.* Lond. 1668.

Hill, *Econ. Prob.:* Christopher Hill, *Economic Problems of the Church*. Oxford, 1956.

Hill, *Society:* Christopher Hill, *Society and Puritanism*. Lond. 1964.

Hill, *T.R.H.S.:* Christopher Hill, 'Puritans and the Dark Corners of the Land'. *Transactions of the Royal Historical Society*, 5th series, vol. xiii, pp. 77ff.

Hinde: J. Hodgson Hinde, 'The Old North Road'. *Archeologia Aeliana*, New Series, vol. iii, pp. 237 ff.

Hobbes, *Works:* Thomas Hobbes, *The English Works*. Edited by Sir William Molesworth. 11 vols., Lond. 1839–45.

Homans: George C. Homans, *English Villagers of the Thirteenth Century*. New York, 1970.

Hooker: Richard Hooker, *Of the Laws of Ecclesiastical Polity*. Edited by John Keble. 3 vols., Oxford, 1841.

Hoskins: 'Harvest' W. G. Hoskins, 'Harvest Fluctuations and English Economic History'. *Agricultural History Review*, vol. xii, pp. 28 ff.

Hoskins, 'Rebuilding': W. G. Hoskins, 'The Rebuilding of Rural England'. *Past and Present*, No. 4, November 1953, pp. 44 ff.

Howell: R. Howell, *Newcastle upon Tyne and the Puritan Revolution*. Oxford, 1969.

Hughes: Edward Hughes, *Studies in Administration and Finance*. Manchester, 1934.

Humphrey: Laurence Humphrey, *The Nobles or Of Nobilytie*. Lond. 1563.

Hutch.: W. Hutchinson, *History and Antiquities of the County Palatine of Durham*. 3 vols., Newcastle, 1785–94.

James: M. E. James, *A Tudor Magnate and the Tudor State* . . . University of York, Borthwick Papers; No. 30, 1966.

James, 'Obedience': M. E. James, 'Obedience and Dissent in Henrician England . . .'. *Past and Present*, No. 48, August 1970, pp. 3 ff.

Jenison: Robert Jenison, *The Return of the Sword, or a Divine Prognostick Delivered in a Sermon at Newcastle*. Lond. 1648.

Kearney: Hugh Kearney, *Scholars and Gentleman: Universities and Society in Preindustrial Britain*. Lond. 1970.

Kenyon: J. P. Kenyon, *The Stuart Constitution*. Cambridge, 1966.

Knowles: David Knowles, *The Religious Orders in England*, vol. iii, *The Tudor Age*. Cambridge, 1959.

Lapsley: G. T. Lapsley, *The County Palatine of Durham*. Lond. and New York, 1900.

Laslett: Peter Laslett, *The World we have lost*. Lond. 1965.

Laud: William Laud, *A Relation of the Conference between William Laud and Mr. Fisher*. Edited by C. H. Simpkinson, Lond. 1901.

Laws: A. R. Laws, *Schola Novocastrensis*. Newcastle, 1925.

Leland: *The Itinerary of John Leland*. Edited by L. Toulmin Smith. 5 vols., Lond. 1906–8.

Leonard: E. M. Leonard, 'The Inclosure of the Common Fields in the Seventeenth Century'. *Transactions of the Royal Historical Society*, New Series, vol. xix (1905), pp. 111 ff.

Levy: F. J. Levy, *Tudor Historical Thought*. San Marino, California, 1967.

Lilburne, *A Worke:* John Lilburne, *A Worke of the Beaste.* Lond. 1638.

Lilburne, *Innocency:* John Lilburne, *Innocency and Truth Justified.* Lond. 1645.

Lilburne, 'Letter': John Lilburne, 'Letter to the Apprentices', 10th May, 1639. Published in *The Prisoner's Plea for a Habeas Corpus,* Lond. 1648.

Logan: F. D. Logan, *Excommunication and the Secular Arm in Medieval England.* Toronto, 1968.

Longstaffe: W. H. D. Longstaffe, 'The Attempt to Annex Gateshead to Newcastle in 1575'. *Archaeologia Aeliana,* New Series, vol. ii, pp. 215 ff.

Lumley Inv: The Lumley Inventories, by L. Cust; *A Lumley Inventory of 1609,* by M. F. S. Harvey. The Walpole Society, vol. vi (1917–18), pp. 15 ff.

Lydgate, *Fall:* John Lydgate, *The Fall of Princes.* Edited by H. Bergen. 4 Parts, 1918–19. Early English Text Society, Extra Series, vols. 121–4.

Lydgate, *Thebes:* John Lydgate, *Siege of Thebes.* Edited by A. Erdmann and E. Ekwall. 2 Parts, 1911 and 1920. Early English Text Society, Extra Series, vols. 108, 125.

Lydgate, *Troy Bk.:* John Lydgate, *Troy Book.* Edited by H. Bergen. Early English Text Society, Extra Series, vol. 126, 1920.

MacCaffery: W. MacCaffery, *The Shaping of the Elizabethan Regime: Elizabethan Politics, 1558–72.* Lond. 1969.

McCall: H. B. McCall, 'The Rising in the North'. *Yorkshire Archaeological Journal,* vol. xviii, 1904–5, pp. 74 ff.

Macfarlane: A. Macfarlane, *The Family Life of Ralph Josselin.* Cambridge, 1970.

Macpherson: C. B. Macpherson, *The Political Theory of Possessive Individualism.* Oxford, 1965.

Markham: Gervase Markham, *A Health to the Gentlemanly Profession of Serving Men.* Lond. 1598. Edited by W. H. C. for the Roxburghe Club, 1868.

Milner: E. Milner, *Records of the Lumleys.* Lond. 1904.

Minstrelsy: Sir Walter Scott, *Minstrelsy of the Scottish Border.* Edited by T. F. Henderson. Lond. 1902.

Mulcaster: R. Mulcaster, *Positions, wherein those Primitive Circumstances be Examined, which are necessary for the training up of Children.* Lond. 1581.

N.C.H.: The Northumberland County History Committee, *A History of Northumberland.* 15 vols., Newcastle, 1893–1940.

Nef: J. U. Nef, *The Rise of the English Coal Industry.* 2 vols., Lond. 1932.

Peacock: M. H. Peacock, *A History of the Free . . . Grammar School at Wakefield.* Wakefield, 1892.

Pevsner: N. Pevsner, *The Buildings of England: County Durham.* Lond. 1953.

Pickthorn: K. Pickthorn, *Early Tudor Government.* 2 vols., Lond. 1949.

Pilbin: P. Pilbin, 'A Geographical Analysis of the Sea-Salt Industry of North-East England'. *Scottish Geographical Magazine,* vol. li, 1935, pp. 22 ff.

Pilkington, *Works:* James Pilkington, *Works.* Edited by J. Scholefield. Parker Society, 1842.

Power: Henry Power, *Experimentall Philosophy, in Three Books. . . .* Lond. 1661.

Raine: J. Raine, *History and Antiquities of North Durham.* Lond. 1852.

Raistrick: A. Raistrick and B. Jennings, *A History of Lead Mining in the Pennines.* Lond. 1965.

Rastell: John Rastell, *A Confutation of a Sermon Pronounced by M. Jewell.* Antwerp, 1564.

Reid, *Council:* R. R. Reid, *The King's Council in the North.* Lond. 1921.

Reid, 'Pol. Infl.': R. R. Reid, 'The political influence of "The North Parts" under the later Tudors'. *Tudor Studies,* edited by R. W. Seton-Watson. Lond. 1924.

Richardson: G. B. Richardson, *Plague and Pestilence in the North of England.* Newcastle, 1852.

Robson, 'Furniture': H. L. Robson, 'The Cosin Furniture in Durham Churches'. *The Antiquities of Sunderland,* vol. xxiv, 1969, pp. 1 ff.

Robson, 'Lilburne': H. L. Robson, 'George Lilburne, Mayor of Sunderland'. *The Antiquities of Sunderland,* vol. xxii, 1960, pp. 86 ff.

Rudyerd: Sir Benjamin Rudyerd, *Memoirs.* Edited by J. A. Manning, Lond. 1841.

Rushworth: John Rushworth, *Historical Collections.* 6 vols., Lond. 1721.

Scott: W. R. Scott, *The Constitution and Finance of English, Scottish, and Irish Joint-Stock Companies to 1720.* 2 vols., Cambridge, 1910–12.

Sharp, *Hartlepool:* Cuthbert Sharp, *History of Hartlepool.* Lond. 1816.

Shrewsbury: J. F. D. Shrewsbury, *A History of the Bubonic Plague in the British Isles.* Cambridge, 1970.

Simon: Joan Simon, *Education and Society in Tudor England.* Lond. 1966.

Smart: Peter Smart, *The Vanitie or Downe-fall of Superstitious Popish Ceremonies . . . A Sermon preached in the Cathedrall Church of Durham . . .* Edinburgh, 1628.

Spearman: John Spearman, *An Enquiry into the ancient and present state of the county palatine of Durham . . .* Edinburgh, 1729.

Starkey: *England in Henry VIII's Time. A Dialogue between Cardinal Pole and Lupset,* by Thomas Starkey. Edited by J. M. Cooper. Early English Text Society, Extra Series, vol. 12 (1871).

Stone, *Causes:* Lawrence Stone, *The Causes of the English Revolution.* Lond. 1972.

Stone, *Crisis:* Lawrence Stone, *The Crisis of the Aristocracy.* Oxford, 1965.

Stone, 'Educational Revolution': Lawrence Stone, 'The Educational Revolution in England, 1560–1640'. *Past and Present,* No. 28, July 1964, pp. 41 ff.

Stone, 'Social Mobility': Lawrence Stone, 'Social Mobility in England, 1500–1640'. *Past and Present,* No. 33, April 1966, pp. 16 ff.

Storey: R. L. Storey, *Thomas Langley and the Bishopric of Durham.* Lond. 1961.

Strype, *Annals:* John Strype, *Annals of the Reformation.* 4 vols., Oxford, 1824.

Strype, *Parker:* John Strype, *The Life and Acts of Matthew Parker . . .* 3 vols., Oxford, 1821.

Summers: J. W. Summers, *History of Sunderland.* Sunderland, 1858.

Surtees, *Brancepeth:* H. C. Surtees, *History of the Castle of Brancepeth.* Durham, 1920.

Surtees, *Witton:* H. C. Surtees, *History of . . . Witton-le-Wear,* in *Durham Parish Histories,* by H. C. Surtees. 3 vols, Durham, 1919–29.

Sur. *Hist. Durh.*: Robert Surtees, *History and Antiquities of the County Palatine of Durham*. 4 vols., Lond. 1816–40.

Sykes: John Sykes, *Local Records*. 2 vols., Newcastle, 1833.

Thirsk: Joan Thirsk, 'The Family'. *Past and Present*, No. 27, April 1964, pp. 116 ff.

Thomas, 'Hobbes': Keith Thomas, 'The Social Origins of Hobbes' Political Thought'. *Hobbes Studies*, Edited by Keith Brown. Oxford, 1965, pp. 185 ff.

Thomas, *Religion*: Keith Thomas, *Religion and the Decline of Magic*. Lond. 1971.

Thomson: G. S. Thomson, *Lords Lieutenants in the Sixteenth Century*. Lond. 1923.

T.R.: T.R., *The Origin and Succession of the Bishops of Durham*. Translated into English by John Hall, 1603. Reprinted, Darlington, 1779.

Trans. Roy. Soc.: *Philosophical Transactions of the Royal Society of London*. 29 vols., Lond. 1665–1715.

Trevor-Roper: H. R. Trevor-Roper, 'The Bishopric of Durham and the Capitalist Reformation'. *Durham University Journal*, vol. xxxvii 1945–6, pp. 45 ff.

Tuck: R. F. Tuck, 'The Origins of the Royal Grammar School, Newcastle upon Tyne', *Archaelogia Aeliana*, Fourth Series, vol. xlvi (1968), pp. 229 ff.

V.C.H. Durh.: *Victoria County History of the County of Durham*. 3 vols., Lond. 1905–28.

Wagner: A. R. Wagner, *The Records and Collections of the College of Arms*. Lond. 1952.

Walker Rev.: A. G. Matthew, *Walker Revised*. Oxford, 1948.

Watson: F. Watson, *The English Grammar Schools to 1660*. Cambridge, 1908.

Webster: John Webster, *Displaying of Supposed Witchcraft*. Lond. 1677.

Welford: R. Welford, *History of Newcastle and Gateshead*. 3 vols., Lond. 1884–7.

Williams: N. Williams, *Thomas Howard, Fourth Duke of Norfolk*. Lond. 1964.

Wilson, 'Changes': B. N. Wilson, 'The Changes of the Reformation Period in Durham and Northumberland'. 2 vols. Durham University Ph.D. thesis, 1935.

Wilson, *Plague*: F. P. Wilson, *The Plague in Shakespeare's London*. Oxford, 1925.

Wrigley: E. A. Wrigley, *Population and History*. Lond. 1969.

INDEX

household, the Neville, 32 ff., 100
Howard, Henry, earl of Northampton, 152
Howard, Thomas, 3rd duke of Norfolk, 46 n³
Howard, Thomas, 4th duke of Norfolk, 49, 50, 51, 109
Howard, Thomas, 1st earl of Suffolk, 152
Howson, John, bishop of Durham, 120, 134, 168, 169
Hull family, 72
humanism. See 'rhetoric, humanist'
Humphrey, Laurence, 31, 32, 192
Hunt, Richard, dean of Durham, 120
husbandman, the
    and the family, 22
    housing of, 12
    literacy of, 105, 106
    military equipment of, 37, 38, 79
    middling, 74-5
    substantial, prosperous, 22, 34, 35, 84
Hutton, prebendary John, 72, 118-19
Hutton, Matthew, bishop of Durham, 4, 118, 150, 154, 155, 158
Hutton, Robert, 120
Hutton family, of Houghton-le-Spring, 72, 73, 103, 116

inflation, 80
Ingleby family, 139
Inns of Court, the, 103-4
Interregnum régimes, 90

Jackson family, of Harraton, 88, 90
Jackson, John, 91
James I, King, 113, 116, 142, 143, 152, 154, 156, 157, 166
James, William
    bishop of Durham, 3, 72, 116, 117, 118, 152, 153-4, 155, 164, 165, 166
    dean of Durham, 76
James, prebendary William, 117, 130
James family, 72, 116
Jenison, John, 139, 140
Jenison, Robert, 195
Jenison, Robert, S. J., 142
Jenison, Thomas, S.J., 142
Jenison, William, 165
Jenison family, of Neasham, 140, 142
Jenison family, of Walworth, 16, 99, 142
Jesuits, the, 126, 144

Johnson, John, rector of Bishop Wearmouth, 135

King's Bench, court of, 42

Lambert family, 68
Lambton, colliery at, 87
    house of Lambton family at, 13, 14
Lambton, Sir William, 89, 176
Lambton family, 31, 71, 90, 103, 138 n¹, 188
Lampton, Joseph, 159
landlords and tenants, 38 ff., 79 ff.
Langton, bailiff of, 33
Lanchester, 128, 129, 138, 140
Lapthorne, Anthony, 126, 130 ff., 133, 135, 171, 195-6, 197
Latimer, Lord. See 'John Neville'
Laud, William, archbishop of Canterbury, 85, 89, 117, 120, 124 n³, 134, 162, 168, 169, 171, 174
Lawson, Mrs Dorothy, 137, 139, 140, 141, 143 ff.
Lawson, William, 77
Lawson family, 138
Lawson family, of Usworth, 99
leaseholders, 39
    'customary', 80, 81
lead-mining, 6, 71
Lee, William, of Brandon, 33
Leicester, earl of. See 'Robert Dudley'
Leland, John, 5, 11
Liddell, Thomas, 144 n¹
Liddell family, 69, 104, 146 n³, 160 n²
Lilburne, George, 87, 89, 90, 91, 133, 134, 135, 136, 137, 170, 173, 174
Lilburne, John, 90, 91, 106-7, 197
Lilburne, Robert, 90, 132, 196
Lilburne, Thomas, 91
Lilburne family, 2, 34, 90, 196
Lindsell, prebendary Augustine, 112, 119, 120, 162, 163, 168
lineage society, the, 26, 32, 177, 180, 181, 184, 185, 186, 191, 194
literacy, 63, 105 ff.
lowland, the
    agriculture of, 5
    the family in, 19 ff.
    the parish in, 128
London, 1, 2, 3, 74, 161, 170, 175, 189
Lumley, John, 5th Lord, 44, 46, 46 n³
Lumley, John, 6th Lord, 50, 51, 109 ff., 135, 137, 147

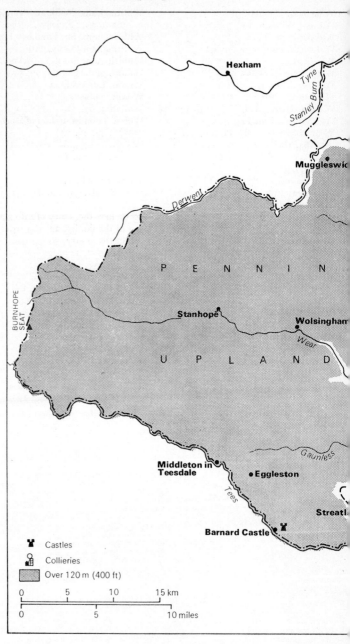